Challenging the Secret Government

D0816725

The University of North Carolina Press   [Chapel Hill and London]

Challenging the

Secret Government

The Post-Watergate

Investigations

of the CIA and FBI

Kathryn S. Olmsted

Library of Congress Cataloging-in-Publication Data

Olmsted, Kathryn S.

Challenging the secret government : the post-
Watergate investigations of the CIA and FBI / by
Kathryn S. Olmsted.

p. cm.

Includes bibliographical references (p.   ) and index.

ISBN 0-8078-2254-x (cloth : alk. paper). —

ISBN 0-8078-4562-0 (pbk. : alk. paper)

1. Intelligence service—United States.   2. United
States. Central Intelligence Agency.   3. United
States. Federal Bureau of Investigation.

4. Watergate Affair, 1972–1974.   I. Title.

JK468.I6045   1996

320.973—dc20   95-23354

CIP

The paper in this book meets the guidelines for
permanence and durability of the Committee on
Production Guidelines for Book Longevity of the
Council on Library Resources.

00 99 98 97 96   5 4 3 2 1

To Bill

You peel off Watergate and you find the Plumbers and the Ellsberg break-in. Peel off the Plumbers and you find the 1970 Huston plan to use the CIA and FBI for domestic surveillance, wiretapping and break-ins. But what would you find if you peeled off another layer and had a close look at that secret world from which these things had been launched?

Daniel Schorr

"My 17 Months on the CIA Watch"

Contents

Illustrations

Acknowledgments

Many people have helped me complete this project. The University of California at Davis provided several research grants and fellowships, and the Gerald R. Ford Foundation and Phi Beta Kappa supplied money for travel and research.

The archivists at the Gerald R. Ford Library were very helpful, especially Helmi Raaska and David Horrocks. I also received cheerful assistance from Mary Carter and Alan Virta at the Frank Church Collection at the Boise State University Library. I wish to thank *Journalism History* for permission to reprint portions of an essay published in volume 19, number 2 (summer 1993).

I am also grateful to all of the people who granted me interviews. I especially thank Doris McClory, who shared her hospitality with me and allowed me to peruse the files of her late husband, Robert McClory.

Roland Marchand, Michael Smith, Paul Goodman, and Larry Berman provided encouragement and constructive criticism along the way. Michael Schudson read an early draft of the manuscript and made some astute suggestions.

I could not have written this book without the loving support of my parents. They made great sacrifices to give me the best education possible. Finally, my largest debt is to my husband, Bill, who read every chapter at least three times. Without his encouragement, interest, and editing skills, my task in writing this book would have been far more difficult.

Challenging the Secret Government

Introduction

When Richard Nixon resigned in August 1974, the United States concluded one of the most traumatic chapters in its history. During the Watergate scandal, Americans had been shocked by the crimes of the Nixon presidency. Investigations by the press and Congress had exposed previously unimaginable levels of corruption and conspiracy in the executive branch. The public's faith in government had been shaken; indeed, the entire "system" had been tested. Now, with Nixon's resignation, two years of agonizing revelations finally seemed to be over. The system had worked.

Yet only four months later, *New York Times* reporter Seymour Hersh disclosed that the government's crimes went beyond Watergate. After months of persistent digging, Hersh had unearthed a new case of the imperial presidency's abuse of secrecy and power: a "massive" domestic spying program by the Central Intelligence Agency (CIA). According to Hersh, the CIA had violated its charter and broken the law by launching a spying program of Orwellian dimensions against American dissidents during the Vietnam War. The *Times* called it "son of Watergate."

These revelations produced a dramatic response from the newly energized post-Watergate Congress and press. Both houses of Congress mounted extensive, year-long investigations of the intelligence community. These highly publicized inquiries, headed by experienced investigators Senator Frank Church and Congressman Otis Pike, produced shocking accusations of murder plots and poison caches, of FBI corruption and CIA incompetence. In addition to the congressional inquiries, the press, seemingly at the height of its power after Watergate, launched investigations of its own. The *New York Times* continued to crusade against CIA abuses; the *Washington Post* exposed abuses and illegalities committed by the FBI; and CBS's Daniel Schorr shocked the nation by revealing that there might be "literal" skeletons in the CIA closet as a result of its assassination plots.

In this charged atmosphere, editorial writers, columnists, political scientists, historians, and even former officials of the CIA weighed in with various suggestions for reforming an agency that many agreed had become a "monster."[1] Several policymakers, including presidential candidates Fred Harris and Morris Udall, called for massive restructuring or abolition of the CIA. Media and political pundits suggested banning CIA covert operations; transferring most CIA functions to the Pentagon or the State Department; or, at the very least, devising a new, strict charter for all members of the intelligence community.[2]

Few barriers seemed to stand in the way of such reforms. The liberal, post-Watergate Congress faced an appointed president who did not appear to have the strength to resist this "tidal shift in attitude," as Senator Church called it.[3] Change seemed so likely in early 1975 that a writer for *The Nation* declared "the heyday of the National Security State" to be over, at least temporarily.[4]

But a year and a half later, when the Pike and Church committees finally finished their work, the passion for reform had cooled. The House overwhelmingly rejected the work of the Pike committee and voted to suppress its final report. It even refused to set up a standing intelligence committee.[5] The Senate dealt more favorably with the Church committee, but it too came close to rejecting all of the committee's recommendations. Only last-minute parliamentary maneuvering enabled Church to salvage one reform, the creation of a new standing committee on intelligence. The proposed charter for the intelligence community, though its various components continued to be hotly debated for several years, never came to pass.

The investigations failed to promote the careers of those who had inspired and led them. Daniel Schorr, the CBS reporter who had advanced the CIA story at several important points and eventually had become part of the story himself, was investigated by Congress, threatened with jail, and fired by CBS for his role in leaking the suppressed Pike report. Seymour Hersh's exposés were dismissed by his peers as "overwritten, over-played, under-researched and underproven."[6] Otis Pike, despite the many accomplishments of his committee, found his name linked with congressional sensationalism, leaks, and poor administration. Frank Church's role in the investigation failed to boost his presidential campaign, forced him to delay his entry into the race, and, he thought, might have cost him the vice presidency.[7]

The targets of the investigation had the last laugh on the investigators. "When all is said and done, what did it achieve?" asked Richard Helms, the former director of the CIA who was at the heart of many of the scandals unearthed by Congress and the media. "Where is the legislation, the great piece of legislation, that was going to come out of the Church committee hearings? I haven't seen it."[8] Hersh, the reporter who prompted the inquiries, was also unimpressed by the investigators' accomplishments. "They generated a lot of new information, but ultimately they didn't come up with much," he said.[9] Why were the early high expectations of Hersh, Schorr, Pike, and Church not met? Why did so little reform result from such extensive investigations?

Scholars have previously examined these investigations as case studies in public policymaking. Loch Johnson has related his personal experience as a Church committee staff member in *A Season of Inquiry: Congress and Intelligence*.[10] Frank J. Smist, Jr., and Rhodri Jeffreys-Jones have included chapters on the Church and Pike committees in their larger studies of congressional oversight of intelligence in the post–World War II United States.[11]

Beyond their obvious importance to policy studies, however, the intelligence investigations of 1975 are significant historical events of post-Vietnam, post-Watergate America. They provide insight into how

Americans understood and reacted to the "lessons" of a very divisive war and their greatest political scandal.

These investigations illustrate a historic moment in post-1945 American history: the breakdown of the Cold War consensus. As Godfrey Hodgson has pointed out, U.S. foreign policy during the 1950s and early 1960s was supported by a broad, almost universal spectrum of Americans from left to right. This was the foreign policy of the "liberal consensus."[12] Conservative Republicans and liberal Democrats alike agreed on the need for an aggressive, anticommunist foreign policy, including overt and covert intervention abroad. Even the most liberal policymakers in this era agreed that the president needed extraordinary power and secrecy to meet the Communist threat.

But the defeat in Vietnam and the humiliation of Watergate shattered this consensus. In Congress and the mainstream media, the boundaries of debate suddenly expanded. Elite opinion leaders were willing to question institutions that had never been challenged before. Nowhere was the resulting excitement, conflict, and confusion more evident than in the intelligence investigations. These inquiries provoked a monumental clash between the legislative and executive branches, raising fears that a system stabilized after Nixon's resignation might now collapse. They also prompted a battle within the media, as journalists were forced to reassess their coverage of national security issues for the past three decades.

The stakes during the "year of intelligence," as the *New York Times* came to call it, were high. The congressional investigators, by exposing the past abuses of the secret government and assessing the risks and benefits of covert action, were challenging the foreign policy of the Cold War. The executive branch, in response, worked frantically to restore the powers of the presidency and to limit the scope of the investigations. Members of the media, for all their enthusiasm about the opportunities to publish prize-winning investigative stories, hesitated to break their long tradition of deference in national security coverage. The public, shocked by the inquiries' revelations, soon became disillusioned with the secret agencies and with the investigators.

The investigations raised basic questions about the nature of power in the post–World War II United States. Had Watergate exposed a systemic problem requiring structural solutions, or was it the unfortunate product of an "outlaw" president and his unethical advisers? After Vietnam and Watergate, should the media and Congress be more skeptical when presidents defended secrecy in the name of national security? Should congressional committees and individual journalists ignore presidential pleas for secrecy? Did the Cold War make it necessary for the government to pursue an amoral, clandestine foreign policy? If so, how could that policy be reconciled with America's view of itself as an open, ethical democracy? After years of accepting governmental secrecy and presidential supremacy in foreign policy, many Americans began asking these questions for the first time in 1975.

Because they confronted these issues, the intelligence investigations can help us understand how members of Congress, the press, and the public interpreted and responded to this moment of crisis for the American system. Despite the transformations caused by Watergate, the inquiries show that American political culture of the 1970s was characterized more by continuity than by change. This resistance to change is shown in three important areas.

First, Congress hesitated throughout the 1970s to assume responsibility for the nation's secret agencies. Immediately after Nixon's resignation, it appeared that members of Congress would reclaim the prerogatives they had conceded to the executive branch after World War II. Many observers have concluded that they were successful in that effort, at least until the advent of the Reagan administration in 1981. Scholars have written of a "resurgence" of Congress during this period, which resulted in a "tethered presidency" or even an "imperiled presidency."[13] As Louis Koenig wrote in 1981, "The question is not whether there is an imperial presidency *but whether there still is a presidency as that office has traditionally been known.*"[14]

But the reports of the demise of the presidency were exaggerated, as this book shows. The post-Watergate Congress may have been more assertive in many areas, but it was ultimately unwilling to shoulder its responsibilities for overseeing the intelligence community. On this issue, at least, there were distinct limits to the "congressional revolution."

Second, the media proved reluctant during the investigations to confront the national security state. Beginning in the early 1970s, many scholars, policymakers, and journalists concluded that Watergate and Vietnam had transformed the media. After these two epochal events, the argument went, the press became an assertive, independent institution, a full-fledged fourth branch of government determined to serve as an extra check on executive authority. While some people celebrated this development, others were terrified by its implications. Political scientist Samuel P. Huntington was one of the earliest proponents of what Daniel Hallin has termed the "oppositional media thesis."[15] Huntington and his successors claimed that the "imperial media" began in the late 1960s and early 1970s to oppose and to question all political authority.[16] Even in the early 1990s, books by Suzanne Garment and Larry Sabato continued to warn of an irresponsible press that pursued political scandals without discrimination.[17]

The journalistic investigations of the intelligence community fit nicely into this paradigm of an aggressive, adversarial press. To many observers, the media's "anti-CIA crusade" of 1975 proved that reporters had a liberal bias and were determined to tear down the nation's defense establishment. The press, in short, had become an arrogant, irresponsible practitioner of "advocacy journalism."[18]

This study, however, demonstrates that there were definite limits to the "adversarial" nature of post-Watergate journalism. The image of the fearless press, determined to oppose political authority and expose incompetence and corruption in government whatever the consequences, is, as Michael Schudson has noted, largely a myth.[19] Like many myths, it has an element of truth. Some Washington journalists were indeed eager to question the government departments that were open to public scrutiny. And a few reporters, like Hersh and Schorr, tried to remove the veil of secrecy from the national security state. But many others were uneasy about the media's post-Watergate power. In the end, when they wrote about the secret government, most members of the press showed great restraint—and they severely criticized their colleagues who did not.

Finally, the American people, acculturated for years to view their country and their leaders as moral and democratic, were reluctant to acknowledge unpleasant truths about their secret agencies. During the Cold War, the United States had used authoritarian tactics to meet the threat of an authoritarian adversary. But, as William W. Keller has explained in *The Liberals and J. Edgar Hoover*, the liberal state did not like to admit that it had violated its ideology in this way.[20] Therefore, the extensive powers of its clandestine agencies were kept secret. This secrecy enabled Americans to assume that the nation's foreign policy goals were compatible with traditional American ideals. But the intelligence investigations brought these secret powers into the open; they forced Americans to acknowledge that their country had tried to kill foreign leaders, had spied on civil rights leaders, and had tested drugs on innocent people. Because this knowledge was very painful, many Americans, including members of Congress, refused to accept it. Secrecy, as journalist Taylor Branch has said, "protects the American people from grisly facts at variance with their self-image."[21] The investigations failed in part because Americans, insulated from painful knowledge about their country's activities during the Cold War, did not want to face those facts.

As the investigations began, a failed war and a momentous scandal had caused many Americans to question Cold War assumptions about secrecy in foreign policy and about the power of the presidency. But by the time the investigations concluded, most members of the press, the Congress, and the public had demonstrated that—even after Vietnam, even after Watergate—they preferred to maintain their basic deference to the secret government.

Within this overall story of continuity, there are two recurring themes. One is the relationship between the players' altruistic motives and their own self-interest. Sometimes these needs were congruent. For example, Senator Church wanted to use the investigation to attract public attention before launching his presidential campaign; he also wanted to mobilize public support for real reforms of the intelligence community, which he had urged consistently since the early 1960s. President Ford tried to protect the Republican Party from further scandal; he also wanted to restore the power of the presidency and safeguard the secret agencies he had defended for twenty-five years.

Sometimes, however, the investigators did not follow their selfish interests. Otis Pike wanted to build public support, possibly before running for the Senate. Yet he continued to hammer away at the secret agencies long after it became apparent that the press and much of the public had turned against him. In several cases, journalists decided to suppress information even though it was clearly in their short-term self-interest to publish it. These examples show that the investigations represented more than mere political posturing, more than the simple journalistic desire to scoop the competition.

Another theme woven throughout this story is the complex, dynamic relationship between the post-Watergate press and Congress. Seymour Hersh's domestic spying stories did not appear in a vacuum. He published his series at a time when Congress was eager to challenge the executive branch, especially the secret agencies. A few months earlier, a Hersh exposé on CIA covert action in Chile had prompted Senate majority leader Mike Mansfield to introduce yet another of his many proposals that the Senate investigate the intelligence community. Hersh's domestic spying articles provided the momentum for the Senate to pass the bill at last.

Throughout the first months of the investigations, the press continued to pressure Congress. A *Washington Post* series on FBI abuses ensured that the congressional investigators would not neglect the domestic intelligence agencies. A CBS report on CIA assassination plots added a new, sensational charge for the committees to investigate. As the months went by, however, the most powerful members of the press and Congress began to worry that the investigations had gone too far. The reform movement faltered simultaneously on the floor of Congress and in editorial board conference rooms.

Chapter 1 provides the background for this study by tracing the history of the intelligence community and its ambiguous relationship with the media and the public. The chapter explains the post-Watergate changes that motivated the critics of the secret agencies—as well as the continuities that would ultimately help the agencies' defenders.

Chapter 2 examines the media's response to Hersh's revelations and analyzes why so many members of the press criticized his stories. As this chapter demonstrates, Hersh's revelations of domestic spying appeared to come at a propitious time for exposés of governmental abuses. But, in fact, many members of the press were alarmed by the role they had played in bringing about Nixon's fall and apprehensive about continued assaults on established institutions.[22]

Chapter 3 turns to the congressional investigations. After looking briefly at earlier congressional attempts to regulate the intelligence community, the chapter examines Congress's motivations and expectations in creating the two investigating committees. Because of institutional differences, the House and Senate took divergent approaches to the investigations.

After the committees were established, they met behind closed doors for many months. Chapter 4 examines the conduct of the press during these months and analyzes three cases of self-censorship by the supposedly aggressive post-Watergate media.

Chapters 5 and 6 analyze the performance of the Pike and Church committees, comparing and contrasting their agendas, styles, and accomplishments. Senator Church chose to focus on the intelligence community's past abuses, thus paving the way for these abuses to be seen as aberrations. Representative Pike took a more systemic and confrontational approach. His committee proved to be more threatening to the intelligence community—and also more vulnerable to charges that it was acting irresponsibly.

Chapter 7 traces the executive branch's strategy in generating a public backlash against the journalistic and congressional investigators. The concluding chapter brings the narrative to a close and seeks to answer the central question of this study: After starting the investigations, why did most members of the press and Congress back away from challenging the secret government?

No major act of the American Congress, no foreign adventure, no act of diplomacy, no great social reform can succeed in the United States unless the press prepares the public mind.

Theodore White, *The Making of the President, 1972*

Secrecy and Democracy

The Press, the Public, and the Secret Government to 1975

The sedate *New York Times* was not known for screaming headlines—especially when the headlines concerned events that had happened years, rather than hours, before. But on 22 December 1974, the *Times* editors gave extraordinary prominence to what they considered to be an explosive story. The four-column headline proclaimed, "HUGE C.I.A. OPERATION REPORTED IN U.S. AGAINST ANTIWAR FORCES, OTHER DISSIDENTS IN NIXON YEARS." The story itself, written by Seymour Hersh, a Pulitzer Prize winner renowned for his scoops on the My Lai massacre, the secret bombing of Cambodia, and the Kissinger wiretaps, was a quintessential example of aggressive, post-Watergate reporting. "The Central Intelligence Agency, directly violating its charter, conducted a massive, illegal domestic intelligence operation during the Nixon Administration against the antiwar movement and other dissident groups in the United States, according to well-placed Government sources," read the shocking lead paragraph.[1]

Hersh went on to claim that the CIA, forbidden by law from operating in the United States, had gathered files on 10,000 American citizens and conducted illegal break-ins, wiretaps, and mail openings. This extraordinary story turned out to be the first of many. In the next eighteen days, the *Times* ran thirty-two CIA-related stories—and managed to mention its own role in uncovering the scandal thirty-eight times.[2] The *Times* had reason to crow; later investigations would prove that its story was accurate.

The Hersh story "triggered a firestorm," CIA director William Colby ruefully wrote later. "All the tensions and suspicions and hostilities that had been building about the CIA since the Bay of Pigs and had risen to a combustible level during the Vietnam and Watergate years, now exploded."[3] The White House, Congress, and the public responded quickly to the story. President Gerald Ford asked Colby to make a thorough investigation of the *Times* revelations. Soon after receiving Colby's report, Ford appointed a blue-ribbon commission headed by Vice President Nelson Rockefeller to examine the allegations further. The House and Senate, undeterred by the presidential commission, both created special investigative committees within two months. What the *Times* variously called "the year of intelligence" and "son of Watergate" had begun.[4]

Hersh's exposé was an unlikely topic for the *New York Times*'s first venture into "advocacy journalism," as *Washington Post* reporter Walter Pincus termed it.[5] The alleged CIA abuses had ended years before; the *Times* was exposing what many considered to be ancient history. But several developments combined to make it an auspicious time for the *Times*'s crusading coverage. Vietnam and Watergate had left many important legacies: a disillusioned, skeptical public; a drastically weakened intelligence community; and a seemingly confident, assertive press. As a result, some journalists abandoned their traditional deference to the nation's secret agencies.

At the same time, however, restraints from the pre-Watergate era continued to exert their power throughout this era of change—restraints that would ultimately serve to limit the media's newfound aggressiveness.

At the time that the *New York Times* published the domestic spying exposé, most Americans had only begun to learn about the secret government agency known as the CIA. The agency had been established with minimal public debate at the dawn of the Cold War era and had taken on unanticipated duties in relative secrecy over the subsequent years. Congress held hearings on the section of the National Security Act of 1947 that created the CIA. But according to historian Harry Howe Ransom, nothing in the published hearings "suggests that Congress intended to create, or knew it was creating, an agency for paramilitary operations."[6] The hearings also never discussed covert operations or psychological warfare. The congressmen believed they were simply creating an agency to gather and evaluate foreign intelligence.

As the Cold War continued, however, presidents secretly began directing the CIA to take on new functions. The CIA's evolving Cold War ethos was best articulated in a secret 1954 report on its covert operations. President Dwight Eisenhower established the Doolittle committee to avoid a planned public examination of the CIA's most secret directorate.[7] The committee, headed by World War II hero General James Doolittle, endorsed an activist role for the agency and advocated methods previously considered "un-American":

> It is now clear that we are facing an implacable enemy whose avowed objective is world domination by whatever means and at whatever cost. There are no rules in such a game. Hitherto acceptable norms of human conduct do not apply. If the United States is to survive, long-standing American concepts of "fair play" must be reconsidered. We must develop effective espionage and counterespionage services and must learn to subvert, sabotage and destroy our enemies by more clever, more sophisticated, and more effective methods than those used against us. It may become necessary that the American people be made acquainted with, understand and support this fundamentally repugnant philosophy.[8]

The president, however, decided not to acquaint the American people with the committee's conclusions. The public was not told that the CIA had begun to intervene covertly in foreign countries and that it might need to abandon "long-standing American concepts of 'fair play' " in the process. By keeping the Doolittle report secret, Eisenhower avoided messy domestic debates about these "fundamentally repugnant" actions and ensured that they would continue. Only a handful of congressmen were informed of the details of the CIA's new duties. From time to time, some congressmen would demand more oversight of the agency, but CIA supporters easily managed to defeat these attempts.[9]

Agency officials appreciated this absence of oversight and accountability. Complete secrecy helped to protect their sources and methods. Moreover, the cloak of national security allowed CIA officials to escape public debate over their actions. But at the same time, this secrecy posed a potentially serious public relations problem. Democratic America's spy agency faced a conundrum: How could it generate public support for its activities when most of the public was not told—and did not understand—what it did?

Initially, what historians have called the "Cold War consensus" in American political culture—the almost universal support for anticommunism—helped the CIA to solve this problem. Because of the CIA's unwillingness to publicize its activities, Americans before the investigations drew most of their knowledge about the agency from popular culture. Throughout the 1950s and the early 1960s, during the height of Cold War culture, the CIA enjoyed a romanticized, heroic image in novels and films. Inspired by author Ian Fleming's success in glamorizing the British secret service, many American imitators portrayed America's secret warriors as unblemished heroes fighting the international menace of communism.[10] The CIA promoted this Cold War tradition of spy fiction by encouraging favored thriller authors, even allowing them access to secret files. The movies and television shows of the 1950s and 1960s—such as *Mission: Impossible* and *The Man from U.N.C.L.E.*—also celebrated America's spies.[11] Popular culture, in short, helped to legitimize the agency.

The Federal Bureau of Investigation (FBI) was another government intelligence agency that enjoyed a glamorous image in popular culture, but FBI officials took a much more active role in creating and shaping this image. Beginning in 1933, bureau boss J. Edgar Hoover turned the FBI into what one scholar has called "one of the greatest publicity-generating machines the country had ever seen."[12] The FBI's responsibilities included law enforcement as well as domestic intelligence and counterintelligence. In contrast to the secretive and anonymous CIA officials, FBI publicists readily shared the bureau's accomplishments in all of these areas with the press. They also tried to damage the public image of bureau targets, like New Leftists or civil rights leaders, by leaking derogatory information about them to reporters. Some friendly journalists even served as FBI informants.[13]

Hoover's public relations unit eventually became one of the most influential divisions within the FBI, helping reporters, film and television producers, and writers over the years to sculpt the popular image of the virtuous "G-man." Hoover decided that publicity, instead of hurting the bureau by exposing its "secrets," actually helped to build public support and to prevent attacks by liberals in Congress.

This popular support for the secret agencies proved strong enough to help them survive the occasional Cold War scandal. The first major CIA embarrassment occurred in 1961, when the Bay of Pigs invasion backfired disastrously. But after the initial calls for reform and restructuring, the agency weathered the crisis with only minor changes. In 1967, the CIA again found itself under attack, this time for domestic improprieties. *Ramparts* magazine revealed that the CIA had secret ties to the National Students Association and other voluntary organizations. Many Americans worried that CIA money and advice for such groups could discredit American organizations abroad and enable the agency to manipulate public opinion at home. President Lyndon Johnson headed off this potential scandal by appointing former attorney general Nicholas Katzenbach to chair a blue-ribbon investigative commission, which recommended that the CIA stop funding such associations. The FBI faced a scare in 1965 when Senator Edward Long of Missouri threatened to investigate and curb the bureau's surveillance of Americans. But Hoover first blackmailed Long over his alleged support from organized crime and then leaked these allegations to the press. The senator's threat was easily contained.[14]

The CIA and FBI thus avoided damaging press and congressional investigations until the early 1970s, when the Watergate scandal transformed American political culture. For reporters and congressmen interested in investigating the CIA, as author Thomas Powers has observed, Watergate was "the foot in the door." The CIA "had been in unwelcome spotlights before, but Watergate did what the Bay of Pigs had not: it had undermined the consensus of trust in Washington which was a truer source of the Agency's strength than its legal charter."[15] It demonstrated that "national security" claims could serve as veils for illegal activity.

Although the CIA was not directly implicated in the illegal burglaries, wiretapping, and cover-up that led to Richard Nixon's resignation, it did have links to some of the principal conspirators. Of the seven men involved in the Watergate break-in, five had worked for the CIA.[16] Two of them, James McCord and Howard Hunt, were twenty-year veterans of the agency. In addition, the agency had supplied Hunt and his colleagues with equipment and services for earlier projects.

CIA director Richard Helms intensified public suspicion of the agency by withholding evidence from the Watergate prosecutors for months. Later, after the Watergate tapes were released, Americans learned that President Nixon had made an enigmatic reference to Helms on the crucial "smoking gun" tape of 23 June 1972. Speaking with his top aide, Bob Haldeman, Nixon explained why he thought the CIA would cooperate in his plan to block the FBI from investigating Watergate. "We protected Helms from one hell of a lot of things," Nixon said.[17] Historians are still not sure what the president meant by that remark.[18]

As the public learned the incredible details of the Watergate affair, no conspiracy seemed too outlandish to believe. Some Americans even speculated that the CIA itself was the mastermind behind the Watergate burglary.[19] Although a Senate subcommittee headed by Senator Howard Baker found no evidence of CIA complicity in the break-in, the general tone of the subcommittee's report implied, as one CIA officer put it, that "there might still be some unseen but noisy creatures in the woods."[20] Baker himself suggested that there was more to the CIA's involvement in Watergate than he was able to prove.

The FBI's credibility was also damaged by Watergate. L. Patrick Gray, Nixon's nominee to head the bureau after J. Edgar Hoover's death, destroyed critical Watergate evidence. When Gray withdrew his nomination under fire, a Nixon aide appeared to play politics with the bureau by offering the directorship to the presiding judge in the trial of Daniel Ellsberg, a Nixon enemy. The Watergate investigation revealed that the Nixon administration had frequently used the FBI for political purposes. These revelations were especially disturbing to Americans because the movies, television shows, radio programs, and books of the Cold War had portrayed secret agents as righteous and incorruptible.

For a brief time, it seemed possible that Nixon's successor might restore the honor of the executive branch and the public's confidence in government. Most Americans extended their goodwill to Gerald Ford, who received a 71 percent approval rating shortly after he was sworn into office.[21] The unpretentious former congressman from Michigan was everything Nixon was not: an honest, open, and accessible man who even toasted his own English muffins. But then Ford gave American citizens a new reason to be cynical about their government: he issued a full and unconditional pardon to Nixon within thirty days of taking office.

Ford's pardon of Nixon accelerated the growing trend of cynicism about government in general and the executive branch in particular. In ten years, the percentage of people who distrusted the government had risen from 22 to 62 percent. Forty-five percent of Americans polled believed that there were "quite a few" crooks in government, up from 29 percent in 1964.[22] The proportion of those who agreed that the country's leaders had "consistently lied to the American people" rose from 38 percent in 1972 to 68 percent in 1975.[23]

The governmental institutions most affected by the "confidence gap," as Seymour Martin Lipset and William Schneider have termed it, were the secret executive branch agencies like the FBI and the CIA. The proportion of Americans who had a "highly favorable" impression of the FBI had fallen from 84 percent in 1965 to 52 percent in 1973. In 1975, that figure dropped again to 37 percent. Although the Gallup organization did not ask Americans about the relatively anonymous CIA before 1973, the agency at that time was held in lower esteem than the FBI: only 23 percent of Americans gave the CIA a highly favorable rating. In 1975, the figure fell to 14 percent. Among college students, the CIA was highly regarded by only 7 percent.[24] The secret agencies' reservoir of support had been seriously depleted.

In the same week that Americans were stunned by news of the presidential pardon, a new CIA scandal erupted. This time it involved agency actions overseas. Chile's elected Marxist president, Salvador Allende Gossens, had been overthrown in a coup the year before. Congressman Michael Harrington, a Democrat from Massachusetts, was deeply suspicious of the CIA's role in the 1970 elections in Chile and in the 1973 coup. He pressured the chairman of a CIA oversight subcommittee, Lucien Nedzi of Michigan, to hold special secret hearings on the matter. Harrington then demanded to see the transcript of those hearings, which included testimony by CIA director William Colby.

In September 1974, Harrington's summary of Colby's secret testimony was leaked to Seymour Hersh, who exposed it in the *New York Times*.[25] He revealed that the Nixon administration had authorized $8 million for covert activities in Chile from 1970 to 1973 in an effort to "destabilize" the Allende regime.[26] Agency and State Department officials had deliberately misled Congress about the extent of this intervention.

The Chile exposé prompted angry congressmen to demand answers from the executive branch. Some legislators called for perjury investigations; others called for a ban on all covert operations. The CIA seemed to have stumbled into the greatest crisis of its short history.

While the secret agencies were at their weakest in the fall of 1974, the advocates of governmental openness and candor had never been more powerful. Many members of the American press were primed to expose the secrets of the previously sacrosanct national security agencies. After Vietnam and Watergate, the media seemed to rediscover their muckraking heritage and cast off the deferential traditions of the more immediate past.

The American press has always viewed itself as performing an essential role in maintaining American democracy. By training its "artillery" on the powerful (as Thomas Jefferson had urged), the press tries to keep the government honest and responsive. In theory, the press serves as a "fourth branch of government," an extra check and balance in the constitutional system.

Journalists have carried out this duty in different ways over time. Up until the early twentieth century, the nation's journalistic "watchdogs" did not hesitate to inject opinion into their stories. Even when the partisan press began to give way to a more "fact-minded" style of reporting in the late nineteenth century, sociologist Michael Schudson has written, reporters still interpreted the news in their own way.[27]

After World War I, journalists started to develop a new system of work ethics: the modern journalistic ideal of objectivity. Because the brutality of the war raised doubts about the reliability of human reason, journalists began to see the need for certain formulas—a credo of "objectivity"— that would enable them to put their biases aside. According to Schudson, the rise of the public relations industry and the persuasive force of wartime propaganda also made journalists "suspicious of the facts and ready to doubt the naive empiricism of the 1890s."[28] This devotion to objectivity would govern the profession for the next fifty years.[29]

While they embraced objectivity, however, twentieth-century American journalists retained their traditional belief in the importance of the "watchdog" role of the press. Modern journalists were not supposed to interpret the news, but they were still expected to curb potential abuses by those in power. Even if they were limited to reporting "the facts," they could continue to strike fear into the hearts of the powerful. As *New York Times* editor and columnist James Reston wrote in 1967, American reporters would never shrink from exposing and criticizing government policies "because, somehow, the tradition of reporting the facts, no matter how much they hurt, is stronger than any other."[30]

In practice, however, American journalists' dual roles as objective observers and watchdogs were not always compatible. Because objective journalists dedicated themselves to presenting all sides of an issue without passing judgment on which side was "the truth," they faithfully reported all statements from top administration officials, whether or not they were accurate. As Tom Wicker has commented, "If the president says, 'Black is white,' you write, 'The president said black is white.' "[31] In renouncing their right to partisan reporting, according to political scientist Daniel Hallin, journalists in turn were granted "a regular right of access to the inner counsels of government, a right they had never enjoyed in the era of partisan journalism." The result of the new doctrine of objectivity was not to free the news of political influence, Hallin states, "but to open wide the channel through which official influence flowed."[32] Objectivity was never the transparent window it claimed to be but rather a means for those in power to dominate the public discussion.

Of course, if Washington power brokers disagreed on an issue, objective journalists were obligated to inform their readers of both sides of the debate. By the end of the 1940s, however, no such debate occurred among political elites on foreign policy. The anticommunist consensus dominated American politics—and the U.S. media, trained to disseminate the statements of policymakers without question, reflected this consensus.

From the 1940s to the 1960s, journalists and politicians alike shared common assumptions about the Communist threat and the need to protect the operations of America's clandestine soldiers in the Cold War. Just as American popular culture echoed and reinforced the Cold War consensus, so the American press eagerly joined the united front against communism. *Washington Post* publisher Phil Graham summed up these views in 1954 when he criticized his editorial writers for recommending a thaw in the Cold War. "A year or so ago it was clear to all of us that the Soviet system was one of total evil—one with which nothing but 'self-enforcing' agreement could be made," Graham wrote in an internal memo. "That, in my opinion, has not changed."[33]

A few individual journalists did challenge Cold War assumptions throughout the 1950s, but they did not work for mainstream publications. Carey McWilliams and his colleagues at *The Nation* analyzed the secret government for their 45,000 readers, publishing special issues on the FBI in 1958 and the CIA in 1962. I. F. Stone, who found himself unemployable during the McCarthy era, wrote biting commentary on

Cold War politics and policy in his newsletter.[34] But comparatively few Americans read these publications, and the general press tended to dismiss them as cranky and irrelevant.

The anticommunist consensus had its greatest impact on foreign affairs reporting. American reporters abroad not only were reluctant to investigate or expose CIA actions but also shared U.S. policymakers' Cold War assumptions and willingly accepted their evaluations of foreign governments. For example, in Iran in 1953, American journalists echoed the U.S. embassy's negative assessments of the nationalist government of Mohammad Mossadegh. When the CIA helped to engineer a coup to overthrow Mossadegh in favor of the shah, the American press overlooked the agency's involvement.[35] Similarly, in Guatemala the next year, historian Richard Immerman has noted, the U.S. press reflected the views of the Eisenhower administration and the United Fruit Company and equated Guatemalan communism with Soviet totalitarianism.[36]

The experiences of the *New York Times* reporters in Iran and Guatemala illustrate the pressures on early Cold War journalists to serve as cheerleaders for U.S. foreign policy. The stories written by Kennett Love, the *Times* man in Tehran, were sufficiently critical of Mossadegh to prompt an anti-CIA group in the 1970s to accuse him of being an American spy.[37] Yet at the time, Love's occasional willingness to report on negative aspects of the shah's regime earned him censure from both the Iranian government and the U.S. embassy. Forced to defend his patriotism to his unsympathetic editors in New York City, Love tried to reassure them by repeatedly pointing out that he had suppressed information about U.S. involvement in the coup.[38]

In Guatemala, *New York Times* correspondent Sydney Gruson was so critical of the new social democratic regime that it expelled him from the country for a few months. But when Gruson wrote a story suggesting that actions by the United States might provoke a nationalist response in Guatemala, CIA officials suspected him of sympathizing with the Guatemalan revolution. The agency asked the *Times* to remove Gruson from Guatemala, and the newspaper complied, according to *Times* historian Harrison Salisbury.[39]

U.S. involvement in the coup against the new Guatemalan government went unreported in the mainstream American press, as did CIA activities throughout the world in the 1950s. American reporters suppressed information about CIA actions in Indonesia, Indochina, and the Philippines. Several American reporters knew about the CIA's secret U-2 spy flights over the Soviet Union for two years before the Soviets shot down one of the planes in 1960 and caused a diplomatic crisis. These reporters never considered writing stories on the program until it became public knowledge.[40]

American reporting on the Bay of Pigs invasion is one of the most revealing cases of journalistic self-censorship. In November 1960, *The Nation* reported that the CIA had established a base in Guatemala where it was training Cuban counterrevolutionaries for an assault on Fidel Castro's government. The magazine notified all of the major news outlets. Most of the general media, however, contented themselves with reporting official denials. When one *New York Times* reporter, Tad Szulc, filed a detailed story on the invasion force, *Times* editors censored the story and did not give it prominent placement.[41] One of the editors involved in this decision, James Reston, would write a book six years later extolling the press's "tradition of reporting the facts, no matter how much they hurt."[42]

After the invasion failed, President John Kennedy warned journalists about the dangers of printing "national security" information. Kennedy reminded reporters that the United States was involved in an undeclared war with the Soviets and asked them to "heed the duty of self-restraint which that danger imposes upon all of us."[43] A few editorial boards made a "feeble" protest against this call for self-censorship, according to journalism historian James Aronson.[44] But most journalists seemed to agree with the president and CIA officials that the press had a responsibility to keep the agency's secrets.[45]

At the height of the Cold War, some journalists not only shared common assumptions with the CIA but also worked actively to further its objectives around the world. The number of journalists and news organizations that helped the CIA is hotly contested, partly because of the secrecy of the records and partly because of definitional battles over what it meant to "work" for the agency. Some media organizations provided "cover" for CIA personnel overseas by allowing CIA officers to pose as reporters, while others used stringers or freelancers who also worked part-time for the CIA. Other journalists received occasional gifts or reimbursements from the CIA in exchange for information. According to the Church committee's final report, approximately fifty U.S. journalists had covert relationships with the CIA, about half of which involved money.[46] Watergate investigative reporter Carl Bernstein charged that the total number of U.S. journalists who worked for the CIA was actually much higher. In a controversial article in *Rolling Stone*, Bernstein claimed that more than 400 American journalists secretly carried out assignments for the CIA from the early 1950s to the mid-1970s. The *New York Times* alone, Bernstein insisted, provided cover for ten CIA officers from 1950 to 1966.[47] Later investigations by *Times* reporters failed to locate the formal agreement that Bernstein claimed existed between the newspaper and the CIA. But the investigations did reveal that some *Times* stringers and staff members had also been paid workers for the agency.[48]

Even when a newspaper or network did not have a formal relationship with the CIA, the agency could still have close ties and mutual interests with its reporters and editors. The early CIA was renowned for recruiting from Ivy League schools. Top agency officials often had attended Princeton or Yale with the publishers or editors of eastern newspapers—and with their reporters as well. Prominent journalists were sometimes friends with CIA officials. For example, *Washington Post* editor Ben Bradlee's brother-in-law was covert operations chief Cord Meyer; *Post* publisher Phil Graham was a close friend of another covert operations chief, Frank Wisner; and the *New York Times* publishing family, the Sulzbergers, socialized with CIA directors Allen Dulles, John McCone, and Richard Helms.[49]

In short, the news media of the 1950s and 1960s had close links with the CIA as an institution and with the Ivy League alumni who ran it. They went to the same colleges, attended the same dinner parties, joined the same country clubs, and shared the same assumptions about the CIA's role in the world. They did not question the existence of the Communist threat or the need for absolute secrecy for the warriors who were fighting that threat. They were not necessarily *conscious* advocates of the Cold War national security consensus; but, as Kennett Love later remarked, "it was the ambient element you lived and worked in. Is a fish aware of water?"[50]

These journalists accepted the statement Richard Helms had made in a 1971 speech to newspaper editors that "the nation must, to a degree, take it on faith that we ... are *honorable men devoted to her service*."[51] Under these circumstances, the media were not likely to undertake an aggressive investigation of the CIA. They were even less likely to endorse an inquiry that could lead to the exposure of past CIA practices—practices such as the agency's use of the American press.

The cozy relationship between the press and the CIA might have continued indefinitely if not for the Vietnam War. In Vietnam, some American journalists first began to question the truthfulness of their government. They were shocked and disillusioned by the wide chasm between the government's official statements on the war and the daily reality they saw around them. "They could see what was really going on, and they refused, in their reporting, to fake it," wrote one of those correspondents, David Halberstam.[52]

The reporters initially found it hard to persuade their editors and producers back home that the government's spokesmen were lying. One such editor was Abe Rosenthal of the *New York Times*, a patriotic son of immigrants who had been expelled from Poland after World War II for his fiercely anticommunist reporting. In Rosenthal's view, one of his Vietnam correspondents wrote, "Communism in Poland and Communism in Indochina were the same."[53] Rosenthal was not alone: other media barons at *Time*, *Newsweek*, CBS, the *Washington Post*, and the *Times* strongly supported the war for several years. The *Post*'s editorialists, for example, were such powerful advocates of the war that they often did "a better job of explaining President Johnson's Far Eastern policies than the president himself," *Time* commented in 1966.[54]

But even the more conservative editors were influenced by the Tet offensive of 1968. The frightening scenes of the Viet Cong besieging the U.S. embassy in Saigon convinced many journalists that the war, if not wrong, was at least unwinnable. As Daniel Hallin's content analysis of television coverage of the Vietnam War has shown, editorial comments by television journalists were 4 to 1 in favor of White House policy before Tet; after March 1968, the ratio was 2 to 1 *against* the government.[55] Walter Cronkite's own pessimistic assessment after his tour of the Tet fighting showed that the mainstream press had turned against the president. It was not so much the actual fighting that distressed Cronkite as the government's lies.[56]

The press's new eagerness to challenge the government was further encouraged by the relaxation of tensions among the superpowers. While the U.S. government was proving itself less deserving of trust, the Communists at the same time seemed less of a threat. Nixon traveled to China in 1972, the United States and the Soviet Union signed the first Strategic Arms Limitations Treaty that same year, and "détente" became part of the 1970s vocabulary. Journalists found a new freedom to question the national security state and to demand that the curtain be lifted on the secret government.

That new freedom was first demonstrated in the Pentagon Papers case. When the *New York Times* and later the *Washington Post* decided to print the top secret study of the war commissioned by Defense Secretary Robert McNamara and leaked to them by Daniel Ellsberg, they crossed a "Rubicon" into a new world of aggressive journalism, according to *Times* reporter Harrison Salisbury.[57] By refusing to accept the government's definition of "secrecy," the newspapers signaled their commitment to a new, independent, and more powerful role for the nation's press.

After Vietnam and détente had weakened the media's deference to the executive branch, Watergate seemed to deliver the coup de grace. With the exception of the *Washington Post* and its two local reporters, Bob Woodward and Carl Bernstein, the press had been slow to realize the importance of the Watergate break-in. But once it became obvious that Nixon had lied to the nation—and to the media—many journalists grew much more skeptical of institutions and authority. Reporters often identified Watergate as a seminal event in their professional development. *Times* columnist Tom Wicker exulted in late 1973 in the new style of tough questioning of the president: "In the last few news conferences, for the first time in my experience, the press has suddenly become what it has touted itself to be all these years—an adversary."[58] Ben Bradlee summed up the changes in American journalism during a panel discussion in late 1973. "To be told when you ask, 'Is it true?'—that the question is character assassination, innuendo, and anyway it's not true, and told again and again that it's not true. And then it's true. That really does something to a man's soul—and to a woman's soul. And to a reporter's soul."[59]

It was against this background that Seymour Hersh's remarkable story appeared. "In it," CIA director Colby later recalled, "all the dreadful fears and suspicions about the CIA, which had been building for years, suddenly crystallized. It suggested a scandal equal in magnitude to the one that just recently had forced a president of the United States to resign on the verge of impeachment."[60] In the new age of "advocacy" or "adversarial" journalism, the CIA was a logical and tempting target.

Even as Vietnam and Watergate continued to transform American journalism, however, many prominent journalists viewed the changes with uncertainty and trepidation. The traditions of the recent past—deference, trust in official sources, a reluctance to challenge the national security mystique—retained their hold over many reporters and their bosses. In the first few months after Nixon's resignation, there were already signs of a coming backlash against the new era of investigative journalism.

Neoconservative intellectuals had criticized the media's emerging spirit of independence for several years. In an important 1971 article in *Commentary*, Daniel Patrick Moynihan claimed that the press had grown "more and more influenced by attitudes genuinely hostile to American society and American government." If the "culture of disparagement" did not end, he predicted, American democracy would be endangered.[61] These complaints in prestigious opinion journals increased during the Watergate scandal. In 1974, for example, Paul Weaver charged that the changes in journalism represented "an incipient retreat . . . from the entire liberal tradition of American journalism and the system of liberal democracy which it has fostered and served."[62]

Attacks on the press served a political purpose for policymakers and intellectuals on the right. By discrediting the men and women who had exposed the lies and scandals of the nation's governmental establishment, they hoped to rehabilitate the establishment itself. But many ordinary Americans also seemed uneasy about the media's role in bringing down a president. In June 1973, one-third of the American people agreed with Vice President Spiro Agnew's charges that the liberal press was out to get the president.[63] Shortly after Nixon's resignation, one angry reader, typical of many Americans who believed that the press had grown too powerful and adversarial, asked the editor of the *Washington Post*: "Now that the *Post* has dispatched Richard Nixon with one-sided journalism, what new crusade will the *Post* undertake?" Many Americans believed that the media had become "wholly unaccountable for their actions," the letter concluded.[64]

Some editors and publishers shared these concerns and truly believed that the profession needed to reform itself. Others worried more about the public's *perception* of their lack of accountability. Journalists were so concerned by the antipress backlash after Watergate, *Time* magazine declared in 1974, that "many are torn between self-congratulation and self-doubt."[65] As *Washington Post* publisher Katharine Graham said in a post-Watergate letter, "A lot of the administration mud and deliberate attacks on the press has stuck—people do think we are unfair and too powerful and that someone should control or at least judge us."[66]

Many publishers also had personal and ideological reasons for restraining their more aggressive reporters after Watergate. Adversarial reporters can offend advertisers, provoke costly libel suits, and anger news sources. They can also irritate the publishers' friends. As Tom Wicker has written, the press, as a member of the establishment, does not want to risk the establishment's disapproval. Elite journalists fear "not just government denunciation but a general attitude among 'responsible' people and groups, even other journalists, that to 'go too far' or 'get too involved' is bad for the country, not team play, not good form, not *responsible.*"[67]

Because of these deeply held beliefs, many editors and publishers grew apprehensive about the "advocacy journalism" of the 1970s. Echoing the concerns of policymakers and conservative intellectuals, some powerful journalists began to express doubts about the new trends.

Among the most prominent to voice this anxiety about the changes in journalism was a woman who had done much to bring them about: Katharine Graham. Woodward and Bernstein's boss caused a mild sensation in the fall of 1974 when she cautioned reporters against becoming too skeptical of officials and "too much a party to events, too much an actor in the drama." In an address before the Magazine Publishers Association, Graham warned the media that excessive distrust of the government could be dangerous: "To see conspiracy and cover-up in everything is as myopic as to believe that no conspiracies and cover-ups exist."[68]

In the same month, the editors of the *Columbia Journalism Review* expressed a similar concern that the press might "overreach" itself after Watergate. The magazine, published by the prestigious graduate school of journalism at Columbia University, noted that the press had been cast, by default, in the role of the political opposition during Vietnam and Watergate. As a result, politicians and judges might retaliate against the press, the editors wrote. They warned that the media could become too intoxicated with power—a hubris that could lead to a precipitous fall.[69]

Many members of the "fourth branch of government," in short, were afraid of appearing too adversarial and irresponsible. CBS reporter Daniel Schorr first noticed this on the night of Nixon's resignation. Early in the evening, CBS refused to air Schorr's "political obituary" on Nixon. He then overheard producers discussing the need to emphasize "nation-healing" stories. The network, relieved that Nixon had not launched a last-minute attack on his media enemies, decided to begin a "mission of conciliation" that night. Schorr, the CBS reporter most identified with the Watergate story, was not allowed to participate in the panel discussions of the resignation. His bosses apparently feared that he might seem too vindictive.[70]

Ben Bradlee, now retired from his job as editor of the *Washington Post*, has come to believe that the press in general and the *Post* in particular pulled back after Watergate. "I think the press was appalled at what had happened as a result of the Watergate investigation," he says. The

Post and its competitors "never had the slightest clue it would end with impeachment." Before Nixon's resignation, the press had not known the extent of its power—and after his resignation, it was not certain that it *wanted* that power. Subconsciously, editors began to limit the scope of their reporters' investigations. "Editors said, 'Let's watch out for reporters who try to act like Woodward and Bernstein,'" Bradlee notes.[71]

As one of the primary architects of Nixon's downfall, the *Washington Post* in particular wanted to appear responsible. William Greider, a former reporter for the *Post*, has written in a 1992 book that the *Post* took itself much more seriously after Nixon's resignation. "Watergate . . . ironically, became the high-water mark for Bradlee's provocative form of newspapering—the beginning of the *Post*'s retreat to a safer tradition," he claims.[72]

Other news organizations were also beginning to retreat to this safer tradition after Watergate. Many journalists did not want to treat their former friends in government like adversaries, Greider wrote in a 1975 magazine article. "There is a strong wish all over town, a palpable feeling that it would be nice if somehow this genie could be put back in the bottle. It is a nostalgic longing for the easy consensual atmosphere which once existed among the contending elements of Washington." As a result, Greider states, "the press especially tugs back and forth at itself, alternately pursuing the adrenal instincts unleashed by Watergate, the rabid distrust bred by a decade of out-front official lies, then abruptly playing the cozy lapdog."[73]

This ambivalence is illustrated by the coverage of the intelligence investigations of 1975. As Seymour Hersh and Daniel Schorr were enthusiastically gearing up for a post-Watergate investigative frenzy, other, more powerful voices in the press were calling for a retreat to the old norms of deference and objectivity. The final result would be disappointment for Hersh, disaster for Schorr, and victory for the advocates of a "responsible" press.

Many observers in Washington who are far from

naive about the CIA nevertheless consider its past

chiefs and most of its officials highly educated,

sensitive and dedicated public servants who would

scarcely let themselves get involved in the kind of

massive scheme described.

"Rattling Skeletons in the CIA Closet,"

Time, 6 January 1975

Trusting the "Honorable Men"

The Post-Watergate Press

and the CIA

According to standard accounts of the intelligence investigations, the sharks of the press reacted to Seymour Hersh's domestic spying exposé with a feeding frenzy that did not subside for nearly a year. CIA director William Colby recalls that "the media seized on the CIA with an investigative intensity and preoccupation comparable only to Watergate."[1] Other participants and scholars have also described the media's role in the scandal as uniformly aggressive, at least during the early stages.[2]

But a close analysis of the press coverage of the intelligence community in 1975 shows that the true picture is more complicated. Journalists reacted to Hersh's stories in different ways and at different paces. Many reporters and editors, acutely aware of their role in bringing down President Nixon, were afraid of the potential costs to the country and to their own profession if they continued to attack the government. They questioned whether the "sensitive and dedicated public servants" at the secret agencies deserved such treatment from the press. As reporters like Hersh tried to push the media to be more adversarial and aggressive, other journalists began to call for a return to a more "responsible," objective press—a press that respected and tried to stabilize the weakened national institutions.

When Hersh began checking into rumors about CIA domestic spying, he followed the tracks left by an internal agency inquiry. Ironically, the CIA itself had compiled the documentary evidence that would lead to the intelligence investigations and to the agency's greatest crisis. In the spring of 1973, Director of Central Intelligence James Schlesinger, who had replaced Richard Helms earlier that year, was infuriated to read in the newspaper that the CIA had helped some of the Watergate conspirators. Schlesinger himself had not known of this aid. As an outsider to the CIA, Schlesinger was already "hypersuspicious" of the old-boy network at the agency, according to his covert action chief, William Colby. He threatened to tear the place apart and "fire everyone if necessary" to find out if other grim surprises awaited him.[3]

Schlesinger and Colby issued a directive ordering all CIA employees to report to the director *any* questionable activities, past or present. They were stunned by the response. The resulting 693-page list included Operation CHAOS, the code name for the domestic spying program; the surveillance and bugging of American journalists; an illegal mail-opening program; drug experiments; and assassination plots, among other activities. Agency employees jokingly called the list "the family jewels."

Colby, who succeeded to the directorship when Schlesinger was named secretary of defense in June 1973, responded by writing several internal directives prohibiting such abuses in the future. He hoped that these directives would end the matter. He realized, however, that now that all of these secrets were gathered in one place, it was likely they would be discovered.

That likelihood increased when Seymour Hersh heard of the story. Regarded by many of his peers as the best investigative reporter in the world, Hersh never had any hesitation about going after the CIA—or any other powerful institution. He had quit the Associated Press in disgust in 1967 when his editors refused to run his investigative piece on U.S. chemical and biological warfare. As a freelancer, he had penetrated the secretive army bureaucracy to uncover the massacre at My Lai. He had established himself as the nemesis of one of the most powerful men in Washington, Henry Kissinger—a man he privately called a war criminal.

Although he described himself as a liberal, Hersh insisted that his political beliefs did not affect his reporting.[4] An aggressive, hyperactive, arrogant reporter, Hersh loved to expose wrongdoing in high places, whether it was the business world, the White House, or the intelligence community. "I'm a bitchy sort of kvetch sometimes. So maybe there is something in me that wants to make everybody else look bad," he told *Rolling Stone* in 1975. "It's not the world's worst fault."[5]

But Hersh was more than just a persistent "kvetch"; he also had a keen mind and a critical, some would say leftist, political outlook. Unlike many reporters, trained from journalism school to transmit rather than to challenge policymakers' opinions, Seymour Hersh analyzed the way his government worked—and found it wanting. Although many reporters fear expressing political opinions in public, Hersh spoke at anti–Vietnam War symposia, worked briefly for antiwar presidential candidate Eugene McCarthy, and participated in antiwar demonstrations. As an admiring reviewer of one of his later books concluded, "He believes that there is an objective truth that is independent of, and generally contrary to, the perceptions of high officials."[6] Bob Woodward, the *Washington Post*'s more conservative investigative journalist, described Hersh as "an old-line radical in a way." According to Woodward, Hersh was "interested more in the abuse of really big power, concentrated power, in the military and international capitalism. That's why he got so deep into the national-security stuff like the wiretaps and the plumbers."[7]

Indeed, Hersh had been fascinated by the national security state in general and the CIA in particular since the mid-1960s, collecting clippings, books, and sources. After the Watergate story began demanding less of his time in the spring of 1974, he started working in earnest on tips he received from inside the CIA, probably from disaffected, younger employees. As *New York Times* reporter and historian Harrison Salisbury has commented, it was as though Hersh had been "born" for this moment, "as though he could not wait for the end of Watergate and the advent of the Ford presidency to throw himself into the CIA story."[8] By the fall of 1974, after six months of intense reporting, Hersh believed that he had uncovered enough details of the agency's domestic spying program to write the story for which he had been preparing his entire career.

Hersh was confident that his employer would print his CIA exposé. At first glance, this confidence might seem misplaced. The *New York Times*, as noted in Chapter 1, had taken a hard-line, anticommunist stance during the Cold War and had formed at least an informal cooperative arrangement with the CIA during those years. But despite its cooperation with the agency, the *Times* in 1975 was actually the most likely mainstream vehicle for an investigative report on the CIA. Since the 1950s, the nation's most important newspaper had shown signs that it would not ignore improprieties and illegalities committed by the agency.

The *Times* put itself on the record in support of closer oversight of the CIA by Congress as early as 1954, when Senator Mike Mansfield introduced one of a series of bills to that effect.[9] The paper consistently maintained that position. Then in 1966, the *Times* created panic within the CIA when it launched the first mainstream press investigation of the agency. Managing editor Turner Catledge ordered the investigation in late 1965 after he heard of a CIA scandal in Singapore. Two bumbling CIA agents had been arrested when their lie detector machine, brought in to test a local source, blew a fuse in a hotel. Singapore's prime minister claimed that he had rejected a $3.3 million bribe from the CIA for the release of the agents. When the State Department first denied, then apologized for, the incident, Catledge was appalled by the government's incompetence and its lies. Was the CIA out of control, he wondered. He assigned his reporters to find out.[10]

More than twenty *Times* correspondents participated in the 1966 probe of the CIA. One of these reporters, Harrison Salisbury, proudly characterized the resulting series as "the first big venture by the *Times* into the new journalism of the sixties and seventies."[11] By today's standards, the series seems rather tame. Former CIA director John McCone read the articles before they were published, and the editors modified them in several places in line with his suggestions. Tom Wicker, the *Times* editor in charge of the series, later wrote that McCone did not have to argue to suppress much; there simply wasn't that much in the series "to cause the CIA undue alarm—much less to threaten national security."[12] Although the articles questioned whether the United States used too many "dirty tricks," the authors concluded that Kennedy had thoroughly reformed the agency after the Bay of Pigs. The CIA was described as a "tightly controlled" agency that performed a "vital and daily service as an accurate and encyclopedic source" of news and information.[13] Despite the mildness of the articles, however, the agency regarded any investigation of its duties as suspect, and CIA officials tried mightily to persuade the *Times* to suppress the series.[14]

Therefore the *Times*, despite its Cold War connections to the CIA, was a logical vehicle for Hersh's story. Similarly, Hersh's top editor, though an avid anticommunist, was in fact a likely man to approve publication of an exposé on domestic spying. Executive editor A. M. Rosenthal's feelings about the United States and its institutions "bordered on the reverential," according to David Halberstam.[15] He had been uneasy about publishing the Pentagon Papers and uncertain about committing resources to investigating Watergate. But Rosenthal considered himself a true antiauthoritarian who opposed all attacks on freedom and democracy, including those by the CIA.[16]

Rosenthal also had a less idealistic reason for wanting to print Hersh's exposé: he wanted to beat the *Washington Post*. During Watergate, many press critics had considered the *Times* the nation's number two newspaper. This had angered and frustrated the *Times* reporters and editors.[17] As a result, Rosenthal was inclined to give controversial reporters like Hersh—and, in foreign affairs, Cambodian correspondent Sydney Schanberg—more latitude in these early post-Watergate days than he would allow a few years later.[18] Hersh, Rosenthal once said, "is like a puppy that isn't quite housebroken, but as long as he's pissing on Ben Bradlee's carpet, let him go."[19]

When Hersh was not given as much space for his story as he wanted, he complained to Rosenthal. Rosenthal gave him an entire page. Hersh later said that the paper was very supportive of his exposé. "I didn't have people cluck-clucking, or saying, 'Is this gonna be good for America?' They said, 'This is too important; we've gotta publish it.' And they published it, as simple as that."[20]

It was lucky for Hersh that his editors gave him so much support, because he received almost none from his colleagues in the print media. Although Hersh's reporting would be vindicated later in the investigations, his early determination to carry the Watergate mentality into the post-Watergate era made his colleagues uncomfortable and even angry.

Hersh's first story on 22 December charged that a special unit of the CIA had conducted a "massive" spying program against domestic antiwar groups and collected files on 10,000 American citizens. The story alluded to the "family jewels," the list of "dozens" of other illegal CIA activities including mail opening, wiretaps, and break-ins that Schlesinger had compiled.[21] This initial article did not name specific groups or individuals who had been the targets of domestic spying. A week later, however, Hersh provided a fairly detailed case study of CIA surveillance of dissidents in New York City in the late 1960s and early 1970s.[22]

Hersh remembers well his colleagues' reactions to his stories. "I was reviled," he comments with more than a hint of satisfaction.[23] As *Times* reporter Harrison Salisbury has written, the journalists of Washington "did not rush to verify" the charges. "Instead word circulated in Georgetown that Hersh had put the *Times* out on a limb. Ben Bradlee of the Washington *Post* had said, so the gossip went, that Sy's story was overwritten and under-researched."[24] Hersh's competitor on the intelligence beat at the *Washington Post*, Laurence Stern, wrote an article on Hersh's stories for the *Columbia Journalism Review* under the condescending headline "Exposing the CIA (Again)." Stern criticized Hersh for the "dearth of hard facts," which "stood in sharp contrast to the article's page-one display." Furthermore, Stern wrote, Hersh had followed his initial story with a "remarkably febrile succession of follow-ups."[25] Stern's employer, the *Post*, editorialized that the *Times* had used too many anonymous sources—a surprising charge from the newspaper that had relied on Deep Throat.[26]

Newsweek agreed that Hersh's stories were "sparse in detail" and quoted several sources scoffing at his revelations. "There's something to Hersh's charges, but a hell of a lot less than he makes of it," one source said.[27] *Time* magazine was the most blunt of Hersh's critics, suggesting that "there is a strong likelihood that Hersh's CIA story is considerably exaggerated and that the *Times* overplayed it." *Time* reminded its readers that Hersh had made "one beaut of a mistake" the year before when he reported that John Dean had not implicated Nixon in the Watergate cover-up.[28]

CIA officials and conservative columnists also attacked Hersh by name, with James Kilpatrick claiming that since "no one ever named Hersh a federal judge," he had no right to call CIA acts illegal.[29] CIA counterintelligence chief James Angleton, who was fired by Colby shortly after the Hersh stories broke (though for unrelated reasons), got even more personal. Not content with calling Hersh a "son-of-a-bitch," he implied that the reporter was making money off the articles and criticized Hersh's writing and his allegedly poor speech.[30]

The anonymous intelligence sources quoted in *Time*, *Newsweek*, and the *Washington Post* agreed that Hersh had exaggerated a simple "jurisdictional" problem between the CIA and the FBI, with the CIA straying into a "gray area" in its charter when it could not cooperate with the FBI on counterintelligence. The *Post* and columnist Jack Anderson even suggested that the thousands of alleged CIA files on American citizens had been developed originally by the Justice Department and given to the CIA only when the individuals involved went overseas.[31] The *Post's* editorial board warned of confusing these jurisdictional problems with illegalities. Through the strategic placement of quotation marks, the *Post* questioned the credibility of Hersh's reports: "While almost any CIA activity can be fitted under the heading of 'spying,' and while CIA activities undertaken on American soil can be called 'domestic spying,' it remains to be determined which of these activities has been conducted in 'violation' of the agency's congressional charter or are 'illegal.' "[32] Later, when Hersh was unexpectedly denied a Pulitzer Prize for the story, conservative columnist John D. Lofton wrote that the Pulitzer jury had turned down the story because it was "over-written, overplayed, under-researched and underproven."[33]

Television reports on the domestic spying charges were also skeptical of Hersh's stories. The *CBS Evening News*, the highest-rated news program of that era, emphasized denials by agency officials and, at this early stage, did not encourage its own reporters to advance the story. Intelligence reporter Daniel Schorr gave a rather sympathetic report on the fired head of counterintelligence, James Angleton.[34] Commentator Eric Sevareid, the CBS equivalent of a columnist, tempered his call for an investigation of the *Times* charges with the observation that "old hands here" doubted that the CIA had threatened Americans' civil liberties.[35]

Although Hersh's fellow investigative reporters did not rush to confirm his story, he did find vindication in a different—and completely unexpected—quarter: the CIA itself. William Colby acknowledged to the Senate on 15 January 1975 that the agency had indeed sent out undercover agents to infiltrate dissident groups in this country and had collected close to 10,000 files on American citizens.[36] Although Colby flatly denied the accusations in the *Times* story in his statement—clinging to the position that the extent of this domestic spying was not "massive"— his remarks corroborated the essence of Hersh's revelations. The *Washington Post* reported that Colby's disclosure had "confirmed major elements" of Hersh's stories, and *Newsweek* agreed that Colby's testimony had substantiated "many basic elements of the original story—if not all the adjectives."[37] The adjective in question was, of course, "massive," and no one in the intelligence community, the executive branch, or the news media, except for the *Times*, would ever concede that Hersh was correct in using it. The blue-ribbon panel appointed by President Gerald Ford to investigate the charges, however, would later use the words "considerable," "large-scale," and "substantial."

Despite this confirmation, the other elite media outlets still did not join the *Times*'s crusade. From the time Hersh's first story appeared on 22 December until the end of January, CBS News aired only fifteen stories on the scandal, none of which gained billing as the top story of the newscast. *Time* and *Newsweek* ran one or two stories per week through the end of January, but neither magazine featured the scandal on its cover.

Many observers were particularly surprised by the rather passive performance of the newspaper most identified with Watergate and the revival of adversarial journalism, the *Washington Post*. During the first six weeks after Hersh's stories appeared, the *Post* ran only thirty-nine CIA-related stories compared to the *Times*'s sixty-four. Moreover, the *Times* stories were generally longer, were displayed more prominently, and were echoed by hard-hitting editorials inside.

William Safire, a conservative *New York Times* columnist who had served in the Nixon administration, was appalled by the *Post*'s lack of enterprise on the CIA scandal. "With heavy heart," Safire wrote, the *Post* "trudges along after the *New York Times* on the CIA probe, reminding us constantly of the danger of doing damage to institutions in all this investigating of past abuses." With Nixon gone, Safire charged bitterly, the thrill was gone for the investigative journalists at the *Post*.[38]

But finally, on 19 January, nearly a month after Hersh's first story was published, the *Post* displayed some initiative in exposing improprieties and abuses in an intelligence agency. This time, however, the agency in question was the FBI, not the CIA.

Confirming rumors that had circulated for years, reporter Ronald Kessler revealed that the FBI under J. Edgar Hoover had compiled files on the personal lives of congressmen. For the first time, two former Hoover assistants were willing to go on the record verifying the charges.[39] A week later, the *Post* further disclosed that the FBI had wiretapped Martin Luther King, Jr., at the 1964 Democratic convention.[40]

The *Post*'s decision to go after the FBI rather than the CIA is revealing. The bureau, by and large, had been as free from press scrutiny as the CIA during the height of the Cold War. A few journalists, notably Fred Cook, author of an exposé for *The Nation*, had written of the FBI's abuses throughout the 1950s and 1960s. As Arthur Schlesinger, Jr., has observed, however, "one would search the *New York Times* and *Washington Post*, *Time* and *Newsweek* of the 1950s in vain for the exposure and disapproval such journals lavished on Hoover twenty years later."[41] For example, in 1954 *Post* publisher Phil Graham refused to print an editorial criticizing the FBI written by his famed editorialist, Alan Barth.[42] In 1964, Ben Bradlee, then at *Newsweek*, learned of the FBI's bugging and harassment of Martin Luther King, Jr. Bradlee warned the president (who, unbeknownst to Bradlee, already knew about and approved of the program) but did not write a story.

Now, more than ten years later, managing editor Bradlee finally decided to run the story. Certainly much had happened in the years between 1964 and 1975 to change his opinion of the newsworthiness of FBI improprieties. Vietnam and Watergate had given Bradlee a broader view of the public's "right to know." And Hoover, who had died three years earlier, was no longer as revered as he had been in 1964.

But the *Post*'s decision to give the story such prominence at this time was undoubtedly related to its rivalry with the *Times*. At first, the *Post* had tried to deny that it had been scooped by its rival by downplaying Hersh's stories; now it attempted to get back in the game by coming up with a new angle.

The FBI angle was not only new but also safer. Throughout the investigations, both journalists and congressmen would find it much easier to attack the FBI than the CIA. In 1975, the FBI's responsibilities for countering the demoralized remnants of domestic communism did not seem as essential as the CIA's foreign duties. Moreover, official sources had recently admitted that the FBI had used improper and illegal methods in the 1950s and 1960s. In 1971, after activists had stolen and then made public documentary proof of the bureau's "counterintelligence" programs against domestic dissidents, the attorney general had condemned the programs.

As Taylor Branch has noted, abuses like the bugging of Martin Luther King, Jr., and maintaining files on congressmen were clear violations of the FBI's high standards.[43] It was difficult to argue that the bureau was not violating the law or the bounds of propriety by bugging a civil rights leader. By contrast, it was harder to define what constituted a "violation" or "illegality" by the CIA, an agency designed for deceit and dirty tricks.

The *Post* had reshaped the "year of intelligence" by adding the FBI to the investigative agenda. Up to this point, the spotlight had been on the

CIA alone. Now Congress would be sure to scrutinize all intelligence agencies as it embarked on a historic investigation.

Why were Hersh's colleagues so skeptical of his trailblazing scoop? Why were they so determined to knock down a story that, if true, had such momentous implications for the future control of the nation's intelligence community?

Some journalists may have attacked the reports simply because they did not like Seymour Hersh. Hersh himself admits that he has a healthy ego: "I'm perfectly more than aware of my talents. I mean, I'm not retiring, I can be awfully difficult."[44] It was tempting for journalists who had been beaten by an arrogant competitor to belittle that competitor's work.

These journalists' perception of Hersh as their competitor rather than their colleague is also crucial to understanding their response. It was embarrassing to miss such a significant story; that embarrassment could be lessened if Hersh's rivals could show that the story was not so important. *Post* ombudsman Charles B. Seib, who criticized his newspaper for its sparse domestic spying coverage, concluded that the *Post* had underplayed the story mainly because of its reluctance to credit its rival.[45]

In addition, the type of story Hersh wrote—with its anonymous sources and alarming conclusions—was difficult to duplicate. Hersh had spent years developing his sources. The reporters competing with him could not quickly come up with their own sources, nor could they obtain a secret agency phone directory and randomly call CIA officers to verify the story. They could only report what was being said publicly. And the agency's defenders made certain that there were plenty of public denials to report.

Moreover, many reporters did not seem to *want* to believe that Hersh's reporting was accurate. Like the journalists at *Time* who found it hard to believe that the "highly educated" officials at the CIA would permit any abuses, many reporters and editorial writers preferred to trust the "honorable men" rather than their own colleagues.

Times reporter Leslie Gelb, struggling to understand the harsh reaction to Hersh, concluded that the domestic spying stories endangered many deeply held beliefs of the establishment press. "For these people what Hersh was attacking was not simply the agency, but a history going back to the days of the OSS, a culture, and highly prized, long-established social relationships. Theirs was a reaction of sentimentality, of a world being destroyed."[46] For journalists who had done favors for the

CIA in the 1950s, who had gone to the same schools and the same parties as top CIA officials, it was hard to believe that these men could be threatening the Republic. It was one thing to attack Richard Nixon; Richard Helms, and all he symbolized, was another matter.

Finally, many reporters seemed to believe that Hersh was endangering not only the nation but also the profession of journalism. After Watergate, the press felt exposed and vulnerable. Conservatives charged that the media were responsible for the fall of a president; media critics worried that journalists had abandoned their proper "objective" role. Now muckrakers like Hersh were giving these critics new ammunition.

This widespread anxiety about the aggressiveness of the post-Watergate press was vividly demonstrated in the pages of the *Columbia Journalism Review*, the profession's most prominent journal. In the midst of the intelligence investigations, the review printed a polemic by a liberal and a good friend of the press, J. William Fulbright. The senator, whose hearings on the Vietnam War had done much to create the current cynical attitude toward government, passionately urged journalists to abandon what he called their "inquisition psychology." Among other things, Fulbright was worried by the exposure of the CIA. The revelations may be true, he said, "but I have come to feel of late that these are not the kind of truths we most need now; these are truths which must injure if not kill the nation." Instead, the American people required "restored stability and confidence," he argued. No matter how many skeletons still lurked in the closet, the media should exercise "voluntary restraint" and reaffirm their "social contract" with the government and the public.[47]

Seymour Hersh, always an iconoclastic and abrasive reporter, was pushing the tolerance of men like Senator Fulbright to the limit. This frightened Hersh's colleagues; they believed that his muckraking crusades were bad for the country and bad for the profession. Hersh was attacking not just one individual president but the very institutions of the national security state. The implications of Hersh's stories were far greater than those of Watergate. Hersh seemed to be implying that it wasn't just Nixon but the entire system that was out of control. The "stain of Watergate," Leslie Gelb noted, was "spreading out to the past, to the pre-Nixon years, and to the future. The dream of being able to make Nixon vanish and keep almost everything else intact was coming into jeopardy."[48] If the nation and the professional standing of journalists were to survive in these perilous times, the establishment press was apparently saying, then investigative journalists had better stop attacking the "honorable men" of the CIA.

Rarely has a journalistic enterprise been rewarded

by such a swift and dramatic flow of governmental

responses.

Laurence Stern, "Exposing the CIA (Again)"

The Meat Ax or the Scalpel?

The Congressional

Investigations Begin

Seymour Hersh's competitors may have belittled his domestic spying exposé, but that did not prevent many alarmed policymakers from believing the stories. Angry congressmen expressed shock and outrage over Hersh's revelations. They demanded Justice Department investigations, special congressional inquiries, and the resignation of former CIA director Richard Helms from his ambassadorial post in Iran. The press had exposed the abuses; now it was up to the policymakers in the White House and on Capitol Hill to investigate those abuses and suggest remedies.

While four standing committees announced that they would launch inquiries, Senate majority leader Mike Mansfield predicted that in January the new Congress would appoint a special investigating panel. The opinion pages of the *Washington Post* and the *New York Times* were filled with speculation on the far-reaching reforms these committees might propose.

The two houses of Congress had differing views on the extent of the reforms needed, however. The Senate shared the desire of most of the establishment press to stabilize the nation's institutions. But many members of the House, more affected by the changes in the political culture, tried to sustain the spirit of Watergate and strictly limit all forms of secrecy in government. These divergent approaches would lead to very different outcomes for the two investigations.

By demanding an investigation of an executive agency, congressmen were exercising an important duty of the legislative branch. One of Congress's most significant functions in the system of constitutional checks and balances is to oversee the president's bureaucracy. As Morris Ogul has written, legislative oversight is "one means by which competitive leadership can remain a reality in American politics."[1]

Congressional oversight of the CIA, however, had always been "sporadic, unsystematic, incomplete," according to historian Harry Howe Ransom.[2] The Armed Services and Appropriations Committees of both houses had oversight subcommittees, but these panels met infrequently, had little or no staff, and never issued reports on their findings until Watergate. When Frank Church entered the Senate in 1956, he later recalled, "some of those senior senators who did have this so-called watchdog committee were known to say in effect: 'We don't watch the dog. We don't know what's going on, and furthermore, we don't want to know.'"[3] One overseer, Republican senator Leverett Saltonstall, once commented: "It is not a question of reluctance on the part of CIA officials to speak to us. Instead it is a question of our reluctance, if you will, to seek information and knowledge on subjects which I personally . . . would rather not have."[4] Ransom concluded in 1975 that the committees "appear to have been co-opted by the intelligence system and do not seem to function as independent critics."[5]

This lethargic attitude toward intelligence oversight did not go entirely unchallenged. A few congressmen had tried over the years to expand and improve the oversight system, introducing more than 400 bills on this subject between 1947 and 1974.[6] None of these attempts was successful, however, partly because of the irresponsibility of one of the CIA's early congressional opponents. In 1954, Senator Joseph McCarthy threatened to investigate the CIA as part of his crusade to expose Communists in government. President Eisenhower deflected McCarthy's demand for a congressional CIA investigation, but the specter of the Wisconsin Republican's reckless and destructive investigations of the executive branch would haunt Congress for years. Eisenhower started the popular executive practice of charging would-be congressional investigators with "McCarthyism."

One such investigator was Mike Mansfield of Montana. In the 1955–56 legislative session, the freshman senator proposed that a joint congressional committee to oversee the CIA be created. This committee, similar in structure and concept to the Joint Committee on Atomic Energy, would have a permanent staff and subpoena power. Initially, thirty-four senators cosponsored Mansfield's bill. But Eisenhower vehemently opposed it, claiming that McCarthyites would dominate the committee.[7] The president's opposition convinced fourteen cosponsors of the bill—all but one of whom were Republicans—to change their minds and oppose the measure. Ultimately, the bill was defeated by a 59–27 vote, with liberal Democrats and right-wing McCarthyites forming an uneasy and unsuccessful alliance in support of greater oversight.[8]

Ten years later, another congressional initiative to strengthen CIA oversight reached the Senate floor. Senator Eugene McCarthy sponsored a bill in 1966 to add three members from the liberal Foreign Relations Committee to the existing oversight subcommittees. McCarthy's effort, however, gained the support of only twenty-eight senators. Once again, a majority of senators agreed that the existing "watchdog" subcommittees were adequate.[9]

Congress's failure to monitor the intelligence agencies was just one example of its increasing reluctance to challenge the executive branch. Since World War II, the rise of what Arthur Schlesinger, Jr., has called "the imperial presidency" had steadily eroded Congress's power.[10] With the advent of the Cold War and the nuclear age, President Harry Truman and his successors made unilateral foreign policy decisions, withheld information from Congress, and centralized power under the president's control.

As James Sundquist has demonstrated, however, Congress often gave up its power willingly. Legislators realized that they could not act as quickly or as efficiently as the executive branch; furthermore, they did not want to take responsibility for potentially controversial foreign policy decisions.[11]

As the president grew more powerful and Congress more deferential, the legislative branch proved increasingly unwilling to investigate the executive branch. Of thirty-one congressional probes from 1946 to 1990 studied by David Mayhew, sixteen took place under Truman and Eisenhower, ten under Kennedy/Johnson and Nixon/Ford, and only five under Carter, Reagan, and Bush.[12]

Mayhew also discerned an interesting trend within this overall decline. He found two "clusters" of investigations in which congressmen "waged assaults against U.S. national-security policy and the central state apparatus that presidents had been using to conduct it."[13] The first cluster took place from 1948 to 1954, as conservatives questioned the loyalty of executive branch bureaucrats. The second occurred from 1966 to 1975, as liberals attacked the imperial presidency. The Indochina hearings conducted by Senator William Fulbright, the Watergate hearings, and the intelligence investigations fit into this second cluster.

This second series of inquiries was sparked by congressional anger over repeated attempts by the executive branch to increase its powers. President Nixon had challenged Congress by impounding appropriated funds, secretly bombing Cambodia, and asserting unlimited executive privilege. The CIA itself had angered many members of Congress by its secret actions in Indochina and by withholding crucial information about Watergate. Political scientists agree that if congressmen do not trust a particular agency, they will oversee it more vigilantly.[14] After years of acquiescence, many in Congress were now ready to begin a new, more aggressive era of oversight.

Viewed in this perspective, the Church and Pike committees represented the last major battle of a liberal crusade against executive branch secrecy. This crusade began with Vietnam, continued through Watergate, and ended with an assault on the institutions of secrecy themselves.

Congress's first serious attempt to limit the post-Vietnam CIA came in 1973, as legislators angrily reasserted their power against a deceitful and discredited executive. A bipartisan group of senators, hoping to restrict the president's power to conduct military operations without congressional approval, introduced the War Powers Bill. Senator Tom Eagleton objected, however, that the bill had a major loophole: it did not apply to the nation's secret warriors. He introduced an amendment to extend it to include the CIA. When his amendment was decisively defeated, the Missouri senator decided to oppose the bill, arguing that it was useless without constraints on the CIA.[15]

Although the CIA easily survived this first salvo, it would continue to fight a defensive battle against congressional assaults for the next two years. In 1974, Senator Howard Baker and Representative Lucien Nedzi headed separate inquiries into the agency's murky role in Watergate. Neither committee was able to solve this mystery definitively. But Baker's report implied that there was a good deal more to the CIA's involvement in the scandal than was then known. Baker believes that his report was the beginning of a new era of congressional oversight of intelligence. "I don't think there ever would have been a Church committee without that [report]," he says.[16] When hawkish Republicans like Howard Baker doubted the CIA's truthfulness, the agency had good reason to worry.[17]

Then in the fall of 1974, Seymour Hersh revealed that the White House and the CIA had lied to Congress about U.S. involvement in Chile. Mike Mansfield, now Senate majority leader, tried to use Congress's outrage over Chile to win approval for another of his periodic proposals to increase oversight of the CIA and to investigate the intelligence community. This time a liberal Republican, Charles Mathias, cosponsored his effort. Other congressmen introduced similar proposals.

Two liberal legislators, Senator James Abourezk of South Dakota and Representative Elizabeth Holtzman of New York, attempted to do more than investigate: they wanted to ban all covert operations. Abourezk believed that the CIA would never inform Congress of its most secret actions, even if the oversight system were reformed. So, he concluded, "since they are never going to tell us, the only real alternative is to take away their money, abolish their operations so that we shall never have that kind of immoral, illegal activity committed in the name of the American people."[18] Abourezk's bill gained the support of only seventeen senators. Holtzman's similar bill in the House lost 291–108.[19]

Although the Ninety-third Congress refused to ban covert actions, it did decide to enact the toughest oversight bill in history. The Hughes-Ryan amendment to the Foreign Assistance Act, named after Representative Leo Ryan and Senator Harold Hughes, expanded the number of congressional committees to be briefed by the CIA from four to six, adding the more liberal Senate Foreign Relations and House Foreign Affairs Committees to the list. Most important, the amendment attempted to improve accountability by requiring the president to make a "finding" that covert action was necessary for national security before reporting it "in a timely fashion" to the six committees. It was widely understood that this meant within forty-eight hours.

The Hughes-Ryan amendment was more significant than anything that would later come out of the Pike and Church committees. It substantially increased the amount of control Congress exercised over the CIA and, indirectly, the nation's foreign policy. By forcing the CIA to brief six (and later eight) congressional committees, and by demanding timely notification of covert actions, the Hughes-Ryan amendment gave Congress more oversight power than it had possessed before—or than it would have after the amendment was gutted in 1980.

Yet this amendment passed almost unnoticed by the press—and, more important, by the White House. Neither the Ford administration nor the CIA made any serious effort to organize opposition to the amendment. One Republican moderate on the House-Senate conference committee was amazed by the lack of resistance to the sweeping proposal. "They [the White House] were shell-shocked from the Chilean exposé, and just couldn't come to grips with the fact that in this thing they were playing with fire," he told conservative columnists Rowland Evans and Robert Novak.[20] Indeed, Henry Kissinger, the president's chief foreign policy adviser, was more worried by the Foreign Assistance Act's limits on aid to Cambodia and Chile and its threatened cutoff of aid to Turkey than the expanded reporting requirements for covert action. Kissinger did suggest that Ford consider vetoing the measure because of several "deficiencies," including the Hughes-Ryan amendment. CIA director William Colby also wrote to Ford expressing concerns about the reporting requirements. But the president, deciding that this was the best foreign aid bill he could get out of a hostile Congress, signed it into law.[21]

The swift, almost unchallenged passage of this radical expansion of congressional oversight illustrates the extraordinary opportunity for change that existed in the fall of 1974. Congress was on the attack, while the CIA was weak and battered. The White House also felt besieged and demoralized, unable to mount an effective defense against a historic erosion of its foreign policy powers. When the Church and Pike committees issued their reports in a much different climate some fifteen months later, they must have longed for that immediate post-Watergate atmosphere.

In late 1974, as the *New York Times* edition carrying Seymour Hersh's domestic spying series hit the streets, Congress was prepared to act. It had seen the CIA misused—or out of control—in Vietnam, in Watergate, and in Chile. Congress had shown its willingness to impose controls on the agency by passing the Hughes-Ryan amendment. Now Hersh's stories would provide the final incentive to launch special investigations.

President Ford heard of the *New York Times* exposé on his way to a skiing vacation in Vail, Colorado. At first, he seemed to hope that the scandal would disappear on its own, without tainting the office of the president. A frantic Colby found the silence from Vail "deafening" and concluded that the White House was "going to draw the wagons around—leaving me isolated and exposed on the outside."[22] But when it became obvious that Congress planned to respond whether the president did or not, Ford's aides began to worry about the consequences of leaving the investigation to the post-Watergate Congress.

Gerald Ford had not been responsible for what Colby called "almost thirty years of CIA's sins."[23] But he was also not inclined to let his former colleagues in Congress attack what he considered to be an essential guardian of the nation's security. As a congressman, Ford had been a member of the intelligence oversight subcommittee of the House Appropriations Committee from 1956 to 1965. He had taken pride in belonging to the privileged club that knew some of the CIA's secrets.[24] Like all congressional overseers of the time, he did not look at those secrets too closely. Ford also enjoyed a close relationship with the FBI, which had helped to arrange support for his first campaign in 1946. He had served as J. Edgar Hoover's informant on the Warren Commission inquiry into John F. Kennedy's assassination and had received the bureau's help during his unsuccessful effort to impeach liberal Supreme Court justice William O. Douglas in 1970.[25]

In public, Congressman Ford had always been quick to defend what he regarded as the nation's frontline troops in the Cold War. Although the CIA had experienced "difficulties and failures," he assured one constituent in 1967, it also had made "a major contribution to the well-being of our nation in this critical 'Cold War' era."[26] In a 1967 newsletter to his constituents, Ford criticized those who had revealed the CIA's ties to domestic organizations. He wrote: "To 'expose' and condemn the CIA and call for major restrictions may only weaken a necessary international operation. As one who served for some years on the congressional committee supervising the CIA, I can say that I have more confidence in the patriotism and competence of men like Allen Dulles, John McCone, Admiral W. F. Raborn and Richard Helms than I have in some of those

Americans who delight in 'exposing' the CIA."[27] Ford's position in 1975 would be essentially the same.

However, Congressman Ford was not always a defender of the CIA's right to absolute secrecy. As an overseer, he believed that the select group of men responsible for oversight should be trusted, and he was enraged when they were not. In 1962, the office of General Lyman Lemnitzer, the chairman of the Joint Chiefs of Staff, infuriated Ford by deleting some of his questions on the U-2 spy plane program from the transcript of a defense appropriations hearing. The deletion implied that Ford was disclosing secret information. In response, Ford delivered an impassioned speech on the House floor proclaiming that "the dissemination of information on governmental activities" was a "vital cornerstone of any free society." Ford charged that the deletion of his questions seemed "like the attempt of the totalitarian government described in George Orwell's book '1984' to rewrite history to suit the viewpoint of the government."[28]

Ford was upset because Lemnitzer's office had questioned his own patriotism and judgment. In this case, he believed, the censors had clearly gone too far. But throughout his congressional and presidential careers, Ford always believed in keeping "national security" secrets from people with less discretion than himself.

The Ninety-fourth Congress was in that category, Ford believed. Conservative senator Barry Goldwater called the new Congress that took office in January 1975 "probably the most dangerous Congress" the country had ever known.[29] The "fighting Ninety-fourth" Congress, as it was called, had been elected in November 1974, just three months after President Nixon resigned. Ten new senators won seats in that election, but the greatest changes occurred in the House. Not only did the Democrats hold an overwhelming advantage of 291–144 in the House, but they also had within their ranks 75 freshmen determined to exert their new power against the executive—and against the traditional, hierarchical Democratic leadership. As the House organized for the next term, these upstart freshmen combined to shake up business as usual in Washington. The Democratic insurgents deposed four elderly committee chairmen, including longtime CIA friend and overseer Edward Hébert of the Armed Services Committee. William Colby watched this Congress with growing dread. The new members, he wrote, seemed "exultant in the muscle that they had used to bring a President down, willing and able to challenge the Executive as well as its own Congressional hierarchy, intense over morality in government, [and] extremely sensitive to press and public pressures."[30]

The White House did not want this newly powerful and radicalized Ninety-fourth Congress to investigate and reform the executive branch's secret agencies. Ford later said in his memoirs that he feared a congressional investigation would result in "unnecessary disclosures" that could "cripple" the CIA.[31] He and his aides quickly decided that "distancing" the White House from the scandal was not enough. The president needed to preempt a congressional inquiry.

Beyond his ideological reasons for opposing a CIA investigation, Ford was also influenced by partisan and institutional considerations. Hersh's initial stories had accused Richard Nixon's CIA of domestic spying—not Lyndon Johnson's CIA or John Kennedy's CIA. If, indeed, the improprieties took place on the Republicans' watch, then too much attention to these charges could hasten the GOP's post-Watergate slide and boost the careers of crusading Democrats. Ford also opposed wide-ranging investigations because he felt responsible for protecting the presidency. "I was absolutely dedicated to doing whatever I could to restore the rightful prerogatives of the presidency under the constitutional system," he recalls.[32] His aides list Ford's renewal of presidential power after Watergate as one of the greatest achievements of his administration.[33] This lifelong conservative believed that he had a duty to control the congressional investigators and restore the honor of his new office.

Within days of Hersh's first story, Ford's aides recommended that he set up an executive branch investigative commission to avoid "finding ourselves whipsawed by prolonged Congressional hearings."[34] In a draft memo to the president written on 27 December, Deputy Chief of Staff Richard Cheney explained that the president had several reasons to establish such a commission: to avoid being put on the defensive, to minimize "damage" to the CIA, to head off "Congressional efforts to further encroach on the executive branch," to demonstrate presidential leadership, and to reestablish Americans' faith in their government.[35]

Ford's aides cautioned that this commission, formally called the Commission on CIA Activities within the United States, must not appear to be "a 'kept' body designed to whitewash the problem."[36] But Ford apparently did not follow this advice. His choice for chairman, Vice President Nelson Rockefeller, had served as a member of the President's Foreign Intelligence Advisory Board, which monitored the CIA. Members Erwin Griswold, Lane Kirkland, Douglas Dillon, and Ronald Reagan had all been privy to CIA secrets in the past or noted for their strong support of governmental secrecy.

In a revealing move, the president also appointed General Lyman

President Gerald Ford meets with Vice President Nelson Rockefeller in the Oval Office in December 1974. (Courtesy Gerald R. Ford Library)

Lemnitzer, the same chairman of the Joint Chiefs whose office in 1962 had been charged by Congressman Jerry Ford with a "totalitarian" attempt to suppress information. In short, Ford's commissioners did not seem likely to conduct an aggressive investigation. Of the "true-blue-ribbon" panel's eight members, only John Connor, a commerce secretary under Lyndon Johnson, and Edgar Shannon, a former president of the University of Virginia, brought open minds to the inquiry, according to critics.[37]

Many congressmen, including GOP senators Howard Baker and Lowell Weicker, found the commission inadequate. Some supporters of the CIA, such as columnist Joseph Kraft, worried that many Americans would view the commission as part of a White House cover-up. Although Kraft personally admired the commissioners, he feared that their findings would not be credible and therefore would not reduce "the terrible doubts which continue to eat away at the nation."[38] A public opinion poll confirmed these reservations. Forty-nine percent of the people surveyed by Louis Harris believed that an executive commission would be too influenced by the White House, compared with 35 percent who supported Ford's action. A clear plurality—43 percent—believed that the commission would turn into "another cover-up," while 33 percent had confidence in the commission and 24 percent were unsure.[39] The *New York Times* editorial board, also suspicious of the panel, urged congressmen not to allow the commission to "become a pretext to delay or circumscribe their own independent investigation."[40] A week later, the *Times* again reminded Congress of its duty to conduct a "long, detailed" examination of the intelligence community: "Three decades is too long for any public institution to function without a fundamental reappraisal of its role."[41]

The fighting Ninety-fourth was listening. Shortly after the new Congress was sworn in, the House and Senate moved to establish special investigating committees. Although both houses were determined to mount thorough investigations, they took markedly different approaches. The Senate, with only one-third of its seats up for reelection in 1974, had fewer post-Watergate reformers who wanted to make radical changes. In addition, because they represented larger and more diverse constituencies, the senators had to be more moderate in their approach. Throughout the entire inquiry, the Senate investigators proved more willing to compromise and more determined to attain bipartisan agreement. By contrast, the House investigators, whose two-year terms made them more accountable to their smaller and more uniform districts, were less accommodating and more partisan.

The Senate acted quickly, taking a final vote to create a special committee on 27 January. During the two-hour debate, both Democrats and Republicans tried to find common ground. Most Senate Democrats echoed John Pastore's call to use the investigation to strengthen "the confidence of the people" in the intelligence agencies, "these great arms of Government."[42] The American people had lost faith in the CIA and the FBI, several senators contended, and a congressional investigation was the only way to regain their trust. As moderate Democrat Walter Huddleston of Kentucky said, "In this year—so soon after Watergate—we cannot leave in doubt the operations and activities of agencies involved in such sensitive and significant endeavors."[43] The Democrats, in short, were conscious of the need to sell the investigation as a means to restore confidence in the CIA and the FBI, not as a way to restructure these institutions.

Indeed, the most radical statements in the Senate debate came not from Democrats but from liberal or moderate Republicans. Richard Schweiker of Pennsylvania raised the specter of a "shadow government" that Congress needed to identify and restrain.[44] Howard Baker, who had not resolved his doubts about CIA involvement in Watergate, confessed that he had a "shuddering fear" that the White House could not control the CIA.[45]

Summing up the mood of the inquiry's Democratic supporters, Pastore heatedly denied that the investigation would dismantle the intelligence agencies. "Nobody is out to destroy the CIA," he said. "All we are saying is that there are some things that have been wrong, and under the pretext of either national security or secrecy, private rights are being violated unnecessarily. That is all we are trying to eliminate."[46]

This moderate theme satisfied even the most conservative Republicans. John Tower of Texas, known as a hawk on defense issues, praised Pastore for setting "the right tone for the conduct of this investigation and the subsequent conclusions to be drawn from it."[47] Even John Stennis of Mississippi, the conservative CIA overseer who fought fiercely to keep the responsibility for the investigation in his own committee, finally voted for the measure.[48] But the hard-liners warned that they would be watching the investigators closely to ensure that the inquiry did not get out of control. Barry Goldwater of Arizona, soon to become the most conservative member of the new committee, cautioned that "if surgery is required, let it be performed only after the most careful diagnosis. And if there is surgery, let us use a very sharp scalpel—not a meat ax."[49]

In this spirit of compromise and bipartisanship, the Senate voted 82–4 to establish the Select Committee to Study Governmental Operations with Respect to Intelligence Activities. The senators appointed to this panel represented a broad ideological spectrum. Minority leader Hugh Scott named both liberal Republican Richard Schweiker and his moderate colleague, Howard Baker. They joined liberal Republican Charles Mathias of Maryland, who was a cosponsor of the resolution that established the investigation.[50] John Tower and Barry Goldwater would serve as the committee's conservatives, but Tower, at least, had indicated a willingness to listen to his less hawkish colleagues. In the months ahead, Tower, as vice chairman, would work diligently with the chairman to maintain an atmosphere of bipartisanship.[51]

The Democratic members of the committee also represented an ideological mix. Both Philip Hart of Michigan and Walter Mondale of Minnesota came from the liberal wing of their party, as their 100 percent ratings from the liberal Americans for Democratic Action (ADA) showed.[52] Gary Hart, a freshman from Colorado who had managed George McGovern's presidential campaign, could also be expected to vote on the left. Two additional freshmen gave the committee more balance: Walter

Huddleston was a moderate southern Democrat who had spoken out eloquently for the committee during the debate; and Robert Morgan was a conservative, law-and-order former state attorney general from North Carolina.

In selecting a chairman, majority leader Mike Mansfield faced an unexpected problem. He had intended to appoint Philip Hart, but the Michigan senator was ill with terminal cancer.[53] Mansfield therefore turned to a man who had actively sought the post—perhaps, observers said, as a means to improve his chances in the next presidential race. Frank Church of Idaho, a longtime critic of the CIA, now had the opportunity to begin the most significant investigation of his distinguished career.

Called "Frank Sunday School" and "Frank Cathedral" by those in Washington who found him a bit stuffy, Church was a bright, conscientious senator known for his flowery speeches and heartfelt morality. After conquering what his doctors thought was fatal cancer at age twenty-three, he was not afraid to take chances. He had launched a long-shot bid for the Senate in 1956 and shocked the state by becoming at age thirty-two the fourth youngest person ever elected to the U.S. Senate.[54]

No one ever doubted the integrity of "the boy wonder from Idaho," but some were irritated by his aloof, moralistic style. Many career spies and foreign policy "realists" found him, as one CIA officer said, "a decent and sincere man, but . . . also sanctimonious and self-righteous."[55] To the real-world pragmatists at the CIA, used to deceiving and being deceived, the intense moral vision of the former choirboy from Idaho seemed alien indeed.

Although Church had begun his career as a strong supporter of the Cold War consensus, he moved steadily leftward as the 1960s progressed. The Vietnam War prompted him to reassess his previous endorsement of an aggressive, interventionist foreign policy. Church expressed antiwar views in an interview in *Ramparts* magazine as early as January 1965.[56] By 1966, he was one of the leading Senate "doves," attracting nationwide attention for his tough questioning of administration officials during the televised hearings of the Foreign Relations Committee. By 1972, according to his biographers, he had come to view the war as nothing less than "a monstrous immorality."[57]

The Vietnam War also convinced Church that Congress needed to reclaim the powers that it had ceded to the executive branch since World

Senator Frank Church of Idaho. (Courtesy Frank Church Collection, Boise State University Library)

War II. In addition to cosponsoring a series of resolutions forcing the president to limit the war in Indochina, he tried to renew and restore Congress's power of investigation. In 1972, Church initiated a Foreign Relations subcommittee inquiry into multinational corporations and their effect on American foreign policy. The subcommittee's findings were explosive. Church proved and expanded upon columnist Jack Anderson's charges that ITT had offered vast sums of money to the CIA to topple the leftist Allende regime in Chile. In 1975, his subcommittee would uncover a bribery scandal with global repercussions. Church's revelation that American corporations had bribed foreign leaders prompted investigations in the Netherlands and Italy and led to the arrest of a former Japanese prime minister.[58]

In his speeches and writings, Church often condemned indiscriminate interventionism and emphasized the need for a moral foreign policy. The idol of his boyhood years, he said in 1971, was the isolationist Republican senator from Idaho, William E. Borah. Church wrote in an article intended for *Family Weekly* magazine that he admired Borah because he "placed great emphasis on public morality. He modeled himself after Abraham Lincoln with whom he shared the premise that the proper political move is always to do the honorable, the ethical, and the right." Church admitted that some of Borah's views "now are out-dated" but contended that in some ways Borah had been ahead of his time. "In particular, I think of his antipathy toward the use of force against small countries, his anti-imperialism, and his willingness to tolerate diversity in the world at large."[59] Borah had warned that intervening in foreign countries could erode liberty here at home. This was a theme that Church would sound throughout his post-Vietnam career.

Defenders of an interventionist CIA were troubled by Church's admiration for Borah but even more alarmed by the senator's views on oversight. Frequently critical of the secret government, Church had supported Senator Eugene McCarthy's attempts to strengthen the oversight committees.[60] In 1967, Senator Church's responses to constituents' inquiries about CIA funding of voluntary organizations were notably different from those of Congressman Ford. Church assured one constituent that "I will do whatever I can, as one Senator, to bring about a full-scale Congressional investigation of the CIA."[61]

Frank Church therefore wanted to head the intelligence investigation because of his sincere belief in making the secret agencies more accountable. He also saw an opportunity, as his biographers have written, to "combine principle with ambition."[62] For Church was planning to run for president the next year. As early as January 1975, the same month he was appointed chair of the committee, he received a memo from a campaign consultant on possible strategies for the 1976 election.[63] The consultant later urged Church to use the investigation to "maximum advantage," while striving to appear as nonpolitical as possible.[64] Church's desire to avoid the appearance of playing politics with the inquiry led him to delay his entry into the race until after Jimmy Carter had earned a commanding lead. When the senator did finally announce his candidacy in March 1976, he emphasized his role as investigator of the secret government. "In 1976 vote for the man who saved us from 1984," read one of his brochures.[65]

Because of Church's presidential aspirations and his liberal politics, Vice President Rockefeller reportedly complained bitterly about his appointment as chairman.[66] But his fears were unwarranted. Church, after all, would have to work with conservative and moderate colleagues on the committee. Moreover, though he impressed many observers as inflexibly moralistic, he had also earned a reputation as a compromiser. Many of his friends on the left were distressed by what they viewed as his eagerness to accommodate the opposition.[67] Indeed, Church would demonstrate several times during the investigation that he valued consensus over confrontation. Rather than worrying about the liberal in charge of the Senate investigation, Rockefeller and other CIA defenders should have been more concerned about developments on the other side of the Capitol.

In contrast to the Senate, the House was more divided, more partisan, and more lively in its debate over the proposed intelligence investigation. The senators, in the spirit of bipartisan consensus, had amicably accepted Republican requests to tighten the security of the committee, to limit its budget to $750,000, and to request its report by 1 September 1975 (a deadline that was later extended). But in the House, John Anderson of Illinois, the point man for the administration in these battles, faced a more inflexible opposition.

The White House congressional relations office had pinned its hopes on Anderson's ability to place "constraints" on the investigation.[68] Anderson did manage to win passage of two amendments, one limiting the panel's funds and the other prohibiting the unauthorized disclosure of information gathered by the committee—a key point of contention later.

Anderson, however, could not persuade the House to make its investigation more bipartisan. The rules of the Democratic Caucus required that Democrats be represented on committees in proportion to their numbers in the House. In the Ninety-fourth Congress, that meant two Democrats for every Republican. Anderson battled mightily to convince the House to make an exception for the intelligence committee, but his amendment was defeated 265–141. Anderson also failed in his bid to require the committee to report on 1 September, as the Church committee planned to do. Instead, House investigators would have until 31 January 1976 to complete their work.

In contrast to their Senate colleagues, few House members argued that an investigation was necessary to "restore confidence" in the intelligence community. Instead, they emphasized the need for a "thorough housecleaning" of agencies that had violated the law.[69] House Democrats indicated that they planned to take up where the *New York Times* had left off. Longtime foes of the CIA like Michael Harrington of Massachusetts, who would soon face a House Ethics Committee inquiry into his earlier alleged leak of information about CIA intervention in Chile, saw the investigation as a chance not to restore the CIA but to expose it further. The country's security, Harrington argued, "depends just as much on the maintenance of a rule of law as it does on the preservation of diplomatic secrets."[70] In response, House Republicans contended that an uncontrolled investigation—one perhaps led by congressmen who shared Harrington's definition of national security—could become "the greatest fishing expedition since Moby Dick," as Anderson put it.[71] The final vote of 286 to 120 illustrated the lack of consensus for a House inquiry.

The new committee reflected these bitter ideological divisions. Because of the proportional representation rule, only three Republicans were allowed on the ten-member panel. The GOP leaders tried to minimize this disadvantage by appointing conservatives: Robert McClory of Illinois, David Treen of Louisiana, and Robert Kasten of Wisconsin.

By contrast, four of the panel's Democrats—Michael Harrington, Ron Dellums and Don Edwards of California, and James Stanton of Ohio— had voted with the liberal Americans for Democratic Action more than 90 percent of the time in 1974.[72] The fifth Democrat on the committee, Robert Giaimo of Connecticut, was more moderate, but he had distinguished himself during the debate on the proposed covert action ban by castigating the "nefarious" and "outrageous" covert activities of the CIA.[73] The committee's lone middle-of-the-road Democrat was Morgan Murphy of Illinois.

The House Select Committee on Intelligence, in short, had five harsh critics of the CIA, three hard-line defenders, and only one moderate Democrat who might go either way. This was quite different from the Church committee, which counted moderate southern Democrats and liberal Republicans among its members.

Adding the final spark to this already volatile mix, Speaker Carl Albert then named as chairman of the committee the very man who had overlooked the alleged abuses to be investigated. Lucien Nedzi, Democrat of Michigan, was known as the most liberal member of the House Armed Services Committee.[74] Despite his early opposition to the Vietnam War, he had been chosen by conservative Armed Services chairman Edward Hébert to head the committee's oversight subcommittee in late 1971. By appointing Nedzi, Hébert was apparently signaling that he would accept more oversight of the CIA. And, in fact, one scholar has concluded that Nedzi effectively "created intelligence oversight in the House Armed Services Committee."[75]

But in the view of the CIA critics on the committee, Nedzi had several black marks against him. His subcommittee's investigation of the CIA-Watergate links was not as aggressive as the one conducted by Republican Howard Baker in the Senate.[76] He had initially disparaged Hersh's domestic spying stories, saying they were exaggerated.[77] He had only agreed to hold special secret hearings on Chile after Michael Harrington had pressured him.[78] After the CIA's intervention in Chile became public knowledge, Nedzi, unlike his five liberal colleagues on the new committee, had voted against abolishing all CIA covert actions. He had introduced legislation designed to preempt the historic Hughes-Ryan amendment.

Most important, though it was not known at the time, Nedzi had heard about domestic spying and other improper activities by the CIA long before Hersh exposed them. Along with Senator John Stennis, Senator Stuart Symington, and Representative Hébert, Nedzi was one of the key congressional overseers who had been briefed by Colby on the "family jewels." Significantly, Nedzi was the only one of the four who was upset by this 693-page compendium of CIA abuses and improprieties. Colby had been impressed by Nedzi's conscientiousness as an overseer: "He insisted on reading the individual items in the family jewels list in great detail, asked very specific follow-up questions in regard to them and demanded repeated assurances that these kinds of activity would never be carried on in the future." Nedzi urged Colby to make the "jewels" public, but the CIA director convinced him that such a "catharsis" would cause irreparable damage to the agency.[79]

Nedzi may indeed have been more assertive than previous overseers. He says now that he was under many constraints in his role as chairman of the Armed Services subcommittee: Hébert had power over him, and the other members of the subcommittee were not interested in aggressive oversight. He sought the chairmanship of the investigating committee because he wanted to have a free hand in examining the abuses.[80] Nevertheless, whatever Nedzi's intentions, his liberal colleagues on the new committee believed he was not aggressive enough. He had agreed to suppress previous evidence of CIA abuses; now he was chairman of a committee packed with congressmen who were determined to expose and eliminate all such abuses. It was a recipe for disaster.

But these problems were in the future. For the moment, amid tension on the House committee and excitement on the Senate panel, the two sets of investigators began their inquiries with a sense of the historic significance of their task. Their mission seemed clear. They could not know that the press, which had prompted them to start their inquiries, would again intrude to change their agendas.

No one in television really knows how to handle a

reporter like Daniel Schorr because there are so

few, if any others, like him.

Leonard Downie, Jr., *The New Muckrakers*

Sensational Scoops and Self-Censorship

The Journalistic Investigations

In the middle of the half-hour newscast on 28 February 1975, the *CBS Evening News* broadcast a report that was to transform the "year of intelligence." Veteran correspondent Daniel Schorr told viewers that President Gerald Ford had "reportedly warned associates that if current investigations go too far, they could uncover several assassinations of foreign officials in which the CIA was involved." Although details of the assassinations were "closely held," Schorr said, apparently at least three had occurred in the late 1950s or early 1960s. The grizzled correspondent ended his report with deadly serious irony: "Colby is on the record saying, 'I think that family skeletons are best left where they are, in the closet.'He apparently had some literal skeletons in mind."[1]

With this report, Daniel Schorr not only uncovered a new abuse for the investigators to examine but also injected some cloak-and-dagger sensationalism into the already titillating CIA story. William Colby was alarmed and depressed; now, he feared, his crusade to save the intelligence community from the investigators would almost certainly fail. "There was no stopping the press or Congress now. . . . A hysteria seized Washington; sensation came to rule the day."[2] The story drastically changed the agendas of both the Rockefeller Commission and the Church committee, as they were forced to spend months investigating the assassination plot charges. The intelligence committees now "approached the morning newspapers gingerly, wondering what new revelations would be added to our already weighty mandate," according to staff member Loch Johnson.[3]

Both Colby and Johnson have portrayed the press as united in its determination to investigate the intelligence community. And certainly the media gave prominent coverage to intelligence issues *once they were exposed*. But, in fact, few journalists were actively trying to expose the CIA in early 1975. Those few brave reporters who violated the post-Watergate consensus by aggressively pursuing national security stories had to negotiate a minefield. A perfectly executed course through that minefield could bring them fame; but, as Daniel Schorr discovered, the slightest mistake could provoke an explosion of animosity both from the administration and from colleagues in the media.

The media's ambivalence regarding the intelligence community is best shown in three stories that appeared between the creation of the investigating committees and their first public hearings some six months later. In their coverage of CIA assassination plots, the *Glomar Explorer* affair, and the spying charges against Alexander Butterfield, the national media proved to be seriously divided over how to cover the national security state. Although some reporters were quite adversarial, others were reluctant to question the wisdom of government officials—even to the point of suppressing stories. The few journalists who tried to report on Gerald Ford's CIA the way that Woodward and Bernstein had covered Richard Nixon's White House were quickly punished for transgressing the limits of "responsible" post-Watergate journalism.

Schorr's assassination story had a bizarre genesis. Like many of the stories during the intelligence investigations, it began with a leak, but this one was a different sort of leak: it was inadvertent, and it came from the president himself. The occasion was a White House luncheon for *New York Times* publisher Arthur Sulzberger and his editors. The purpose of the informal gathering, according to a memo sent to the president by press secretary Ron Nessen, was "to expose top officials of the *Times* to you in a relaxed, informal setting in hopes that they will recognize your qualities and be more understanding in future editorials." The goal was to persuade the editors that "you have a keen grasp of the problems facing the nation, a clear understanding of how to solve those problems, and the determination to solve them."[4] As it turned out, the president may have been too eager to impress his guests. Ford apparently tried so hard to convince the *Times* editors of his "keen grasp" of national problems that he temporarily forgot he was talking with reporters.

Seven *Times* executives attended the luncheon. Sulzberger was accompanied by managing editor A. M. Rosenthal, Washington bureau members Clifton Daniel and Scotty Reston, and editors John Oakes, Tom Wicker, and Max Frankel. Three aides accompanied Ford, including Nessen. Much of the meeting was uneventful. But toward the end of the luncheon, the subject of the Rockefeller Commission came up.

The *Times* had criticized the dominance of conservatives on the commission. Ford explained that he needed men who could be trusted not to stray from their narrow mission of investigating the CIA's domestic activities. Otherwise, he said, they might come upon matters that would "ruin the U.S. image around the world" and harm the reputation of every U.S. president since Truman.[5]

"Like what?" asked Rosenthal, always the hard-nosed reporter. "Like assassinations!" Ford blurted out, quickly adding, "That's off the record!"[6]

Ford's slip confronted the *Times* editors with a dilemma. They were the elites of the media, flattered by the private presidential luncheon and not inclined to repay Ford's hospitality by ignoring his request for confidentiality. Now, through the president's own error, they had been entrusted with a fascinating confidence from the president himself. Was it their duty to tell the story to the public? Or should they keep secret the issues that Ford had belatedly determined were "off the record"?

Wicker argued for writing the story. It was odd, he noted, for the president to say that he did not want his handpicked commission to explore certain issues and then to explain those issues to the editors of the *New York Times*. Wicker was sure that Ford had been around Washington long enough to know what he was doing and that he must, for whatever reason, want the story to get out. The slip had not been a slip, and the story was certainly not "off the record."

Rosenthal supported Wicker, but Reston and Oakes strongly opposed publication. Their word of honor was at stake, they believed. The other editors were reluctant to take sides. Daniel finally resolved the controversy by asking Nessen whether the paper could use the information. No one was surprised when the press secretary said the entire discussion was privileged information.[7]

Rosenthal and Wicker were upset by the decision not to print the story, but neither one felt he could unilaterally violate the decision made by the *Times*'s inner circle. Rosenthal, in particular, seemed to feel guilty about not alerting Seymour Hersh to the potentially sensational story. After the luncheon, Rosenthal reportedly called Hersh and told him, "Keep on working." "On what?" Hersh asked. "Never mind," Rosenthal said. "Keep working." Hersh realized that his editors were trying to tell him something, but he could not figure out what it was.[8]

Rosenthal's behavior was positively straightforward compared to the approach taken in a rare article by Washington bureau chief Daniel four days after the luncheon. That article, labeled a "news analysis" and buried deep inside the paper, seemed to try to introduce the assassination issue without directly using the information from the luncheon. Headlined "The Rockefeller Panel and Its CIA Mission," the article noted that the conservative commissioners were not likely to pry into the CIA's foreign activities. Some of these alleged foreign activities included assassination, Daniel wrote. But he did not give any source for this alarming charge except a fictional movie.[9]

Daniel could not bring himself to violate the president's confidence (or, alternatively, to take advantage of his slip). Instead, he tried to raise the issue by attributing assassination charges not to the president but to a film. The effect was not the same. Even as informed a reader as Seymour Hersh could not understand the article's stumbling attempt to call attention to a new issue.

In short, some of the *Times* editors obviously felt ambivalent about their paper's decision to suppress the assassination story. Given this ambivalence, it is not surprising that the story leaked. Significantly, the *Times* editor or editors who decided to leak the story gave the tip not to a rival newspaper, but to an aggressive and well-respected television reporter. Once Daniel Schorr got involved in what he later liked to call "son of Watergate," neither the investigations nor his own career would ever be the same.

During his four decades in daily journalism, the fifty-eight-year-old Schorr had built a reputation as a newsman who was willing, even eager, to defy authority. He had worked as a reporter—first for newspapers and later for radio and television—since junior high school, only interrupting his journalistic work for service in army intelligence during World War II. After the war, he worked as a stringer in Europe for both newspapers and radio. In 1953, he began his quarter-century affiliation with CBS News.[10]

Schorr was an unusually assertive man in a profession known for its assertive personalities. While in Moscow for CBS, he was periodically cut off the air and finally kicked out of the country for defying censorship. But it was Schorr's talent for angering American officials that solidified his reputation as one of the most contentious men in American journalism. In 1962, President John Kennedy asked CBS to remove Schorr from Germany because of his reports on German criticism of Kennedy's foreign policy. Lyndon Johnson called Schorr a "prize son-of-a-bitch" after the newsman reported that the president was shortchanging his ambitious social goals.[11] Schorr almost lost his job in 1964 when his story on Barry Goldwater's proposed postnomination trip to Germany seemed to imply that the senator would be warmly welcomed by neo-Nazis. After Schorr aired that controversial piece, CBS News president Fred Friendly personally cleared all of Schorr's reports from Germany on American politics.[12]

No one, though, hated Schorr with quite the same passion as did Richard Nixon. Not only was Schorr personally attacked by the president on one of the Watergate tapes, but he also had the honor of provoking one of the examples of abuse of power listed in the second article of impeachment against Nixon. In August 1971, Schorr's unfavorable analysis of a Nixon speech angered the White House. Shortly afterward, Chief of Staff Bob Haldeman ordered the FBI to conduct an extensive investigation of Schorr. The bureau interviewed twenty-five of Schorr's friends, employers, and family members. The agents tried to persuade these people to agree to interviews by claiming that Schorr, who was actually number 17 on Nixon's enemies list, was being considered for a White House job.[13]

In Schorr's opinion, it was his newspaperman's taste for blunt, investigative pieces that made him stand out amid the blandness of television journalism and thus provoked such unusual hatred from government officials. He claimed that he had "a newspaperman's antagonism to the stage-craft, image-making and slogan-selling to which television seemed so susceptible."[14] Schorr did seem out of place among the beautiful, young, and glib correspondents who dominated television news. A *New York Magazine* profile described him as "gray, grouchy, and pouchy, looking like a refugee from an Alka-Seltzer ad."[15]

But Schorr's critics contended that it was his abrasiveness, not his investigative skills, that made him enemies. And those enemies included Schorr's colleagues as well as his adversaries in government. He was accused of stealing stories that properly belonged to other reporters and of hyping his reports to get undeserved airtime. The *New York Magazine* profile, based on interviews with several critics, maintained that Schorr tended to have "minor-key accomplishments that, through the sheer force of his personality . . . get major-key amplification."[16]

Schorr also annoyed his bosses. CBS managers initially praised his assertive style when they assigned him to cover Watergate full-time in the summer of 1972. As the story continued, however, Schorr's pointed reports seemed to make the CBS brass uncomfortable. Although he was never reproved for his biting analyses of Nixon speeches, he found himself increasingly relegated to the sidelines. To his chagrin, he was not assigned to participate in panel discussions on the night of Nixon's resignation. CBS, he discovered, wanted to emphasize "nation-healing" stories and apparently did not want to take the chance that Schorr might seem vindictive.[17]

Schorr's worst crime, as far as his bosses were concerned, actually came when he was off the air. On 17 January 1975, Schorr met with Duke University students in an event billed as "Press the Press." In response to a question, Schorr blasted his network's resignation-night coverage. CBS officials were so relieved that Nixon didn't attack the press in his resignation speech, Schorr said, that they "reciprocated by soft-pedaling Nixon's wrongs and establishing a general atmosphere of sweetness and light."[18]

Schorr suffered grave repercussions from that moment of candor. Three of the CBS correspondents who covered the resignation—Eric Sevareid, Walter Cronkite, and Dan Rather—charged that Schorr had slandered them.[19] CBS News management sent Schorr an unprecedented memo demanding that he clear any public remarks with his bosses in advance. They eventually relented on this form of prior restraint. But

Schorr knew that he would never be forgiven for breaking "the cardinal rule of avoiding public criticism of my employers."[20]

In this atmosphere, Schorr began his historic involvement with the intelligence investigations. This unusually blunt, aggressive reporter would not be easily deflected from uncovering all that he could find. This persistence would eventually cost him his job.

During the first few months of the Ford administration, Schorr's career seemed stalled. He was not an anchor; he had no regular beat; and his big story, Watergate, was now finished. His bosses were at best ambivalent about him. Bill Small, president of CBS News, had told him in 1972, "Schorr, you're a son-of-a-bitch, and I only wish I had half a dozen sons-of-bitches like you." By the fall of 1974, Small "had seemingly changed his mind about the latter half of that observation," Schorr wrote later.[21] The self-described "aging, rather square" reporter was desperate to find a sensational new story that could translate into a regular beat and regular airtime.[22] In early 1975, he heard about the soon-to-be-famous *New York Times* lunch with the president.

When Schorr heard of Ford's slip at the luncheon, he assumed that the assassinations in question were domestic. Accordingly, he looked for clues to unsolved murders that might have had a connection to the CIA. He spent much time investigating suspicious deaths of Soviet diplomats in the United States.

Schorr was about to give up when he finally had a bit of luck: Colby consented to an interview on 27 February that Schorr had requested months before. Schorr spent about thirty minutes of the interview discussing the CIA and Watergate. Finally, at great pains to appear casual, he told Colby that Ford was reportedly concerned about CIA involvement in assassinations.

"Has the CIA ever killed anybody in this country?" Schorr then asked directly. Colby was so stunned by Ford's incredible slip that he decided to answer only the specific question asked. "Not in this country," he replied.[23]

"Not in this country!" For the second time in the assassinations story saga, an ill-conceived statement by an administration official had alerted reporters to a story they had not known existed. Schorr was shocked by Colby's response. "I stared at Colby as it sank in on me that I had been on the wrong track, but had now been put unintentionally on the right one." Still trying to sound casual, he asked the names of the targets.

"I can't talk about it," Colby said. Schorr was undaunted. "Hammar-skjöld?" he asked, referring to the United Nations secretary-general killed in a plane crash. "No, of course not!" Colby replied. Schorr tried again. "Lumumba?" he asked. The leftist leader of the Congo had been killed in 1961. Colby refused to talk about Lumumba or any other possible past CIA murders, but he did confirm that the CIA had banned assassination as a method since 1973.[24]

Schorr decided that he knew enough about these alleged assassinations to go on the air. Although CBS News officials scrutinized his script, he wrote later, "no one questioned that, however explosive, it had to be broadcast." His producers allotted him two minutes, which was "un-usually long" for a story without compelling visuals.[25]

Once again, as after Hersh's exposé of CIA domestic spying in Decem-ber, the other media were reluctant to acknowledge a scoop by a rival. The *Washington Post* put an Associated Press summary of Schorr's revela-tions on page 3; the *New York Times*, still cautious of violating its agree-ment with the president, summarized the report on page 30. William Colby tried hard to ensure that other reporters remained suspicious of the story. "From the moment of Schorr's broadcast," he wrote later, "I flung myself into a struggle to prevent an investigation into the subject of assassinations."[26]

Colby's efforts were only temporarily successful. Although the as-sassinations story did not hit the front pages of the prestige newspapers for an entire week, additional revelations by the *Washington Star* fanned new enthusiasm for the story. The story soon became "Topic A" of intelligence coverage, in Schorr's words.[27]

As a result of public and congressional pressure, the Rockefeller Com-mission soon embarked on the very course President Ford had hoped to avoid: a thorough investigation of these attempted murders. The Church committee added assassinations to its already lengthy agenda. Many reporters tried to advance Schorr's story by finding out who had been assassinated. Over the next few months, periodic front-page articles trumpeted new aspects of the story: the involvement of the Mafia in the Castro plots; the attempts on the lives of Lumumba, Ngo Dinh Diem of Vietnam, and Rafael Trujillo of the Dominican Republic; and alleged attempts to kill Sukarno of Indonesia and Duvalier of Haiti.[28]

The most dramatic reaction to Schorr's exposé came in late April, two months after his original report aired. The Rockefeller Commission called Richard Helms back from Tehran, where he was serving as U.S. ambassador, to answer questions about the assassination plots. Schorr, along with three or four other reporters, waited in the corridor for Helms to emerge. When Helms walked into the hallway, Schorr offered his hand in greeting and said, "Welcome back."

Helms exploded. "You killer! You cocksucker! 'Killer Schorr'—that's what they ought to call you!" he yelled at the newsman.[29] The former CIA director, previously famous for his discretion, then strode angrily to the press room, where he issued a more temperate denunciation of Schorr for the benefit of the cameras. "I must say, Mr. Schorr, I didn't like what you had to say on some of your broadcasts on this subject. I don't think it was fair, and I don't think it was right. As far as I know, the CIA was never responsible for assassinating any foreign leaders." Another reporter then asked if the CIA had discussed assassinations. Helms lost his temper again. "I don't know whether I've stopped beating my wife, whether you've stopped beating your wife. In government, there are discussions of practically everything under the sun." The reporter persisted: "Of assassinations?" "Of everything," Helms snapped.[30]

The next day, the confrontation was on page 10 of the *New York Times* and the front page of the *Washington Post*. Schorr maintains that he reconciled with Helms immediately after his outburst. Nevertheless, the encounter in the hallway earned Schorr fifteen minutes of fame—and a tip for another story. One television viewer, retired air force colonel Fletcher Prouty, was so incensed by the "verbal abuse" directed at Schorr that he called CBS and offered to tell about his involvement in a 1960 plot to kill Castro. Prouty, relating his story on television the next night, insisted that Helms knew of this particular plot.[31]

As a result of Helms's attack on him, Schorr was no longer just reporting the story—he had *become* the story. Even more than Hersh, Schorr became identified in the public's mind with journalistic exposés of the intelligence community. He had earned a reputation for stopping at nothing to expose executive abuses. With Nixon gone, this was not always seen as a virtue.

The *New York Times* had also played an interesting role in the assassinations story. The vehicle of Hersh's domestic spying exposé—the media leader in investigating the intelligence community—had censored itself. This decision was not at all unusual, as became clear in the next major intelligence story of 1975: the *Glomar Explorer* affair.

In the fall of 1973, Seymour Hersh first heard of a CIA plan to salvage Soviet nuclear secrets from the sea. As he understood it at the time, the

CIA wanted to recover Soviet missiles that had been test fired in Asia and had landed in the Pacific Ocean. But before he could learn much about the program, code-named Project Jennifer, the CIA's censors swung into action.

According to internal documents, top CIA officials became aware of Hersh's inquiries about Project Jennifer in January 1974. Alarmed, Colby decided to approach one of Hersh's bosses and urge the paper not to pursue the story. The editor—whose name was excised from the documents—was "delighted to be trusted," Colby reported.[32] The CIA director then met directly with Hersh and tried to convince him of the project's importance for national security. Hersh was uncharacteristically easy to convince. Since he had been unable to find out much about the top secret project, Hersh decided that his time was better spent on covering the Watergate affair.

Journalists often find it hard to decide whether to publish national security stories. On the one hand, reporters believe that it is their duty to inform the public of official misconduct and policy mistakes; but on the other, the media's pursuit of genuine national security secrets could alienate the public and bring about government censorship. The trick lies in distinguishing a *genuine* secret from official bungling that has been labeled a "national secret" by the bunglers. Reporters must ask themselves: Would the security of the nation truly be jeopardized by the exposure of this secret? Or have government officials made decisions here that could not stand the light of day—decisions that the American people, as citizens of a democracy, have the right to know about? Project Jennifer proved difficult to define. At this early stage, with little information to go on, the *Times* decided that the public did not need to know about this particular CIA operation.

Although Colby may have been able to influence the *New York Times*, he could not control a group of enterprising southern California criminals. In June 1974, burglars broke into the Los Angeles office of Summa Corporation, a Howard Hughes company. Among other items, the thieves absconded with two footlockers full of documents. One of those documents, the Hughes people believed, detailed the true story of Project Jennifer.[33] The CIA had agreed to pay Hughes more than $350 million to construct a deep-sea salvage ship called the *Glomar Explorer*. The ship had a special mission: to raise a sunken Soviet submarine from the floor of the Pacific Ocean. The diesel-powered sub, now fifteen years old, had exploded and sunk for unexplained reasons in 1968. The Soviets had been unable to recover it. The CIA, using the Summa Corporation as cover, was hoping to succeed where the Russians had failed. Disguised as a mining vessel, the ship had already made one unsuccessful attempt to raise the submarine. The crew had managed to recover one-third of the sub but not the part containing codebooks or missiles.[34]

As the Los Angeles police began investigating the burglary and subsequent ransom demands for the return of the stolen items, a garbled version of Project Jennifer leaked to the *Los Angeles Times*. The paper had heard that the *New York Times* was also on the story and therefore decided to rush its account into print. On Saturday, 8 February 1975, the first edition of the *Los Angeles Times* trumpeted its scoop in a banner headline with four-inch letters: "U.S. Reported after Russ Sub." The story did not mention the Project Jennifer code name, and it wrongly placed the sub in the Atlantic, not the Pacific, Ocean.

Nevertheless, the CIA immediately swung into action. Before all of the papers had hit the streets, an agency official rushed over to the *Los Angeles Times* building to meet with editor William Thomas. He argued that Project Jennifer was a continuing military operation; the agency planned to try to raise the submarine again. The official predicted "grave harm to national security" if the story continued to run.[35]

Thomas proved to be very receptive to national security arguments. Saying that he regretted printing the story at all, he moved it to page 18 in subsequent editions and promised not to publish any future stories on the subject. The CIA official reported to Washington: "I do not doubt that Mr. Thomas is on our side and will do what ever [*sic*] he can, with this most unfortunate development."[36]

Back in Washington, Hersh was furious with himself for allowing the *Los Angeles Times* to beat him on the story. "I hit my head and said, 'Dumbbell,'" he recalled later.[37] On Monday morning, he called the CIA and tried to threaten and cajole the agency into helping him advance the story. He implied that he would write a positive article on the project if Colby would give him more details. "I have no problem writing a good story about CIA, believe it or not," he told an agency official.[38] Later that day, Colby tried to mollify Hersh. "You have been first class about this thing for a long time. You remember I came down and talked to you about it one time. You have been damn good." Hersh replied: "It is not a question of being good. I am a citizen too."[39] Although both men were trying to influence the other with reassurance and flattery, it was clear that they did not trust one another. Colby, who closely tracked Hersh's progress during the investigation, suspected that he had no intention of writing a positive story.[40]

But this time the CIA had more to worry about than Seymour Hersh. As a result of the *Los Angeles Times* story, *Time*, *Newsweek*, CBS, National Public Radio, and *Parade Magazine* were trying to learn the truth about Project Jennifer. Colby, who somewhat unconvincingly maintained that the *Los Angeles Times* story had not destroyed the project's cover, tried frantically to keep any further information on the venture from becoming public. "I found myself racing around from newsrooms to editorial offices to television stations, trying desperately to plug any leaks on the story and feeling as if I were rapidly running out of fingers and toes with which to do the job," he wrote later.[41]

And the post-Watergate press, the institution credited with the downfall of President Nixon, the very people criticized by Senator Fulbright for practicing "advocacy journalism" and dealing cavalierly with national secrets, listened to the CIA director. All of the editors approached by Colby agreed to suppress the story. At one point, when Colby received an alarming phone call from General Brent Scowcroft of the National Security Council about Hersh's plans for a follow-up article, Colby said, "I cannot believe his boss would let him run a story."[42] *Washington Post* publisher Katharine Graham agreed that Project Jennifer did not sound like "anything we would like to get into." Colby praised her restraint and patriotism, saying the self-censorship was "a great tribute to our journalists."[43]

As more details about the project emerged, however, a few journalists began to question the wisdom of suppressing the story. The Soviets, after all, knew about the operation—probably before the *Los Angeles Times* story but certainly afterward.[44] The only interested parties unaware of the project were the American people, who had spent $350 million— more than President Ford had requested for aid to Cambodia as it fell to the Khmer Rouge—on a failed project to recover old missiles and outdated codes. As Senator Frank Church later said, "If we are prepared to pay Howard Hughes $350 million for an obsolete Russian submarine, it's little wonder we are broke."[45] For these reasons, a few independent-minded reporters believed that Project Jennifer was *not* a genuine national security secret and that the American people needed to be informed about it.

American editors decided not to question the CIA's national security arguments, however. Typical of many editors across the country, *New York Times* editor A. M. Rosenthal informed Hersh that the paper preferred to suppress his story. Hersh would be allowed to publish only if the CIA completed its second attempt at raising the *Glomar*, if the attempt was abandoned, or if someone else published the story.[46] Hersh responded with a three-page memo arguing that the Vietnam War had been an ongoing military operation when the *Times* published the Pentagon Papers.[47] Rosenthal was not moved. Hersh was convinced that his editors were wrong, but he did not think the issue was worth quitting over.[48]

As the weeks went by, Colby stepped up his efforts to keep Project Jennifer out of the news. On 17 March, he held three separate meetings with officials from National Public Radio, CBS, and United Press International to persuade them to suppress the story. The CIA chief was finally reduced to issuing preemptive warnings to the major news organizations that had not yet contacted him. He called one NBC official to ask that "if you hear anything about CIA and the ocean, you sit on it until you have had a chance to talk to me." The understandably confused NBC official replied, "Oceans, as in water?"[49]

For his part, Colby was "totally surprised and pleased" by the media's self-censorship.[50] He had engineered "the weirdest conspiracy in town . . . an American conspiracy."[51] The most interesting part of the affair, he thought, was "the way the American press showed its great responsibility."[52]

Indeed, "responsibility," not aggressiveness, was the watchword of the post-Watergate press in the case of Project Jennifer. Far from playing the mythic role popularly assigned to them after Nixon's fall, the nation's editors seemed terrified of the potential risks of defying the government. "I would just as soon not be in the position of getting credit" for releasing the submarine story, one *Los Angeles Times* editor told Colby.[53]

Yet at the same time, journalists were afraid that one of their competitors would have more courage or less faith in national security arguments than they did and thus scoop them. As a result, these editors nervously informed the CIA every time they heard that a competitor was working on the story. They demanded that the agency tell them immediately if anyone broke the self-imposed ban on publication. Colby carried around a list of phone numbers in his wallet "because if it goes, I am committed to tell everyone."[54]

The journalists in this drama had to balance their natural desires to inform the public (and, of course, beat the competition) with their need to appear "responsible." All of the editors, publishers, and producers contacted by Colby decided to err on the side of caution: they preferred to risk giving their competitors a scoop rather than seem "unpatriotic" to their readers and viewers.

One Washington reporter, however, had no editors, publishers, or producers to constrain him. Jack Anderson was the author of the most popular syndicated political column in the United States, "Washington Merry-Go-Round." He had taken over the column in 1969 after the death of his partner and the column's originator, Drew Pearson. From the 1930s until his death, Pearson had cultivated a reputation as a fearless muckraker, exposing so many greedy congressmen and incompetent bureaucrats that he became "the most intensely feared and hated man in Washington," according to *Time*.[55] Pearson was known both for his liberal commentary and for his brashness in an age of deferential reporters. When Anderson took over the column, he placed more emphasis on investigative reporting and fact checking and less on liberal crusading. Still, his client newspapers counted on Pearson-style bombshells from the column seven days a week, and Anderson strove to deliver them.[56]

Since Pearson's death, Anderson had established his own reputation for fearlessness by printing secret Nixon administration documents on U.S. aid to Pakistan during the India-Pakistan war. He also exposed ITT's alleged bribing of the Nixon administration in exchange for the favorable settlement of an antitrust suit against it. In another series of columns based on stolen ITT memos, Anderson revealed that the multinational corporation had offered money to the CIA to prevent Salvador Allende from taking office in Chile. Anderson's scoops prompted the CIA to spy on him—he was one of the targets of the domestic spying program exposed by Hersh. Nixon's plumbers even discussed killing him.[57] Other journalists in Washington might hold back at the request of a government official, but Anderson—as his own boss—was willing and able to write the type of story that his clients had come to expect from him.

Anderson learned of the *Glomar* project from an attorney with the American Civil Liberties Union, Charles Morgan, who was trying hard to persuade journalists to run it. Colby tried just as hard to persuade Anderson to join the crowd of distinguished journalists who had agreed to suppress the story. Colby told Les Whitten, Anderson's associate, *"Everyone else is sitting on it. That is one of the most fascinating parts of it—the whole press . . . has been just splendid."* Whitten was not impressed. "We are all doing a half-assed job," he replied.[58]

A few hours later, Colby tried to persuade Anderson himself. The columnist told Colby that he wanted to cooperate with the CIA, "but we have to be guided by what we think is in the public interest." Colby responded that the public would not be served by this particular disclosure. "If there were anything bad about this, I could not argue with you," he said.[59] Anderson was not convinced, however, and he broke the story that evening in his radio broadcast. An hour before he went on the air, Colby called "my friends on the *New York Times*" and other newspapers to alert them.[60]

As if to justify their long collaboration with the CIA, most of the press presented the sub story as a triumph for the national security establishment. According to the media, Project Jennifer was a daring, high-tech success story that demonstrated just how competent the agency could be.[61] The *Washington Post* editorialized that the project showed the CIA "performing its prime function brilliantly."[62] The *New York Times* editorial board also used the adjective "brilliant" to describe the "complex and fascinating undersea adventure."[63] *Time* called Project Jennifer "the great submarine snatch" and characterized it as "a clean, highly creative enterprise that had served its purpose."[64] *Newsweek* declared that the besieged CIA "had shown it could take on a real-life Mission Impossible—and make it nearly possible after all."[65] The *Los Angeles Times*, invoking Jules Verne and Ian Fleming, proclaimed that "the feat must rank with the greatest exploits in the history of espionage."[66]

There were, however, a few critical notes in the press coverage. Both Hersh's story for the *Times* and Anderson's column criticized the project as a $350 million boondoggle, a silly, expensive, and dangerously provocative experiment that had predictably failed.[67] Schorr on CBS similarly described the project as an expensive failure that had produced a "meager payoff so far."[68] But the majority of the Project Jennifer coverage was overwhelmingly favorable. In fact, some observers theorized that Colby, despite appearances to the contrary, had *wanted* to get the story out to give the agency a public boost at the time of its greatest crisis.[69]

Once the dust had settled from the *Glomar* revelations, media critics began a fascinating process of self-examination as they attempted to understand the mass self-censorship in the wake of Watergate. Most of those who had joined the embargo defended their decision to do so. The *Washington Post*, typically striking a note for "responsible" journalism after Nixon's fall, proclaimed in an editorial that its suppression of the *Glomar* story was not inconsistent with its devotion to a free press. "On the contrary, a willingness to make such exceptions when confronted with compelling arguments from a government in exclusive possession of all the facts of the matter is a mark of a *responsible* free press," the paper intoned.[70] *Time* castigated the media for jeopardizing the national security by writing about CIA secrets; the continuing intelligence controversy, "of which Project Jennifer is only the latest fuel," could irreparably damage the agency.[71] In another article, the magazine praised the journalists who, like the *Time* editors, had practiced "restraint" by shelving the story.[72]

But even as editors defended their decisions on the *Glomar* story, other voices in the media expressed dismay over the craven submission of the post-Watergate press. Tom Wicker was one of the few syndicated columnists to come to Anderson's defense. The unanimous decision of the nation's editors to suppress the story demonstrated that the press was indeed a monolith, he wrote. And, contrary to myth, that monolithic press was *not* "anti-Government, anti-security, anti-conservative or 'pro-leftist.'"[73] A *New York Times* editorial writer agreed that the media cooperated with Colby "to prove in the wake of Watergate that they were not irresponsible, that they did have a real sense of the national interest."[74] The media review *MORE* was blunt: the submarine case suggested that "the lessons of Vietnam and Watergate still need to be driven home to most editors and publishers."[75]

Anderson himself charged that the post-Watergate press seemed more concerned with restoring its reputation for "responsibility" than with exposing government wrongdoing. "The old pre-Watergate, pre-Vietnam ideals of partnership with government, of cozy intimacy with the high and mighty," appealed to a press "concerned that its abrasive successes have earned it a bad name and a hostile reception," he wrote.[76] As a result, he told a reporter, journalists were trying too hard to prove "how patriotic and responsible we are, prove that we're not against the establishment, the government, that we're not all gadflys."[77]

William Greider, a *Washington Post* reporter, said the *Glomar* story demonstrated that the post-Watergate press was uncertain whether to play watchdog or lapdog. Early in the year, "the press snarled at the CIA with its new ferocity," he wrote, but when Colby "came up with a small bone (the Howard Hughes submarine caper), it rolled over on its back to have its tummy rubbed."[78]

Seymour Hersh was one reporter who refused to roll over for the agency. Hersh had been willing to go along with Colby early in the *Glomar Explorer* saga, but only because he was distracted by Watergate and uncertain of his facts. Once he realized the importance of the story, Hersh again proved to be an ardent advocate of publishing something the government wanted suppressed. Although this posture made him legendary among the press corps, it sometimes proved costly to his career. Just how costly became obvious in the spring of 1975, when he lost an almost certain Pulitzer Prize and then was nearly subjected to government prosecution.

Hersh's domestic spying stories made him the clear front-runner for the Pulitzer Prize for national reporting.[79] The post-Watergate climate, however, was not favorable for an iconoclast like Hersh. The Columbia University Board of Trustees, which oversees the award selection, had publicly rebuked its Pulitzer advisory board in the past two years for picking controversial winners. In 1972, the board had honored the *New York Times* for its publication of the Pentagon Papers and Jack Anderson for his columns on the Nixon administration's secret policies in the India-Pakistan war. The trustees were also annoyed when a *Providence Journal-Bulletin* reporter won the next year for revealing Nixon's minimal income taxes. This year, apparently sensitive to past criticism, the fourteen journalists on the Pulitzer board "seemed to go out of their way . . . to find relatively noncontroversial subjects" for their awards, according to *Time*'s press critic.[80] Passing over Hersh, the board awarded the Pulitzer for national reporting to Donald Barlett and James Steele of the *Philadelphia Inquirer* for a series on unequal enforcement of tax laws.

That same month, Hersh faced a much greater career crisis than the denial of his second Pulitzer, though he was not aware of it at the time. Hersh had continued his aggressive coverage of the intelligence community for the *New York Times* with a May article about a U.S. submarine spying program. This navy project, called Holystone, used special submarines to spy within the three-mile limit of the Soviet Union.[81] Hersh wrote a critical story about Holystone, quoting sources who believed that it was an unnecessarily risky operation.

For reasons only they understood, the Soviets did not take any action as a result of the story. Nor did the U.S. Navy. Despite its "exposure" by Hersh, Holystone continued until 1981, when spy Ronald Pelton sold detailed information about it to the Soviet Union.[82] Perhaps, as Hersh believed, the Soviets already knew about the program; or perhaps his story did not contain enough details for them to act. Nevertheless, the members of the Ford administration were determined to think of some way to punish Hersh for exposing secrets.

In two secret meetings at the White House, Ford's top aides considered several alternatives. Richard Cheney, the deputy chief of staff, outlined the options in his handwritten notes from the meetings. The easiest, least confrontational solution would be to discuss the issue informally with the *New York Times*. More drastic alternatives included an FBI investigation of the *Times* and of Hersh; convening a grand jury to seek indictments; and getting a search warrant to go through Hersh's papers in his apartment.[83] Very quickly, however, the administration decided not to prosecute Hersh. The White House feared that any sort of government investigation would alert the Soviets to the importance of the story.[84] Moreover, Attorney General Edward Levi advised that the law was unclear and that the pursuit of Hersh's sources would turn the case into "a journalistic *cause celebre*."[85]

This, obviously, was the last thing the White House wanted. The Ford advisers had hoped to find a way to use this incident to turn public opinion against all of the CIA's inquisitors, not to make Hersh a martyr. In his notes on White House discussions of Hersh's story, Richard Cheney wondered: "Can we take advantage of it to bolster our position on the Church committee investigation? To point out the need for limits on the scope of the investigations?"[86]

The case against Hersh was abandoned. Several months later, however, administration officials would discover other targets in the press who would better serve their purposes.

The last major press exposé before the opening of the public congressional hearings did not involve any enterprising reporting. Instead, the story was based on a deliberate leak by embattled members of the House intelligence committee. As a result of internal strife within the committee, the House was considering abandoning its intelligence investigation in the early summer of 1975.[87] The committee members were desperate to save their inquiry. As the Rules Committee held hearings to determine the future of the investigation, two members of the imperiled committee made some sensational charges. Republican Bob Kasten and Democrat Ron Dellums claimed they had evidence that the CIA had "infiltrated" the White House without the president's knowledge. With such potentially explosive information to explore, they argued, the committee must continue.[88]

The two congressmen could not have asked for better coverage of their charges. Both the *New York Times* and the *Washington Post* placed the allegations on the front page. On CBS, Daniel Schorr described what he called the "years-long CIA penetration of the White House," which he said had ended on Colby's orders in 1973. The CIA reacted with outrage, with Colby calling the charges "vicious nonsense."[89]

The allegations later proved to be significant but exaggerated. Dellums and Kasten had based their charges on an entry in the "family jewels" list of CIA abuses. According to this item, the CIA had "detailed" employees to other executive offices, including the office of the president. This practice was worthy of investigation, for it allowed executive departments to escape budget constraints and in at least one case gave the CIA power to influence executive branch policies regarding the agency. But the stories of "infiltration" and "penetration" of the executive, implying that the CIA was an omnipotent and omniscient agency spying on the president himself, were overblown. The agency employees had never spied on their White House colleagues or secretly reported back to their CIA bosses. In any case, Colby had ended the practice after Watergate.[90]

But all of this was not clear in July 1975, and the picture became even more clouded when retired air force colonel Fletcher Prouty decided to enter the controversy. Prouty was a disillusioned military man who had been a CIA "liaison" in the Pentagon from 1955 to 1963. He had published a book in 1973 called *The Secret Team: The CIA and Its Allies in Control of the United States and the World*. The book contended that the CIA was behind a massive conspiracy designed to subvert American democracy. In a little-noticed passage in his generally little-noticed book, he charged that Allen Dulles had "positioned CIA personnel and agency-oriented disciples inconspicuously throughout the Government" as part of a vague but malevolent plot.[91] Prouty was also a Kennedy assassination conspiracy theorist; the character played by Donald Sutherland, Mr. X, in Oliver Stone's 1991 movie *JFK* was based on him.[92] Prouty had contacted Daniel Schorr back in May 1975 with a credible, and apparently true, story about his involvement in an assassination plot against Castro. When he told Schorr on 11 July that he knew the identity of the CIA's "man in the White House," the veteran correspondent believed him.

That White House contact, according to Prouty, was none other than Alexander Butterfield, the man who had revealed the existence of the White House tapes. The implications, as Schorr realized, were explosive: if Butterfield was a CIA spy, then Watergate might have been a CIA plot. Maybe Butterfield had been acting on agency orders when he disclosed the Oval Office taping system to Congress.

Schorr was spurred on to broadcast this story by competitive pressure, for an NBC correspondent had scheduled a taped interview with Prouty for the *Today* show of 11 July. To beat the competition and burnish his reputation as the television reporter with the best intelligence contacts,

Schorr invited Prouty to the CBS studios that morning and put him on the air live shortly after 7 A.M. He had spent only fifteen minutes questioning the colonel before putting him on national television. Prouty explained that when he had needed help from the White House in 1971, he had been told by Howard Hunt, the Nixon plumber and ex–CIA officer, that Butterfield served as a liaison for the CIA in the White House.

The subsequent flurry of Butterfield stories never explained the functions of a "liaison" for the CIA. Prouty himself did not charge Butterfield with spying, although he implied that he had been up to no good. Schorr, for his part, did point out in his report on the *CBS Evening News* that viewers had to weigh the word of one retired colonel against a "sweeping" denial by the CIA. (Butterfield himself was traveling and could not be reached by reporters.)[93]

Prouty's story quickly fell apart. He repeatedly contradicted himself, and no one else would confirm his charges. CBS interviewed Howard Hunt in his Florida jail cell, where he denied referring Prouty to Butterfield.[94] The network also gave Butterfield a forum on *60 Minutes* to deny the allegations categorically. A few days later, Senator Church announced that an intelligence committee inquiry had not been able to substantiate Prouty's accusations.[95]

More interesting than the short-lived Butterfield story itself, however, was the attack launched on the story's primary exponent, Daniel Schorr, by his colleagues in the media. A *Time* profile of Schorr described the correspondent as "too eager" to get scoops, a man inclined to cut corners and make mistakes.[96] The *Washington Post* ombudsman, Charles Seib, excoriated both Schorr and NBC correspondent Ford Rowan for engaging in "careless" journalism that had caused unjustifiable harm to Butterfield's career.[97] The lengthiest and most detailed attack came in the *Columbia Journalism Review*. The review's story, which was much more critical of Schorr than of Rowan, ended with an ominous speculation: "One shudders to think what would have happened if television in 1950 could have as easily put a source on live as it can today and Daniel Schorr had made an appointment to meet a man named Joseph R. McCarthy at 6:45 A.M. to put him on the air at 7:00."[98] That analogy would soon become popular: shortly after the article appeared, Henry Kissinger and others would begin attacking the *congressional* investigators as proponents of a new type of McCarthyism.

For his part, Schorr was unrepentant. He told the *Columbia Journalism Review*: "We live in a time when, until the dust settles some, we cannot discard allegations made by people who are not frivolous. Until a balance is restored, I guess we'll just have to live through incidents like this. The lesson I do *not* draw is 'don't put guys like Prouty on the air.' "[99] In a 1992 interview, Schorr was a little more regretful. He explained that he had come to believe that Prouty was "flaky" and that he looked back on the story with "less than complete satisfaction."[100] But at the time, he had considered Prouty a good source and saw no reason to ignore his charges.

The media pundits, however, insisted that Schorr had a responsibility to ignore men like Fletcher Prouty. Schorr's decision to air Prouty's charges was seen as emblematic of the media's unrestrained, sensationalistic, and adversarial coverage of the intelligence community. Six months later, columnist and former CIA officer Tom Braden was still citing the Butterfield incident as an example of the media's overeager and error-ridden reporting on the intelligence community.[101]

But Daniel Schorr's persistent, aggressive, and occasionally careless reporting on the Butterfield charges was the exception rather than the rule. More typical was the *New York Times* editors' reluctance to tell the public what the president had told them about CIA assassinations. More typical than Schorr's eagerness to expose some spy secrets was the eagerness of elite editors to keep those secrets—and then, when secrets like the *Glomar Explorer* were exposed, to praise the brilliant and competent men of the CIA who had conceived of them.

Harrison Salisbury has characterized the *New York Times* in particular and the press in general during the intelligence investigations as "a half-trained colt, speedy, intelligent but skittish on the track, quick to shy and uncertain of staying the course."[102] This metaphor implies that the press was one monolithic institution, alternately charging ahead and shying away. In reality, the journalistic investigations of the intelligence community were more like a race course filled with different types of horses: some chomping at the bit but most reluctant to leave the safety of the gate.

Only a few individuals in the press—Seymour Hersh, Daniel Schorr, and Jack Anderson—persistently tried to create a new relationship between the press and the secret government. As a result of their assertiveness, they encountered almost unanimous disapproval from their colleagues in the media establishment. They didn't win any prizes for their investigative triumphs. Instead, they risked prosecution by the government, contempt from their colleagues, and, as Daniel Schorr would soon discover, retaliation from their employers.

American foreign policy must be made to con-

form once more to our historic ideals, the same

fundamental belief in freedom and popular

government that once made us a beacon of hope

for the downtrodden and oppressed throughout

the world.

Frank Church, speech at Idaho State University,

18 February 1977

Abuses and Aberrations

The Church Committee

Investigation

As chairman of the Senate intelligence committee, Frank Church was charged with investigating past abuses by the secret agencies. Central to this investigation was the question of responsibility: Just who was to blame for these abuses?

At first, this question did not seem very controversial or politically dangerous. The story that had launched the Senate intelligence investigation—Seymour Hersh's December 1974 exposé—had described CIA domestic spying during the Nixon years. When Church sought the chairmanship, he must have assumed that the inquiry would focus primarily on the administration of the recently discredited president. But then came the allegations of FBI abuses and CIA assassination plots. Suddenly, the Senate inquiry was redefined to include critical examinations of at least four presidencies, including that of the martyred John Kennedy. The crimes, it seemed, could not be blamed on Richard Nixon alone.

The inquiry, in short, would be much broader than originally planned. In the course of the investigation, Church and his colleagues would be forced to reexamine their ideas about the power of the presidency and the role of the United States in the world. They would need to question their assumptions about the Cold War and covert action and their own support for postwar U.S. policies. Most important, they would need to examine their beliefs about America's "historic ideals." Were these ideals myths or realities? If they were more than myths, why had they been abandoned?

In essence, the committee members needed a model for their investigation. They had to determine whether these crimes and improprieties were unfortunate deviations from the normal course of U.S. foreign policy—the course that had made the United States a "beacon of hope" for the world—or whether they signaled more systemic flaws. Ironically, the committee's insistence that the abuses were aberrations would undermine its own efforts for reform.

At the start, it was not clear how the Rockefeller Commission—the executive branch's own inquiry into the Hersh charges—would affect Church's investigation. The White House had initially hoped that a thorough executive branch examination of CIA abuses would preempt at least part of Church's inquiry. As the Senate committee set about hiring its 135-member staff and negotiating for the release of documents from the executive branch, the Rockefeller Commission planned to produce a quick report on domestic spying to reassure the public that the White House was not covering up any abuses. If the administration's plan had worked, the commission's report might have undermined the strong public and press support for Church's investigation.

But all did not go according to plan. The commission faced its first public relations problem when Daniel Schorr revealed on the *CBS Evening News* that the president did not want the commissioners to investigate assassination plots. Embarrassed, the president now had to expand the commission's jurisdiction and extend its deadline so that it could examine those very plots.

The commission staff members proceeded to unearth compelling evi-

Vice President Rockefeller presides over a meeting of the President's Commission on CIA Activities within the United States on 13 January 1975. (Courtesy Gerald R. Ford Library)

dence on attempted assassinations, according to David Belin, executive director of the commission and former counsel for the Warren Commission. Most of the commissioners, including Ronald Reagan, agreed that the final report should include a chapter on the plots.[1] At a press conference on 12 May, commissioner Douglas Dillon said that the public report would indeed discuss assassinations.

At this point, however, the commissioners created their second public relations disaster: they voted to suppress this part of their investigation. It is unclear why the commissioners changed their minds. Belin believes that Henry Kissinger convinced them to remove the chapter on assassination plots; White House counsel Roderick Hills claims he was responsible for excising what he considered an incomplete and inflammatory account.[2]

In any case, the White House informed the press on 6 June that the final report would not contain any material on assassinations. Instead, the White House would pass the issue to the Church committee, which would receive all of the commission's assassination files. Moreover, the rest of the report would not be released as scheduled. President Ford wanted to review it before he decided whether the public should be allowed to see the fruits of his commission's inquiry.

The White House could not have chosen a more provocative or suspicious course of action. The media had been promised a complete, official report on sensational abuses; now, at the last minute, that promise had been broken. Outraged, the members of the press corps demanded an explanation. At a press conference, reporters called press secretary Ron Nessen a liar and accused him of covering up abuses. One reporter snidely asked if former president Richard Nixon had been consulted on the cover-up.[3] After an hour of this sharp questioning, Nessen—who had been a member of the White House press corps just ten months earlier—slammed shut his briefing book, marched angrily from the room, and went into seclusion to consider quitting his job.[4]

The administration's "fantastic screw-up" on the Rockefeller report, as columnist John Osborne termed it, undercut the commission's main goal: to reassure the public.[5] The front pages of the nation's newspapers chronicled the White House's ineptitude, while the editorial pages smoldered with distrust. The New York Times, for example, charged that the Ford administration's reputation for "fidelity to principles of openness and candor" would be imperiled if the White House did not release the entire report immediately.[6]

Stung by the criticism, Ford quickly decided to release the part of the report that did not involve assassinations.[7] To many observers' surprise, it was not a whitewash. In addition to extensive descriptions of the domestic spying activities exposed by Hersh in December, the report disclosed a few abuses for the first time. The most explosive revelation concerned the CIA's drug tests on unsuspecting Americans from 1955 to 1966. One scientist had killed himself after the agency slipped LSD into his drink, and his aggrieved family was the focus of many subsequent negative stories about the CIA. The report was so complete that Hersh's main source for his original story said that 90 percent or more of the abuses he knew about were included.[8]

Once the president released the report, the press abruptly changed course and praised the candor of the Ford administration. The New York Times editorial board, for example, called the report "a trenchant, factual and plain-spoken document" and ran seven stories on its contents the first day.[9] The Times was most pleased by the commission's apparent vindication of Hersh's original story—and thus the paper's own news judgment. In addition to two stories favorably comparing Hersh's charges to the activities described in the report, the newspaper ran a column by Anthony Lewis headlined "The Teller of Truth" stressing Hersh's critical role in revealing the abuses. The politicians, Lewis said, "did nothing until Seymour Hersh forced their hand."[10] Hersh himself did not hesitate to point out how misguided his critics had been. "I hope they're all eating crow tonight," he said in a television interview.[11]

Although the report's description of past abuses was thorough, the commissioners proposed relatively weak reforms to guard against future ones. The commission's final recommendations included modest reorganization proposals for the CIA, the creation of a joint oversight committee in Congress, and tighter executive oversight. But the commissioners did not recommend criminal sanctions—except in the case of employees who disclosed secret information. The only officials who would be punished under these recommendations would be Seymour Hersh's sources. Moreover, the commission did not, as Tom Wicker pointed out, contemplate changes in the CIA's mission. Instead, it proposed "measures of limited efficacy for the closer supervision of the existing agency with its existing mission and its existing operational abilities."[12] Hersh agreed that the commission had failed to make real recommendations for change, such as banning covert action.[13] His main source for the original story was skeptical that the report would have any lasting effect. "They'll clean up their shop a little, but in 10 or 20 years it'll start again," he said.[14]

The controversy over the release of the report had two significant results. Because of the administration's inept handling of the report, as well as the mixed verdict given the report by the CIA's critics, Frank Church maintained his clear mandate to continue the Senate investigation. The Rockefeller Commission, despite the executive branch's hopes, had not succeeded in preempting the need for further investigation. The second result was the important public relations lesson learned by the White House. The defenders of the intelligence community had made a colossal blunder by partially suppressing and delaying the release of the report. That mistake would be their last.

The Rockefeller Commission's decision to pass the assassination issue to the Senate presented both risks and benefits for the Church committee. The most obvious benefit was the opportunity for more press coverage. The plots were, after all, the most sensational of all CIA abuses. But the potential disadvantages were considerable. Research on the assassination plots diverted the committee's attention from more systemic analyses of the intelligence community.[15] In addition, the investigation of the plots lengthened the committee's tenure by months—a considerable risk for a special committee faced with the prospect of declining public support.

The revelations of murder plots also posed unexpected problems for the Democrats on the committee. The investigation, of course, had never been a wholly partisan affair. Some liberal Republicans, like Church committee members Charles Mathias and Richard Schweiker, supported the inquiry, while many conservative Democrats opposed it. But at the beginning of the inquest, when the investigators assumed that all of the CIA abuses had occurred during the Nixon administration, it was much easier for Democrats to demand a thorough housecleaning. Now, however, the allegations of murder plots during the Kennedy and Johnson administrations meant that an aggressive investigation could damage Democrats as well.

Finally, the assassination issue forced the liberals on the committee to reexamine their deepest beliefs about the nature of the presidency since World War II. To write a report on the assassination plots, the committee members had to decide who had authorized the plots—and thus to reconsider their perceptions of the Cold War, of the Kennedy and Johnson presidencies, and even of Watergate.

The main obstacle to determining responsibility for the plots was the concept of "plausible denial," which was built into the structure of the National Security Council. Under this doctrine, the secret warriors insulated the president from knowledge of potentially unpopular CIA actions so that he could later deny responsibility for them. As Richard Helms told reporters, "You've got to protect the president from the dirty stuff."[16] Instead of the president, decision makers outside of the Oval Office would pass final judgment on covert action. President Eisenhower made this procedure formal in 1955 by creating the 5412 Group, named after the National Security Council order establishing it. The 5412 Group, which consisted of senior officials from the Pentagon and State Department as well as the director of central intelligence and the president's national security adviser, approved and regulated covert operations. Although it was periodically renamed—the Special Group in the Kennedy administration, the 303 Committee in the Johnson years, and the 40 Committee after 1970—it continued to serve the purpose of preserving the president's deniability while maintaining some White House control over agency operations. Just how much detail these special group members knew about agency operations is unclear, however, as the investigators would discover.

Agency officials like Helms and Richard Bissell, the legendary former deputy director of plans, maintained that the various special groups had authorized the assassination plots at least "in general terms." The committee never found a straightforward, written authorization to kill someone, but Helms explained that it was absurd for the committee to expect a written record. "I can't imagine anybody wanting something in writing saying I have just charged Mr. Jones to go out and shoot Mr. Smith," he testified.[17]

Helms had an obvious interest in portraying his CIA as a tightly controlled agency that faithfully served the president. The advisers of these former presidents had an equally obvious interest in blaming the plots on Helms and a runaway agency. Former high-level aides who might have known about the assassination plots now suffered "an epidemic of amnesia," committee staff member Loch Johnson wrote.[18] Others were outraged by the suggestion that their bosses could have been involved in such scandalous doings—especially if that boss was John or Robert Kennedy. Adam Walinsky, a former Robert Kennedy aide, charged that the CIA and its defenders were trying to save the agency by blaming its "scummy activities" on public officials who were "conveniently dead."[19] The CIA, he said, hoped to show "that it may be a gang of murderers, but it is Our Gang; Killers, but obedient; not independent entrepreneurs, but faithful servants of the Company."[20]

Initially, the committee members ventured no opinions on the presidents' culpability for the plots. Then, shortly after the Rockefeller Commission gave his committee exclusive jurisdiction over the plots, Church hinted at his sympathies. He told the press that the committee had not found any evidence "that would directly link the CIA involvement in this kind of activity with the President of the United States."[21] He obviously did not speak for all members of his committee, however, for three days later Barry Goldwater told the nation on *Issues and Answers* that John Kennedy must have known about the murder attempts.[22] Senator Schweiker echoed Goldwater's sentiments in a *Newsweek* interview early in July.[23] Later that month, in a statement that defined the emerging debate, Church came up with a paradigmatic phrase for the investigation: the CIA, he said, could be compared to a "rogue elephant on a rampage."[24]

Church's refusal to blame the presidents caused his GOP colleagues to charge that he was motivated by partisanship. In their view, the chairman was exaggerating the agency's excesses to save the Kennedys' reputations. The only president he was willing to concede might have acted improperly was a disgraced Republican, they complained. "From the beginning," John Tower wrote later, "it seemed that Frank Church thought that alleged improper and illegal intelligence-gathering activity began with

Richard Nixon."[25] The White House aides who worked with the committee also had their suspicions about the chairman's partisan motives, with one staff member writing his bosses that the Church staff seemed uninterested in abuses connected with Democratic administrations.[26] Columnist William Safire, a former Nixon speech writer, launched a crusade against Church's "cover-up" of Democratic abuses.[27] Safire was incensed by the committee's attempt to hide its discovery that Kennedy had shared a mistress with a mafioso involved in the Castro plots. The committee described the mistress as Kennedy's "close friend" in the assassination report.[28]

The Republicans may have been partly correct in charging that Church used the "rogue elephant" metaphor to protect Democrats. The chairman certainly did not want to antagonize the powerful Kennedy family during his campaign for the presidency. Moreover, he must have realized that his party would win points with the voters in 1976 if his committee found that Republicans were responsible for all of the abuses.

But there is no evidence that Church's partisan loyalties significantly influenced the investigation. The real work of the committee was done by the staff members, and they insist that Church never told them to ease up on the Democratic presidents.[29] Despite Republican complaints that Church was eager to blame Nixon, the chairman defended all of the presidents, including Nixon, during the public hearings.

Ultimately, Church and his committee members were motivated more by ideology than by partisanship. The question of presidential responsibility did not pose a dilemma for the committee's conservatives; they readily believed that the president was completely in charge, and they were not bothered by this assumption. They maintained that the president *should* have expansive powers in foreign affairs—and that those powers sometimes included assassinations. Senator Goldwater defended Presidents Kennedy and Johnson, his political enemies, against liberals who condemned them for the murder plots. Goldwater even said that if he had been elected president instead of Johnson in 1964, he probably would have approved the assassination plots.[30] Conservatives like Goldwater believed that the United States had to emulate the Communists' methods in order to protect the nation's security. As columnist Marquis Childs put it, "No matter what name it goes by, spying is a dirty business, and the chief spy can hardly qualify as a Boy Scout leader."[31]

By contrast, Church was morally repulsed by the idea of officially sanctioned murder attempts, and he did not want to believe that his presidents had endorsed such crimes. Church had served with Kennedy and Johnson in the Senate and had delivered the keynote address at the 1960 Democratic convention that nominated them. He had changed since his New Frontier days, of course, and had become a prominent opponent of the war championed by these two presidents. But it still must have been difficult for him to admit that these two men, the only Democratic presidents he had served under as senator, had been responsible for some of the abuses he was now investigating.

Moreover, along with Kennedy and Johnson, Church himself shared some of the responsibility for the foreign policy of the Cold War that had permitted the abuses. As Godfrey Hodgson has pointed out, U.S. foreign policy of the 1950s and early 1960s was supported by a broad, almost universal spectrum of Americans from left to right: this was the foreign policy of the "liberal consensus."[32] Conservative Republicans and liberal Democrats alike agreed on the need for an aggressive, anticommunist foreign policy, including overt and covert intervention abroad. Even the most liberal policymakers in this era agreed that the president needed extraordinary power and secrecy to meet this Communist threat. "Cold-War liberals liked the CIA in the fifties and early sixties because they liked the imperial presidency then," historian Garry Wills commented during the investigations. "They *wanted* the President to escape the constraints of a fuddy-duddy Congress, just as they wanted the CIA to slip past a muscle-bound Pentagon."[33]

But what did this support of covert intervention really mean? What types of actions did the CIA carry out? Only a handful of policymakers in Washington knew the answer in detail. The rest of the American public, including liberal senators, seemed content to be kept in ignorance. Both the press and the oversight committees in Congress were willing to trust the government to do what was necessary for national defense without asking too many questions. This secrecy allowed liberals to support the CIA while maintaining their belief that Americans were always "the good guys, the white hats, the idealists struggling for democracy and freedom," as columnist Russell Baker wrote.[34] The heroic image of the CIA in the popular culture of the 1950s and 1960s had helped to reinforce this view of American spies.

Now that Vietnam and Watergate had shattered the liberal consensus, Americans learned of the covert operations and dirty tricks that their secret warriors had carried out during the height of the Cold War. And many American liberals were shocked to learn the truth about their government's advocacy of expediency over virtue. "Perhaps at the age of 57 I should know better," one woman wrote Senator Church, "but I really want our country to behave honorably. I never thought the ideals they taught us were just public relations."[35] Playwright Lillian Hellman expressed astonishment at the revelations of 1975. "Murder," she commented in amazement; "we didn't think of ourselves that way once upon a time."[36] A common theme in letters to the editor was the gap between the nation's values to be celebrated in its Bicentennial and the agencies' secret activities. "The CIA abroad and the FBI at home are an affront to the heritage we expect to celebrate in 1976," one writer said. "They have disgraced the flag."[37] Another told the *Washington Post* that the CIA "has taught Americans to live in fear and to think from a premise of fear: what a dastardly way to celebrate our Bicentennial!"[38]

Hellman urged the government to stop using dirty tricks and to begin to practice what it preached. This was typical of the response of many shocked Americans: from now on, they said, the United States should adhere to its true values of liberty and democracy. Americans should put on their white hats again. Prominent liberals insisted that these new tactics were both practical and essential if the country was to regain its soul. The *New York Times* editorial board, for example, declared that morality in government "is not an impractical dream of naive do-gooders. It is the only inherent strength of a self-governing nation."[39] The Church committee assassination report later echoed this judgment: "Means are as important as ends. Crisis makes it tempting to ignore the wise restraints that make men free. But each time we do so, each time the means we use are wrong, our inner strength, the strength which makes us free, is lessened."[40]

But why had the country chosen to sacrifice means for ends? How had Americans come to violate their publicly expressed values? One explanation might be, as Garry Wills suggested, that the Cold War presidents had encouraged the CIA to imitate Soviet methods, regardless of the cost to American values.

This analysis challenged the moral basis of American foreign policy of the Cold War. Acknowledging that the presidents, not an autonomous CIA, had approved assassinations and violated citizens' rights would call into question the morality of the Kennedy-Johnson foreign policy that Church and other liberals had supported in the early 1960s. It would also cast a shadow on a mourned president—and raise the possibility that Kennedy had contributed indirectly to his own death. For if the president had ordered murder plots against Castro, could it be possible that Castro had taken his revenge through Oswald? Finally, blaming the imperial presidency rather than a runaway CIA suggested that the abuses under investigation by the Church committee were more intractable than those exposed by Watergate. If the problem was the presidency rather than the president, if the abuses would not disappear with one man's resignation, then serious, structural reforms would be in order.

But Frank Church and the *New York Times* preferred to believe an alternative theory: that the CIA had run amok. Granted too much secrecy and power, the agency had gone on a rampage and trampled on American values. The problem was one unaccountable agency, not the entire system.

In effect, the "rogue elephant" metaphor became Frank Church's model for CIA behavior. Throughout his committee's public hearings, Church consistently interpreted the agency's past activities through the prism of his favorite theory.

The chairman's conviction that the CIA was out of control, combined with his desire for a sensational topic with which to open his public inquiry, led him to choose an unusual subject for the first set of hearings. For three days, the Church committee members quizzed agency officials about two tiny vials of exotic poisons that had gone astray.

In 1969, in the midst of international treaty negotiations, President Nixon had ordered the destruction of all U.S. chemical and biological weapons. CIA chief Richard Helms told his employees to comply with the order. One middle-ranking CIA officer, however, did not obey. Because the 11 grams of shellfish toxin and 8 milligrams of cobra venom under his control had been difficult and expensive to obtain, this CIA scientist decided to ignore the president's order. When William Colby in 1975 required all employees to inform him of questionable agency activities, another CIA officer told him about the poison cache.

Colby's decision to report this transgression to the Church committee—and his sincere interest in uncovering and reporting similar problems—was part of his strategy for saving the CIA from Congress's wrath. To survive the investigations, Colby believed, the agency needed to reveal all of the CIA's past abuses, while emphasizing that these abuses were "few and far between."[41] Colby believed that the CIA had "bad secrets," such as domestic spying, and "good secrets," such as its sources and some of its methods.[42] Congress would be so impressed by his good faith in disclosing the "bad secrets," Colby hoped, that it would not

A meeting of the Church committee. *Clockwise from Senator Church:* Gary Hart, Philip Hart, Richard Schweiker, Robert Morgan, Walter Mondale, Charles Mathias, Barry Goldwater, Howard Baker, and John Tower. (Courtesy Frank Church Collection, Boise State University Library)

jeopardize the "good secrets" or insist on major reforms. Colby maintained that this approach was not only a tactical but also a constitutional necessity. As a lawyer who had represented the American Civil Liberties Union, Colby believed that he had a duty to cooperate with the congressional investigations, at least as far as the law required. This combination of strategy and scruples led Colby to inform the Justice Department that his predecessor, Richard Helms, might have committed perjury before a congressional committee.[43]

Helms, for obvious reasons, disagreed with this approach, as did other CIA officials and many members of the Ford administration. Former counterintelligence chief James Angleton hinted to friends that Colby might even be working for "the other side."[44] White House officials let Colby know that they disapproved of his accommodating approach. Shortly after Colby first testified to the Rockefeller Commission, the vice president drew him aside and asked, "Bill, do you really have to present all this material to us?" Henry Kissinger once told Colby, who was Catholic, "Bill, you know what you do when you go up to the Hill? You go to confession."[45]

In the case of the shellfish toxin, at least, the White House's doubts about Colby's strategy seemed correct. Church wanted to open the public hearings with an exciting issue; now Colby had handed him "a corker on a silver platter," the CIA chief later conceded.[46] If disseminated through the air, these toxins and other biological weapons could kill many thousands of people. For more precise targeting, the toxins could serve as ammunition in dart guns.[47] Church quickly realized the theatrical possibilities of a hearing that used dart guns and poisons as props. A dramatic hearing would mean lots of media coverage, which in turn would help mobilize support for reform—and possibly for Church's presidential candidacy.

Furthermore, the CIA's failure to destroy these poisons despite a presidential order lent support to Church's rogue elephant theory. Other senators and some staff members did not believe that the small vials of toxins merited such extensive committee attention. "Frank," Senator Mathias told the chairman, "what we have here is a rogue mouse."[48] But Church believed that the toxins helped illustrate a larger issue: the presidents' lack of control over the CIA.

During the hearings, Church presented the toxins as an example of the agency's "insubordination" and its "exceedingly loose" controls.[49] Walter Mondale echoed Church's theme, agreeing that the toxin cache gave him a "gnawing fear" that "things are occurring in deliberate contravention and disregard of official orders."[50] Richard Helms, in contrast, tried to treat the incident as an aberration, saying it was "one of the few instances I knew of in my 25 years where an order was disobeyed."[51]

As he had hoped, Church's poison hearings succeeded in gaining the press's attention. Public television covered the hearings live, and photographs of Church and Goldwater with the dart gun appeared on the front pages of newspapers across the country. The image was not one that the agency wanted to project. As Colby wrote, "The over-all impact was of the wildest hugger-mugger of the cloak-and-dagger world."[52] Moreover, Church seemed to have persuaded many pundits to accept his conclusions about the presidents' control over the CIA. The *New York Times* editorial board agreed that the toxins represented the "most reckless kind of insubordination."[53] Tom Wicker contended that the poisons were "only one more bit of evidence that this agency is a Frankenstein's monster that must be destroyed."[54]

But Church's decision to highlight dart guns and poisons also created some problems for the committee. The executive branch was alarmed and frightened. Many members of the Ford administration became convinced that Church was leading a sensationalistic, irresponsible inquiry that had to be controlled. The toxin hearings, combined with the simultaneous Pike committee decision to confront the executive branch, prompted the White House to begin a coordinated counterattack against the committees.[55]

The hearings also sealed William Colby's fate. Ford had considered replacing him for months. Now, his inability to prevent the embarrassing dart gun hearings—in fact, his indirect responsibility for those hearings—persuaded many in the White House that he had to go. A Ford aide told conservative columnists Rowland Evans and Robert Novak that the photographs of the senators with the dart gun "just about doubled all the damage done to the United States since Congress started investigating."[56] Colby would be fired within two months.

Finally, the toxin hearings served to convince Frank Church that the CIA was indeed a rogue elephant on a rampage. Of his colleagues, only Mondale seemed to agree with him. But Church was certain. "Like other examples discovered in previous executive sessions, and which continue to emerge from the ongoing investigation of the committee," he said in concluding this set of hearings, "the case of the shellfish toxin illustrates how elusive the chain of command can be in the intelligence community."[57] He would continue to find similar cases as his inquiry progressed.

The Church committee's second set of public hearings gave the chairman another opportunity to test his hypothesis. For three days, the committee heard witnesses from the CIA, the FBI, and the Nixon White House testify on what was known as the "Huston plan."

In 1969 and 1970, as young dissidents planned huge antiwar protests in Washington, Richard Nixon decided that his secret intelligence agencies were not doing enough to monitor and control dissent. After chastising his spy directors, he directed Tom Huston, his aide for internal security affairs, to come up with a new master plan for spying on Americans. The Huston plan authorized intelligence agencies to open the mail, examine the cables, eavesdrop on the conversations, and break into the homes and businesses of American citizens who disagreed with their government's policies. The president approved the plan, even though many parts of it were illegal and unconstitutional. The directors of the CIA, the National Security Agency (NSA), and the Defense Intelligence Agency voiced no objections. But J. Edgar Hoover of the FBI demanded that Nixon give him explicit authorization to break the law. The FBI director, now over seventy and threatened with the specter of forced retirement from the bureau he had built, had grown cautious. Nixon refused to sign his name to each case of government lawbreaking, and the plan died.[58]

Or did it? Intelligence agencies had been conducting similar programs since before the Huston plan was proposed and continued to operate these programs after its supposed demise. The CIA operated a mail-opening program from 1955 to 1973, both before and after the Huston plan. The FBI's counterintelligence programs against dissidents, the CIA's domestic spying program, and the NSA's monitoring of overseas cables also took place before and after Nixon's decision to rescind the Huston plan.

In Church's view, the Huston plan hearings reinforced his theory that the intelligence agencies were rogue elephants. As in the case of the shellfish toxin, Church told the committee's audience, the decision of the president on the Huston plan "seemed to matter little."[59] In fact, he concluded, the president almost seemed an "irrelevancy."[60] He angrily told James Angleton, former head of counterintelligence for the CIA, that "the Commander in Chief is not the Commander in Chief at all. He is just a problem. You do not want to inform him in the first place, because he might say no."[61] Angleton's own statements seemed to buttress Church's thesis. "It is inconceivable that a secret intelligence arm of the government has to comply with all the overt orders of the government," he told committee staff members.[62]

On the first day of these hearings, Senator Mondale, the lone committee adherent of Church's rogue elephant theory, continued to agree with Church. At one point, he told Huston that "the only way the President can control these agencies is to get them over to the White House for dinner and spend hour after hour to find out what is going on, and then get on his knees and plead that they might do as he wished."[63]

But on the second day, the committee heard evidence that Presidents Johnson and Nixon had put heavy pressure on the intelligence community to increase domestic spying. Convinced that the antiwar protesters were supported by foreign leaders, the presidents had ordered the intelligence agencies to find evidence of this alleged alien influence.

Mondale seemed persuaded by this new information. On the second day of hearings, he noted that the stimulus for domestic spying "began in the White House." The presidents' paranoia had led to unconstitutional spying on Americans and had delayed the end of the war. Perhaps the country needed laws to limit the powers of the president as well as those of the CIA, he concluded. "Because, really, you were an agent of the President in all of these matters," he told Angleton.[64]

By the third day, Mondale had abandoned Church's metaphor for good. He told his colleagues and the audience that the primary problem seemed to be "presidential unaccountability to the law."[65] Since the blame lay with the president, he wondered what type of reforms could solve this problem: "What do we do to make certain that Presidents in the future do not use these secret agencies to carry out their fantasies, to try to shift the blame from themselves to somebody else, and if possible, to foreigners? I think it is asking a lot of human nature to ask people at the second level of Government to disobey the orders of the President."[66] He reminded his colleagues that "the grant of power to the CIA and to these other agencies is, above all, a grant of power to the President." This power was highly dangerous because the president could exercise it in secret. "And that," Mondale said, "is what I think makes our task so very difficult."[67]

But even as Mondale withdrew his support for Church's theory, the chairman continued to find evidence of the CIA's autonomy. After a one-day inquiry into the political uses of the Internal Revenue Service, the committee held three days of hearings on the intelligence agencies' illegal mail-opening programs. The committee revealed that the CIA had opened more than 200,000 letters and had photographed the outside of 2.7 million pieces of mail sent to and from the Soviet Union during its nearly twenty year program. The FBI had operated a similar project. Richard Helms told the committee that he thought he had informed President Johnson about the CIA's program but couldn't remember if he had notified Nixon. He was sure he had informed Nixon's attorney general, John Mitchell.

In his questioning of the witnesses, Church tried to emphasize the CIA's independence. When Mitchell disputed Helms's contention that he had been informed of the program, Church accepted the Watergate figure's testimony at face value. "How in the world can the President exercise meaningful control when the agencies of the Government are conducting dubious operations and the President has no knowledge of them, the attorney general has no knowledge of them, until after the fact?" he asked. The agencies would recommend programs, the president would turn down the programs, but then "the same practice is continued, just as though he weren't there," Church commented.[68]

Senator Mondale had realized that the Church committee's real mission was to control the president's secret authority. Upon reflection, he had concluded that the members' task was much more difficult than chastising bureaucrats like James Angleton and Tom Huston. But the committee's chairman continued to resist that unpleasant conclusion.

Near the end of its public hearings, the committee turned to the most shocking examples of domestic abuses. The committee's examination of the FBI was one of its most significant contributions to public knowledge. It also unearthed the most persuasive evidence of presidential responsibility for intelligence agency abuses.

The committee began its FBI hearings by presenting the details of COINTELPRO, or counterintelligence program—the bureau's efforts to discredit and destroy dissident organizations. The program had been directed against many groups, including Communists, the Socialist Workers' Party, the Ku Klux Klan, civil rights and black nationalist groups, the New Left, and women's liberation groups. FBI informants would infiltrate these organizations, report on their movements, disrupt their plans, and often attempt to discredit the organizations' members—even, in some cases, to the point of encouraging them to kill one another or destroying their personal lives. For example, one agent tried to break up the marriage of a white woman involved in a black activist group by writing a letter to her husband. Pretending to be a disgruntled black woman in the group, the white agent wrote to the husband in what he presumed was black English: "Look man I guess your old lady doesn't get enough at home or she wouldn't be shucking and jiving with our black man in ACTION, you dig? Like all she wants to integrate is the bedroom, and us black sisters ain't gonna take no second best from our men."[69]

The most egregious example of the FBI's abuse of authority was its harassment of Martin Luther King, Jr. Not only had the bureau bugged and wiretapped the civil rights leader, but it had also engaged in a concerted program to knock him "off his pedestal and to reduce him completely in influence."[70] The FBI warned congressmen, university officials, and even the pope of King's allegedly dangerous and immoral tendencies. The low point of the bureau's harassment campaign came thirty-four days before King was to accept the Nobel Peace Prize in 1964. King received an anonymous tape in the mail that purportedly recorded him engaged in extramarital affairs. The letter that accompanied the tape— written by assistant FBI director William Sullivan himself, it was later revealed—concluded with this suggestion: "King, there is only one thing left for you to do. You know what it is. You have just 34 days in which to do it."[71] King took this to be a suggestion that he commit suicide.

The committee's hearings also revealed that presidents since Franklin Roosevelt had ordered the FBI to wiretap, follow, and compile secret files on American citizens for political purposes. Both Robert Kennedy and Lyndon Johnson had preceded Richard Nixon in ordering the bureau to wiretap or monitor the activities of reporters. President Johnson had asked the FBI for reports on Barry Goldwater's staff in 1964, when the senator was running against him for president, and on Americans who wrote the White House opposing his foreign policy decisions. Even Franklin Roosevelt had asked the FBI to investigate Americans who sent angry telegrams to the White House.[72]

In the view of the nation's pundits, the FBI hearings proved that the president was responsible for many of the intelligence community's abuses. The *New York Times* decided that the latest revelations put Watergate in a new perspective. "By the time Richard Nixon became President, the practiced seaminess had become so entrenched that the deceptions of Watergate flowed with alarming naturalness," the paper's editorial board declared.[73] William Safire tried to use the revelations to revise the historical image of his favorite president. "History will show the Nixon Administration not as the one that invented abuse of power," he wrote, "but the one that gloriously if unwittingly served the cause of individual liberty by the clumsy way it tried to continue the abuses of Kennedy and Johnson."[74] Tom Wicker astutely pointed out that the newest revelations and conclusions about presidential responsibility presented troublesome problems for reformers. "No one in Congress or the executive branch has even begun to face—let alone answer—the consequent philosophical and institutional questions" raised by this new evidence, Wicker wrote.[75]

But the chairman did not seem impressed by the evidence of presidential responsibility for many FBI abuses. Church avoided two of the four days of hearings on FBI abuses—hearings that included many unpleasant revelations of Democratic presidents' sins. Even when he attended, his better-prepared colleague, Walter Mondale, frequently upstaged him.[76] The chairman was conspicuously absent the day his staff presented the report concluding that presidents of both parties had abused the FBI for political purposes, and he seemed resistant to their conclusions. For example, on the second day of FBI hearings, Church noted that the presidentially inspired Huston plan had been far more limited than the routine methods employed by the bureau on its own.[77] In the face of increasingly troublesome evidence, Church refused to abandon his theory of bureaucratic autonomy.

While the Church committee argued over rogue elephants and imperial presidencies, the American public struggled to comprehend the committee's shocking revelations about the nation's spies. Polls showed that the CIA and the FBI had dropped to their lowest approval ratings in history, with most Americans expressing strong disapproval of CIA domestic spying and FBI harassment of Martin Luther King, Jr.[78] The American people had been fed a diet of images of heroic spies and counterspies in movies and novels for years. They had believed that the CIA and the FBI could do no wrong. As a result, most Americans were stunned and horrified by the revelations, and some seemed ready to believe that *everything* they had been told was a lie.

One sign of this cynicism and disillusionment was the renewed popularity of conspiracy theories. After learning that Hoover's FBI had tried to convince Martin Luther King, Jr., to kill himself, that the White House plumbers had plotted to kill Jack Anderson, and that the CIA had drugged unsuspecting citizens, some Americans began to question the official explanation of many recent events. As journalist Rod MacLeish explained, "American society has gone buggy on conspiracy theories of late because so many nasty demonstrations of the real thing have turned up."[79] News articles and op-ed columns pondered possible CIA involvement in everything from the Watergate break-in to the murder of mobster Sam Giancana just days before he was to testify to the Church committee about the Castro plots.[80]

The most popular theories concerned the murders of John F. Kennedy and Martin Luther King, Jr. Many Americans had never been convinced that Kennedy's assassin, Lee Harvey Oswald, had acted alone. When the Church committee revealed that the CIA and the FBI had withheld key evidence from the commission investigating Kennedy's death, the lone-assassin theory was left "almost totally without adherents," according to Gallup pollsters. By 1976, the overwhelming majority of Americans, 81 percent, believed that other people were involved in the assassination, while 8 percent were unsure. Even more surprising, seventy percent of Americans believed that Martin Luther King's assassin, James Earl Ray, was part of a conspiracy, while sixty percent believed that both the Kennedy and King assassinations involved conspiracies. Only 5 percent of the American public accepted the official explanations of both shootings.[81]

Furthermore, some influential Americans openly suggested that the FBI itself had been involved in the King slaying. After the Church committee revealed the bureau's harassment of King, Coretta Scott King and other former King advisers called for reopening the assassination probe.[82] The *New York Times* added its voice to the chorus demanding a review of the investigation, saying that the Church committee's revelations added "grotesque dimensions" to earlier doubts about whether Ray had acted alone. "The very least one can wonder, considering the late FBI director J. Edgar Hoover's feelings about Dr. King," the *Times* wrote, "is whether he could have put his agency's whole heart into the investigation of the assassination."[83] Others wondered more. The *Saginaw News* admitted that it was "chilling" and alarming to believe the FBI played a role in King's death. "Yet it is hardly more chilling than testimony already a matter of record concerning alleged spy network involvement with organized crime in the field of international assassinations," the paper concluded.[84]

As the *Saginaw News* editorial illustrates, speculation about FBI involvement was not limited to the radical fringe. Columnist Mike Royko told of "a middle-aged man with middle-of-the-road political beliefs, a short haircut, a mortgaged house, a midsized car, 9-to-5 job and a couple of kids in college" who had suggested to him that King "had been bumped off by the nation's most respected police agency." The man "almost took it for granted" that even if the FBI had not killed King, it had at least covered up for those who did. Royko explained that he was not shocked. "A few years ago, my answer would have been something like: 'Don't be ridiculous.' But now all I could say was 'I don't know.' "[85]

As Americans braced themselves for more frightening revelations, Hollywood and the publishing industry dramatized their worst fears—and thus reinforced their plausibility. Historian Richard Gid Powers has described how the FBI's image in popular culture shifted dramatically in the mid-1970s. For decades, the bureau's massive public relations machine had projected a positive public image by working with the entertainment industry and with friendly journalists—and by freezing out the few unfriendly journalists. But in the 1970s, the formerly heroic "G-man" abruptly began turning up as the villain in movies, television programs, and pulpy thrillers. For example, in Irving Wallace's 1976 novel, *The R Document*, the evil FBI director planned to kill the president, set up concentration camps, and suspend the Constitution. Thriller author Robert Ludlum wrote of a scheming, blackmailing bureau in his 1977 novel, *The Chancellor Manuscript*.[86] Just a few years before, the bureau had been symbolized by the clean-cut, heroic Efrem Zimbalist, Jr., in *The FBI* television show. In Powers's view, these fictional accounts demonstrate that "popular culture's new devil theory about Hoover and the FBI" had become conventional wisdom by 1976. "Popular fiction does not risk tampering with the public's sense of 'what is,' " he writes. "Pulp writers accept the popular wisdom and manipulate it to suit the conventions of formula entertainment."[87]

Many Americans were so disgusted by the revelations about the bureau and its late director that they demanded a new name for the J. Edgar Hoover FBI headquarters. No public controversy about the $126 million building had emerged when it was dedicated on 1 October 1975. The president and attorney general had appeared at the dedication to eulogize Hoover, and the newspaper stories on the event did not mention the growing shadow over his reputation. But the situation changed the next month when the Church committee revealed Hoover's harassment of King. A few days after the committee's FBI hearings, the *Washington Post* noted the irony of naming the new building after "the perpetrator of massive, systematic and vicious violations of the constitutional rights of American citizens."[88] A week later, Gilbert Gude, a Republican congressman from Maryland, introduced a bill to change the building's name.[89] The *Post* editorial board, op-ed columnists, and other citizens urged Congress to pass the bill. One correspondent, for example, wrote the *Post* that the building should not bear the name of a man who "cared little about the Constitution and laws of the nation, and who never hesitated to bring his enormous power, legal and illegal, down on those he hated."[90] Although Gude's bill attracted twenty-five cosponsors, it died in the Public Works and Transportation Committee. The bill was reintroduced in two subsequent sessions but never made it out of committee.[91]

The CIA's image in popular culture was also damaged by the intelligence investigations. In the agency's case, this image had been under attack before the congressional inquiries. In the early 1970s, a handful of American spy novels and movies had begun to portray the CIA as a callous, amoral, and even murderous bureaucracy.[92] Most notably, the 1973 movie *Scorpio* featured a ruthless CIA director who was willing to sacrifice the lives of his agents and American citizens in order to assassinate a possible Soviet double agent.[93]

Although the trend of demonizing the CIA in popular culture began before the investigations, the congressional and journalistic inquiries clearly intensified it. By 1975 and 1976, as the intelligence investigations proceeded, the portrayal of a paranoid CIA, which tried to murder virtuous agents intent on exposing its perfidy, had become a veritable subgenre of spy literature. In Robert Duncan's *Dragons at the Gate* (1975), the CIA tried to kill an agent who opposed its plan to destroy the Japanese economy; in Brian Garfield's *Hopscotch* (1975), the CIA tried to kidnap and murder a former agent determined to write his memoirs; and in Jim Garrison's *The Star-Spangled Contract* (1976), the CIA, the Pentagon, the Defense Intelligence Agency, and other government officials succeeded in killing an agent who wanted to expose their plot to assassinate the president.[94]

The movie that best exemplified this change in the CIA's popular image—and the investigations' role in accelerating this change—was *Three Days of the Condor*. In the movie, which was released in late 1975, Robert Redford played a CIA analyst who had discovered a renegade group within the agency planning an unauthorized covert action in the Middle East. First the treacherous agents killed all of the analyst's colleagues; then the CIA itself targeted him to hide evidence of the plot. The analyst finally saved himself and, presumably, his country by telling all to the *New York Times*. In the movie's last scene, a CIA official told the analyst that his disclosures would greatly damage the agency. "I hope so," he replied.

Although based on a novel by James Grady written the year before the intelligence revelations, the film included plot changes that demonstrated the influence of the investigations.[95] The film's dramatic ending in front of the *New York Times* building and its unspoken tribute to journalistic heroism were wholly inventions of the movie. In addition, the movie version eliminated the few sympathetic CIA characters who were in Grady's novel. It also changed the central conspiracy from drug smuggling to unauthorized covert action. The villains in the novel were criminals hiding under the cover of the CIA; the villains in the screen version were perfect examples of Frank Church's "rogue elephants." It was not mere greed that led them to murder but their fanatical, misguided patriotism. According to the film's production notes, Redford and the producers "decided to create a film that would reflect the climate of America in the aftermath of the Watergate crisis."[96]

The executive branch was gravely worried by this change in climate. A few negative portrayals of the intelligence agencies in films and novels did not necessarily mean that Americans would now demand far-reaching reforms. But they did indicate that many citizens were starting to question institutions that had never been challenged before. Faced with a disillusioned public and an aggressive Congress, Ford's top advisers decided that the White House needed to take the offensive.[97]

Throughout his chairmanship, Church had tried to avoid confrontation with the executive branch. He attempted to negotiate with the White House staff in order to gain access to documents rather than to issue public threats or take unilateral action. The executive branch was pleased by this approach. The FBI noted that its relationship with the Senate committee was much more "harmonious" than its dealings with the House committee, while the Republican members praised Church's "unfailingly considerate and cooperative" attitude.[98] CIA counsel Mitchell Rogovin found Church to be "rather benign and friendly" in contrast to the pugnacious Pike.[99] But some of the Church committee staff members disagreed with their chairman's conciliatory style. "People will say you're terribly reasonable," one of them said, "but that's only because you haven't found out anything."[100]

When he did confront the White House, Church tried hard to demonstrate his objectivity and fairness. In the midst of profound disagreements with the executive branch over the release of interim reports, he gave a speech on the Senate floor praising the CIA's numerous successes in forecasting world events.[101] By contrast, Otis Pike publicly charged that the CIA was so incompetent that it would not be able to predict an attack on the United States itself.[102] Under Church's watchful eye, his committee's public hearings sparked few controversies like those that regularly flared up during the more colorful House committee hearings. Church's committee did not issue subpoenas for documents until six months into its inquiry, and it never recommended citing any official for contempt. Pike, by contrast, did not shy away from threatening executive officials with contempt when they failed to comply with his numerous subpoenas.

But Church's civil approach did not always persuade the executive branch to surrender documents more readily. From the beginning, the agencies were reluctant to give the committee all of the documents it wanted when it wanted them. As staff member Loch Johnson recalled, "We might have been ready to tango straight to the center of our mandate, but the executive branch preferred to waltz."[103] CIA counsel Rogovin concedes that he was always looking for opportunities to delay, which is the standard legal procedure in such cases. Congressional investigators,

President Ford meets with members of the Church committee on 5 March 1975 to negotiate the committee's access to documents. *Clockwise from President Ford:* Secretary of State Henry Kissinger; Senator John Tower; John Marsh, counselor to the president; Philip Buchen, counselor to the president; Brent Scowcroft, assistant for national security affairs; and Senator Frank Church. (Courtesy Gerald R. Ford Library)

like plaintiffs in a civil case, always try to speed the process along, Rogovin has observed, while "the other side always thinks the schoolhouse may burn down and then you don't have to take the exam."[104]

The Ford administration soon moved beyond passive delaying tactics to a more aggressive, systematic strategy. The first sign of this new combativeness was the executive branch's opposition to the committee's hearings on the National Security Agency. This supersecret bureaucracy, the headquarters of U.S. communications intelligence, had directed two programs of "questionable propriety and dubious legality," in Church's view.[105] In Operation MINARET, the NSA had intercepted and monitored the overseas phone calls of some 1,600 Americans. Operation SHAMROCK had relied on the voluntary cooperation of international cable companies, which had provided the NSA with copies of private cable messages for twenty-eight years.

The administration argued that public hearings on sensitive NSA matters would disclose secret technology and harm national security.

The secretary of defense and attorney general appeared before the committee to warn against public hearings; the president himself phoned key committee members. The committee, deeply divided over the issue, at first decided to allow a limited hearing on MINARET but none on SHAMROCK. To convince reluctant committee members that a SHAMROCK hearing would not endanger national security, Church sent his staff's report on the program to the NSA director and asked him to assess its accuracy.[106] In effect, he was offering the executive branch the opportunity to censor the committee's report in advance. Finally, after a House subcommittee chaired by Congresswoman Bella Abzug began to publicize the program despite executive objections, Church persuaded his committee to hold a narrowly focused hearing on SHAMROCK.[107]

The administration also tried to sabotage the committee's hearings on covert action. The committee wanted to hold public hearings on U.S. intervention in Chile, a recent and illustrative example of covert action. But the administration officials concerned—William Colby and Henry Kissinger—refused to appear at these hearings. Church was reluctant to subpoena them, even though Otis Pike had not only slapped Kissinger with several subpoenas but also threatened him with contempt. "Let's avoid the needless pyrotechnics of the House committee," Church told his staff.[108] As a political pragmatist, Church understood that the Senate would be unlikely to support him on a contempt charge against the popular and powerful Kissinger. Although the committee released a detailed report on Chile, it was forced to hold public hearings on the subject without testimony from the primary policymakers.[109] The members heard from two former U.S. ambassadors who had been largely unaware of major decisions. The committee also tried to persuade former president Nixon to testify but had to settle for his written responses to the committee's questions.[110]

Finally, the administration tried to suppress one of the committee's proudest accomplishments: its assassination report. Ford's decision to attempt to squelch the report surprised many committee members; after all, he had given the Rockefeller Commission's assassination files to the committee in an attempt to reassure the public that the government was not engaged in a cover-up. The committee majority had assumed that its report, though based on secret hearings and documents, could be made public after careful review. But the president insisted that he had never expected the committee to release a catalog of the CIA's murder plots. The members could recommend ways to prevent such abuses in the future, but they were not to dredge up the sins of the past. In a meeting

Senator Church reads his committee's assassination report, which was released on
20 November 1975. (Courtesy Frank Church Collection, Boise State University
Library)

with top aides, Ford repeatedly emphasized his opposition to an official
U.S. government document on assassinations.[111] He ordered his aides to
do everything they could to stop the report.

When his committee showed signs of bending to the president's will,
Frank Church made the most courageous decision of his chairmanship:
he threatened to resign unless the report was released.[112] His stunned
colleagues quickly endorsed a compromise that would mollify their
chairman and avoid a direct confrontation with the president: they would
let the Senate decide. The Senate, however, was equally unwilling to take
a stand on the issue. It refused to block the report's release, but it would
not approve its release, either. The senators' refusal to back Church on
this issue demonstrates how little support existed for more revelations,
even though the investigations would continue for months.

Church finally released the report on the committee's own authority
on 20 November.[113] Nine months after Daniel Schorr had disclosed the
existence of assassination plots, six months after the Rockefeller Commission had suppressed its conclusions on the matter, a thorough exam-

ination of the CIA's involvement in murder conspiracies finally saw the light of day.

Church's determination to release the report was both ideologically consistent and politically astute. Of the twenty-seven newspapers surveyed by *Editorials on File*, only five criticized the committee for releasing the report over the president's objection.[114] The nation's editors found the report's revelations "shocking and disturbing" (the *Rocky Mountain News*), "revolting" (the *Milwaukee Journal*), and "inexcusable by any standards of international morality and diplomatic expediency" (the *New York Times*).[115] The *Times* expressed the consensus of the nation's editorial writers when it called on the committee "not to destroy the intelligence agencies but to put them on a short leash to prevent them from straying beyond the legal and moral limitations essential to preserve a free and lawful society."[116]

The report itself clarified the sordid details of the plots and cleared the CIA of direct responsibility for any successful assassinations. The committee determined that the agency had tried and failed to kill Castro at least eight times, using such exotic weaponry as exploding seashells, toxic diving suits, and poisoned ballpoint pens. The CIA also sent an unnamed "lethal substance" to agents in the Congo to kill Patrice Lumumba, but his Congolese enemies captured and killed him before the American agents could execute their plan.

In these two cases, the committee found direct evidence that the CIA had plotted murder. In three other instances, the investigators determined that the agency had encouraged the killers of foreign leaders but had not been involved in the actual assassinations. American officials in 1961 supplied weapons to dissidents in the Dominican Republic who were trying to kill dictator Rafael Trujillo. These rebels succeeded in killing Trujillo but apparently not with the CIA weapons. U.S. policymakers also encouraged the coup against Ngo Dinh Diem of South Vietnam in 1963 but did not suggest that the coup plotters assassinate him. In Chile in 1970, the CIA aided a group that planned to kidnap General Rene Schneider, whose devotion to constitutional processes made him an obstacle to their plan to overthrow Salvador Allende. The agency did not suggest killing Schneider, but, as Church said in his introduction to the report, "the possibility that he would be killed should have been recognized as a foreseeable risk of the kidnapping."[117]

Daniel Schorr, who had been verbally attacked by Richard Helms for his reporting on assassination plots, maintained that the report vindicated him. "It seems, according to this report, to be true, as ex-director

Richard Helms has said, that the CIA never assassinated any foreign leader," he told his CBS audience. "It seems also to be true that it wasn't for want of trying."[118]

But the report did not end the debate on the "rogue elephant" issue. "Even after our long investigation," the report concluded, "it is unclear whether the conflicting and inconclusive state of the evidence is due to the system of plausible denial or whether there were, in fact, serious shortcomings in the system of authorization" that made it possible for the CIA to plot these murders without express approval from the president.[119] Walter Mondale had summarized the committee's position more succinctly the month before: "Pinning down responsibility for many of the actions the committee has uncovered is like nailing Jello to a wall."[120] The committee did, however, come closer to exonerating some presidents than others. The report concluded that it was a "reasonable inference" to assume that Dwight Eisenhower had authorized the plot against Lumumba, while it absolved Lyndon Johnson from responsibility for the Castro plots.[121]

Despite the report's equivocation on the issue of presidential responsibility, however, Church still seemed inclined to blame the CIA more than the presidents. When a reporter asked why there seemed to be "misunderstanding" between the agency and the presidents on the plots, Church said, "Well, I think if you turn to page 267 and read where 'Agency officials failed on several occasions to reveal the plots to their superiors or to do so with sufficient detail and clarity' I think you'll find the answer to that question."[122] It is interesting that Church chose to highlight this finding of the report rather than the criticism of White House officials that immediately followed it.[123]

Moreover, the report clearly stated that, presidentially directed or not, the plots were "aberrations." The committee "does not believe that the acts which it has examined represent the real American character," the report concluded.[124] The *Washington Post* accepted the committee's judgment on this issue with relief. "To believe otherwise," the paper said in an editorial, "is to assault the basic process of consensus and correction by which a democratic society must proceed."[125] Neither the *Post* nor the committee explained how these "aberrations" had continued through four presidencies.

Church's achievement should not be underestimated. Despite his desire to jump into the presidential race and his time-consuming simultaneous investigation into multinational corporations, he remained committed to the intelligence inquiry. He led his committee in disclosing the details of the FBI's harassment of Martin Luther King, Jr., and other domestic leaders and groups. The committee members exposed the dimensions of the mail-opening programs, the NSA surveillance of Americans, the FBI's illegal break-ins, and the political use of the Internal Revenue Service. They described how presidents since Franklin Roosevelt had misused the FBI for political purposes. They gave the nation its most complete study of covert action in their interim report on Chile. And they detailed the CIA's involvement in various assassination plots, thus raising questions about the completeness of the Warren Commission report and about the historical image of John Kennedy.

Church was also a politically shrewd chairman. He never antagonized individuals in the executive branch, and he labored hard to convince his Republican colleagues that he was a responsible overseer. He proved adept at maintaining the favorable press coverage that was essential for his committee's success. He also persuaded most of the media, with the notable exception of William Safire, that he had not blocked the disclosure of Democratic abuses.

But *abuses* is the key word. Church and his committee focused exclusively on abuses, not on broader problems with the structure and purpose of the intelligence community. As CIA counsel Rogovin has commented, the committee members had the opportunity to make "a much more significant analysis of the intelligence community than some of the episodic abuse issues that they got wrapped up in."[126] These abuses, they determined, were in the past and furthermore were exceptions to the rule. This assessment would subvert the committee's own reform efforts. Why should Congress make fundamental reforms if the past abuses had been aberrations and were thus not likely to happen again? How could the committee legislate against the "odd mistake," in Richard Helms's words?[127] Only systemic problems would merit extensive reforms.

Ironically, the Church committee's final report printed part of a secret Cold War document that contradicted its conclusions on these "aberrations." The 1954 Doolittle committee report had devised an official justification for covert action. Concluding that the United States now faced "an implacable enemy whose avowed objective is world domination," the Doolittle committee argued that "there are no rules in such a game. Hitherto acceptable norms of human conduct do not apply." It urged U.S. policymakers to reconsider "long-standing American concepts of 'fair play.'" The United States must learn to *"subvert, sabotage and de-*

stroy our enemies by more clever, more sophisticated and more effective methods than those used against us."[128]

The Doolittle report was an unpleasant reminder that ends had become more important than means—that in some respects, the United States had become like its enemy. The Church committee rejected its reasoning. "It may well be ourselves that we injure most if we adopt tactics 'more ruthless than the enemy,'" the Church committee's assassination report concluded.[129] But although they condemned this passage of the Doolittle report, the Democratic members declined to grapple with its implications. They failed to realize that this document explained the philosophy behind the abuses.

The Doolittle report proved that the abuses uncovered by the Church committee were far from aberrational; they were natural extensions of Cold War policies. The growth of secrecy and power in the executive branch—as well as the interventionist foreign policy of the Cold War—had made such tactics inevitable. Plausible denial may have obscured the president's responsibility, and the individual agencies may have acted autonomously on minor matters like dart guns and mail opening. But the overall direction of U.S. intelligence activities was consistent. And that direction came from the top.

In the House of Representatives, by contrast, the investigating committee did not concentrate on abuses and did not view intelligence community mistakes as aberrations. As one former CIA official told Seymour Hersh, "The House goes after the arteries, while the Senate goes after the capillaries."[130] In a way, then, the House committee presented a greater threat to the intelligence community. It remained to be seen whether its approach would be any more successful.

It took this investigation to convince me that I had

always been told lies, to make me realize that I was

tired of being told lies.

Otis Pike, quoted in Oriana Fallaci,

"Otis Pike and the CIA"

Challenging the System

Otis Pike's Investigation

Otis Pike was not at all like Frank Church. A moderate Democrat repeatedly reelected by a conservative Long Island district, he had no special love for the Kennedy presidency; in fact, he wasn't even a liberal. And no one could ever accuse Pike of being sanctimonious. He was flamboyantly irreverent, frequently using his legendary wit to ridicule the federal bureaucracy, the military, and even himself.

Above all, Pike developed an agenda for his intelligence investigation that was hailed by friends and foes alike as more substantive and rigorous than that of Church's committee. Instead of focusing on CIA and FBI abuses, Pike led an inquiry that examined the systemic problems of the intelligence community. He wanted to know the answers to three questions: How much does our intelligence community cost us? How well does it perform its job? And what risks does it pose?

The CIA and White House officials who dealt with both committees later commented that they were initially more impressed by Pike's investigation. William Colby respected Pike's "splendid" agenda. "He wasn't after the diddly little abuses," he says.[1] Mitchell Rogovin, the CIA's outside counsel for the investigations, explains that he did not like Pike but respected him more than Church as a committee chairman. "He knew what he was looking at, and he wasn't going to be deflected by poisoned dart guns and shellfish toxins and the silliness of the moment."[2] Even Church committee member Howard Baker concedes that "the House approach was better."[3]

Pike did not believe in examining past abuses for their own sake; he was interested not in the occasional aberration but in the patterns that the abuses disclosed. He did not try to attract public and media attention with dart guns and sensational revelations. His adversaries both respected and feared this approach. Yet unlike Church, at the end of the investigation, Pike was discredited, vilified, and repudiated by his institution. As White House aide James Wilderotter has commented, "The Senate committee, which should have looked worse, wound up looking better than the House committee."[4]

The story of this transformation helps explain the dynamics of Congress after Watergate. Otis Pike, for all his conservative credentials, favored much more substantive changes than did most House members. Ultimately, the post-Watergate House—despite its aggressive reputation—proved reluctant to wrest control of intelligence from the executive.

When Otis Pike assumed the chairmanship of the investigation in July, he also took on the burden of a bitterly divided committee and the pressure of an unrealistic deadline. The House intelligence committee had already existed for six months but had accomplished nothing except its own destruction.

The committee had begun its life under the chairmanship of Lucien Nedzi. In many ways, the Michigan Democrat was a transitional figure in intelligence oversight. His appointment to chair the CIA oversight subcommittee of the Armed Services Committee in 1971 had been widely viewed as a victory for congressional oversight. As a liberal and an early opponent of the Vietnam War, Nedzi strongly disagreed with one of

Challenging the System

his Senate counterparts, John Stennis, who maintained that overseers should protect the CIA, shut their eyes, "and take what is coming."[5] Nedzi demanded many more agency briefings for his subcommittee and was more skeptical of CIA activities than previous overseers had been.

But the subcommittee chairman did not believe that his oversight responsibilities included publicizing past abuses. He wanted to keep the CIA accountable but saw no useful purpose in advertising its failings to the press or the public. Moreover, he felt constrained by his conservative colleagues and small staff. Accordingly, he saw the new special committee as an opportunity to investigate the secret agencies with a free hand.[6]

Nedzi's thorough but cautious oversight had been regarded as responsible, even progressive, in the early 1970s. But by 1975, Vietnam and Watergate had shattered the liberal consensus and polarized the Democratic Party. Many Democrats on Nedzi's committee, radicalized by the war and the revelations of Nixon administration abuses, demanded a more assertive style of oversight.

These new watchdogs were determined to expose policies that had been ignored or even tacitly approved by "responsible" overseers like Nedzi. They remembered that their chairman had voted against banning CIA covert actions and that he had opposed publicizing CIA activities in Chile. They wondered what other dirty secrets he might have overlooked. Some of them suspected that he was more interested in covering up abuses than in exposing them.

Given these profound differences on the committee, it was only a matter of time before the underlying tensions erupted into open conflict. The first sign of trouble appeared when the panel tried to hire a staff director. By early April, the Church committee had hired its committee counsel, staff director, and forty staff members. But the House committee had not made a single appointment. Nedzi complained that there was no consensus for a staff director among his divided committee members. The most liberal members, Ron Dellums and Michael Harrington, wanted former attorney general Ramsey Clark for the post. Other members thought it was important to appoint a Republican staff director. In any case, many members believed that Nedzi was taking too long to make the selection. In mid-May, the committee finally settled on a thirty-year-old Republican lawyer named A. Searle Field. The choice was not entirely a happy one. Harrington charged that Field, who had led his class at Georgetown Law School but was young and comparatively inexperienced, met only "minimal standards" for the position.[7]

A worse crisis rocked the committee the next month. The committee chairman, already under fire from some of his members for the slow pace of the investigation, was the subject of an explosive *New York Times* exposé headlined "Nedzi Is Said to Have Kept House in Dark on CIA Violations." As the article explained, Nedzi had learned about the "family jewels" list of CIA abuses more than a year before and had not informed either the public or his fellow committee members.[8] He had been privy to the CIA's darkest secrets—the secrets that had prompted the whole investigation—and had not told a soul.

Ironically, Nedzi was the only congressional overseer who had been alarmed by the CIA abuses. When CIA chief William Colby had briefed him in 1973 on the 693-page list of company horrors, Nedzi had insisted on reading the entire report and had urged Colby to make it public. He now maintains that he was planning to tell his committee about Colby's secret briefing; in fact, he says, he was in the process of scheduling an intelligence committee hearing on the "family jewels" when the *Times* story appeared.[9] That story, however, destroyed his credibility on the committee. Some of the members were already skeptical of his ability to conduct a fair investigation. After all, the year before he had tried to prevent Michael Harrington from releasing information on CIA intervention in Chile. Now here was more proof that he was not committed to public disclosure of past abuses—that he was a "weak, vacillating presence," in Harrington's words.[10]

All six of the other Democrats on the committee immediately demanded that Nedzi resign or be removed.[11] Insulted and outraged, Nedzi refused to resign, and the House leadership refused to unseat him. Speaker Carl Albert, surprised and angry that these upstarts would attack a respected House member, could not understand the insurgents. "I'm not going to destroy a chairman," Albert told reporters. "What are they so mad about?"[12]

After a long and acrimonious meeting with the committee rebels and the House leadership, Nedzi finally agreed to a compromise. He would appoint a special subcommittee to focus on the CIA. The full intelligence committee would deal with the other agencies. Although the compromise did not satisfy the most liberal members of the Nedzi committee, Speaker Albert was immensely relieved by the arrangement.[13]

But Albert was unduly optimistic. Just days later, the "fragile veneer of accommodation," as one member put it, was stripped away when the members began arguing over who would sit on the new CIA subcommittee.[14] In making his appointments to the smaller panel, Nedzi ignored Democratic seniority and omitted Dellums and Harrington. Although he later capitulated and agreed to appoint Dellums, Nedzi's continued refusal to place Harrington on the subcommittee enraged the other six Democrats. They voted as a bloc to make the new panel a "subcommittee of the whole," which would include all ten members of the committee. This move put Nedzi in the humiliating position of merely sitting in on an inquiry that he was supposed to head. Infuriated, Nedzi charged that the other members had stripped him of all but "a gavel and a title" and promptly resigned.[15]

The old and new styles of oversight had proven to be incompatible. A majority on the Nedzi committee no longer believed that it was a virtue to keep the CIA's dirty secrets. They viewed Nedzi as a slave of the CIA, not as a "responsible" overseer. The problem they faced, however, was that a majority of the House did not agree with them.

The House made its feelings clear on 16 June when it overwhelmingly refused to let Nedzi quit. Although he insisted that he did not seek the vote, Nedzi clearly wanted the House to vindicate him by rejecting his resignation. He successfully framed the issue as a referendum on his "honor and integrity"—and the honor of all congressmen who had kept the CIA's secrets. The fourteen-year House veteran implied that a vote against his resignation was a vote to vindicate his entire generation—a generation of Americans who had come of age before Vietnam and Watergate. "A man cannot choose his time," he told the House. "He must deal with his own times as he finds them. And be judged primarily by the standards of those times as to his courage, wisdom, and moral rectitude."[16] What was he supposed to have done when he learned of the past abuses? "Rent a stadium and reveal all? Call in television cameras and expose things 10, or 15, or 25 years old?"[17] Democrats and Republicans alike responded sympathetically to Nedzi's speech, praising the chairman's integrity and condemning his committee critics as practicing "cannibalism."[18]

In voting to support Nedzi, the House members acted on a variety of contradictory impulses: personal support for a respected colleague; irritation with the rebellious committee members, who threatened the orderly processes of the House; support for a "responsible" investigation; and disapproval of any intelligence inquiry. If the majority's primary motives were unclear, however, it was nevertheless obvious that the investigation had been stopped and the more outspoken critics of the CIA had been discredited. Nedzi's critics on the committee were in a small minority: the final House vote was 290–64 to reject his resignation.[19]

The House as a whole had never been as committed as the Senate to conducting an investigation. Democratic proponents of reform in the Senate had succeeded in persuading Republicans that the investigation would be fair, bipartisan, and designed to restore confidence in government. But the House investigators had been more strident and unwilling to compromise, especially on the House rule giving Democrats a two-to-one majority on the committee. As a result, 120 conservative House members had opposed the creation of an investigating committee from the start. Now, six months later, with nothing to show for its efforts but an embarrassing internal squabble, the House was left with a committee chairman who was despised by most of his members but could not quit. Many observers speculated that the House would let the Senate proceed with the investigation alone.

But the committee continued for two reasons. First, all of the committee members, both Republicans and Democrats, were determined to proceed with the inquiry and launched a campaign to save the investigation. As part of this effort, they detailed the weighty issues they would examine, including charges of CIA "infiltration" of the White House.[20] Secondly, many House members believed that abandoning the investigation would hurt the House's public image. The post-Watergate House, they believed, should not appear to take part in a whitewash of executive branch abuses. As one congressman said during a debate on the future of the committee, "We have been called the aggressive 94th Congress. . . . I know that none of us want the label of the cover-up Congress."[21]

Still, a sizable minority of House members fought hard to end the investigation, 122 congressmen voting to quash the inquiry against 293 opposed, including all of the committee members. A similar attempt to abolish the investigation and establish a joint oversight committee in the future lost by a narrower margin of 230–178. Finally, the House agreed by a voice vote to reconstitute the committee with an "expanded"—and hopefully more collegial—membership.[22]

The new membership became a hotly contested issue. Don Edwards, busy with other tasks, asked to have his name removed from the list of thirteen members. Nedzi's supporters insisted that Michael Harrington also leave the committee. House hard-liners had already begun a campaign against Harrington by denying him access to secret files of the House Armed Services Committee, despite House rules requiring such access. Harrington argued that the supporters of secrecy were using the moribund issue of his alleged leaks on Chile the year before to discredit him and the entire investigation.[23] Harrington's supporters fought to keep him on the committee, but a long and bitter debate on the floor ended in a 274–119 vote against including the Massachusetts congressman on the committee.[24]

The "reconstituted" intelligence panel bore some resemblance to the late, unlamented Nedzi committee. The symbol of past oversight—Nedzi—was gone, as was the most prominent critic of that past oversight. But three liberal critics of the CIA remained: Robert Giaimo, Ron Dellums, and James Stanton. A moderate Chicago Democrat, Morgan Murphy, also stayed on the committee, as did the three conservative Republicans—Robert McClory, David Treen, and Robert Kasten.

The new members were a diverse mix. Two of the Democrats, Philip Hayes of Indiana and William Lehman of Florida, were relative unknowns who would not play significant roles on the committee. But the other new members would help to shape the agenda and control the tone of the investigation. Les Aspin of Wisconsin was an up-and-coming young Democrat known for his zeal in uncovering Pentagon waste and his talent for self-promotion. Aspin's liberal leanings were balanced by the hard-line conservative beliefs of Texas Democrat Dale Milford, a former television weatherman given to frequent patriotic speeches. The new Republican, Jim Johnson of Colorado, was a wild card. He was billed as a moderate, but he would later reveal himself to be more opposed to covert action than most of the Democratic members.

Speaker Albert's choice for committee chair was widely hailed. Otis Pike, Democrat of Long Island, was described by the New York Times editorial board as "a middle-of-the-road Congressman who has never allowed his concern for national security to cloud his perception of excesses in the executive branch."[25] In Pike, the House leadership had found a man who could satisfy both radicals and conservatives—at least at the beginning.

Given his background, the handsome, silver-haired, fifty-three-year-old congressman chosen to head the new intelligence committee did not seem likely to become a CIA critic. A World War II bomber pilot and veteran member of the Armed Services Committee, Otis Pike had represented a conservative district for eight terms. He was a supporter of the Vietnam War for many years, "I guess long after my district told me not to be."[26] The famed Italian journalist Oriana Fallaci described Pike as a "product of the system, and a faithful one."[27] Yet Pike conducted an

Representative Otis Pike of New York. (Courtesy Library of Congress, Prints and Photographs Division, U.S. News and World Report Magazine Collection, LC-U9-31464-A)

aggressive—his critics would say even reckless—investigation. The clues to his chairmanship lay in his fearless, irreverent personality and his impatience with any type of government incompetence.

Unlike many politicians, Pike liked to laugh at himself and at the U.S. government. The *New York Times* called him one of the wittiest members of Congress, and he lived up to the description.[28] "There's adequate room in politics for a man who takes his work seriously but not himself," he once commented.[29] Pike also refused to take anyone else seriously, including Washington power brokers. This irreverence won him fame—and enemies. Unlike the genial Nedzi, Otis Pike would never be an insider.

Pike's awareness of Nedzi's unhappy history as chair only intensified his natural independence. Determined not to appear coopted by the intelligence agencies, Pike refused to agree to many procedures that Frank Church had approved. He declined to examine documents that his full committee could not see, and he resisted any private consultation with the CIA and executive branch. He also tried to keep his investigation as open as possible: he presided over fifty-four public hearings, more than three times the number held by Church.

Pike's critical, inquisitive nature had already earned him a reputation as a tough investigator. In 1969, he had chaired a special investigative subcommittee on the North Korean seizure of a U.S. spy ship, the *Pueblo*. His subcommittee's harshly worded report concluded that the failure of the defense intelligence agencies to disseminate information quickly "necessarily raises serious questions concerning the effective operation and administration of these organizations."[30]

When Pike decided to take this new, potentially dangerous assignment, he may have calculated that it could help him win enough name recognition to become a serious candidate for the Senate in 1976. He denies now that he was considering a Senate bid, but many observers speculated at the time that he hoped the inquiry would help his career as well as his country. Nedzi's example, though, demonstrated that the job could lead to humiliation as well as celebrity.

As the independent-minded, pugnacious chairman settled into his new assignment, he quickly succeeded in impressing both sides of the intelligence debate with his proposed agenda. Pike wanted to examine three areas: the cost of the intelligence agencies, their performance, and the risks that they posed to Americans.

The chairman decided to address the issue of cost first. The intelligence community's budget—the overall amount as well as expenditures for individual agencies and programs—was concealed from all but a few members of Congress. To regain control over the intelligence community, Congress first needed to reassert its budgetary authority, Pike believed. Article 1, section 9, of the Constitution states: "No money shall be drawn from the Treasury but in consequence of appropriations made by law and a regular statement and account of the receipts and expenditures of all public money shall be published from time to time." As Pike noted in his opening statement, "It does not say 'some public money.' It says 'all public money.' "[31] In his first seven days of open hearings, Pike and his committee tried to exercise what they regarded as their constitutional right to find out how that public money was spent.

As the hearings opened in late July, the Pike committee Democrats quickly established a reputation for tough, occasionally abrasive questioning of witnesses. "Mr. Colby, how did we survive as a nation for 175 years without the CIA?" Robert Giaimo snidely asked the intelligence director at one early hearing.[32] Giaimo was no more contentious than the irascible chairman, who set the tone for the hearings with relentless and often sarcastic questioning. Unlike Church, Pike did not try hard to remain civil throughout the hearings. For example, after hearing James Lynn in closed session, Pike characterized the budget director's secret testimony as "miserable and worthless."[33] The chairman also had nasty confrontations with Lynn during the public session, including the following exchange on Congress's ability to make informed choices in the budget process:

> Pike: When Congress wants to choose between national priorities and the amount of money which is spent in area Y is concealed from 90 percent of the members of Congress, how does Congress make the choice?
>
> Lynn: We don't conceal anything from Congress, Mr. Chairman.
>
> Pike: Oh, come on. . . . Does the budget admit that we have a CIA? Is it in the budget?
>
> Lynn: In the budget presentation?
>
> Pike: Is it in the budget?
>
> Lynn: No. We certainly admit it is in there somewhere.
>
> Pike: That's real fine. Can members of Congress find the NSA in the document you prepared?
>
> Lynn: No; it isn't, sir, because 50 U.S.C.—
>
> Pike: You don't need to cite the statute to me.
>
> Lynn: It is not to be put in the budget of the United States.
>
> Pike: I say to you Congress is not aware and not being aware they can't make the choice.
>
> Lynn: What I disagreed with was your word "conceal." We are not concealing anything. This is in conformance with the law.
>
> Pike: When you can't find it in the budget, but you tell us it is there, I submit that it is legitimate to characterize that as being concealed.[34]

Sometimes the committee members' assertive style paid dividends. At one point, Congressman Aspin appeared to fluster Colby into admitting that the National Security Agency occasionally monitored the overseas phone calls of American citizens.[35] With the chairman's encouragement, the committee staff members were also consistently aggressive. Staff member Greg Rushford recalls that Pike told him, "Don't bring back anything the agencies want you to have; just get what they don't want you to have."[36]

That aggressive attitude would generate controversy and hostility throughout the investigation. Many CIA officials and Church committee staff members viewed the House committee members as reckless and their staff as immature and irresponsible. CIA counsel Rogovin now calls the Pike staff "atrocious" and "incompetent."[37] Church committee counsel F. A. O. Schwarz, Jr., says that Pike's staff members thought "they alone possessed virtue. They were all true believers."[38] Jack Boos, Pike's chief investigator, admits that the staff was "green" but insists that they were nevertheless hardworking and appropriately skeptical of CIA assertions.[39] And Pike's chief counsel, Aaron Donner, maintains that the staff had to be "nervy" to discover the truth. "They were not afraid to say the Emperor had no clothes on," he says.[40]

The committee succeeded in uncovering some startling new information about the secret budget. The General Accounting Office (GAO), the independent arm of Congress that audits government agencies, had not been permitted to audit the CIA since 1962, the committee discovered. The GAO had no idea how much money the CIA received or how it was spent. The CIA was, as Congressman William Lehman commented, "an open spigot without accountability."[41] The committee also discovered that executive oversight of the intelligence budget was minimal at best. Only six employees of the Office of Management and Budget scrutinized the foreign intelligence budget, and three of them were former CIA employees.

But the sparks generated by the budget hearings were merely a prelude to the firestorm that would engulf the committee when it returned from its summer break. At that point, the members turned to their second topic—an inquiry that could threaten the very existence of the powerful bureaucracies under examination. Just how well, the committee wanted to know, does the intelligence community do its job?

To analyze the intelligence community's performance, the committee decided to examine six cases, beginning with the recent Mideast war. The Egyptian attack on Israel in October 1973 had come seemingly without warning and had precipitated an international crisis. The Pike committee wanted to know how much the intelligence agencies had known about Egypt's intentions.

It quickly became obvious that they had not known much. A candid, twenty-five-page internal postmortem prepared by the CIA disclosed that several agencies had predicted there would be no war just hours before it broke out. According to the postmortem, the intelligence on the crisis was "quite simply, obviously, and starkly wrong."[42]

To inform the public of the full extent of the intelligence community's incompetence, the committee wanted to release the six-page summary of the postmortem. The CIA, in turn, wanted to keep five paragraphs of the document secret. Suspecting that the CIA's real motive was to hide its own mistakes, the committee found this compromise inadequate. The committee convened in closed session on the afternoon of 11 September to negotiate the release of more information.

That still-secret meeting featured an intense struggle between Pike and CIA counsel Rogovin. After several hours, Rogovin, who repeatedly left the room to call Colby, gave permission to release much of the material. But the CIA still insisted that fourteen words be kept secret. The committee took up those fourteen words one at a time, acquiescing to the agency's desires for secrecy in almost every case. But Pike balked at the CIA's last request. The CIA wanted to delete four words—"and greater communications security"—that appeared in a list of steps taken by Egypt prior to the war. The CIA argued that the words revealed the Americans' ability to eavesdrop on Egyptian communications. To disclose the words, Rogovin argued, would reveal "sources and methods."

But Pike contended that the phrase, far from disclosing a secret technology, demonstrated just how poorly the intelligence agencies had performed. The nation's top spies had not realized the Egyptians were planning to attack even though they had secured their phones and radios in preparation for war. Some intelligence sources later told the *New York Times* that Pike was correct in maintaining that the four words did not reveal a national secret: the Egyptians and Soviets already knew that the United States could eavesdrop on Egyptian conversations.[43] Later, Pike discovered that the supposedly top secret information about Egyptian communications had already been published in a book by Marvin Kalb and Bernard Kalb. The Kalbs' main source for the book—a flattering biography of Henry Kissinger—was the secretary of state himself.[44]

The committee debated the four words for over an hour. According to news reports, Pike had difficulty convincing the members that the issue merited a confrontation with the executive. Even Ron Dellums initially argued against such a move. But Pike was insistent. In the end, the committee voted 6–3 to release the document with the four words included.[45]

That night, deeply disturbed by the committee's action, White House and CIA officials met to plan their reaction. Some White House aides favored moving past the immediate crisis to work out an orderly system for handling such disagreements in the future. Others argued that the committee's access to classified documents should be cut off immediately, partly in retaliation for the four words and partly to teach the committee a lesson for the future. According to CIA counsel Rogovin, these advisers thought, " 'Well, maybe those four words aren't that important, but if they disregard us on this, they'll disregard us on four other words.' "[46]

Ultimately, the hard-liners prevailed. The White House decided to fight back.

The counterattack began the next morning. Assistant Attorney General Rex Lee arrived at the committee's public hearing to deliver a shocking message from the executive branch. Until Pike promised that he would never again release classified information without permission, the president had ordered that the committee would receive no more classified documents, that no executive officials would testify before it on classified matters, and that the committee must return all secret documents in its possession. The executive branch was threatening to close down the entire House investigation.

Stunned by the unexpected announcement, Pike exploded with fury. The attempt to wrest the documents from the committee violated the checks and balances of the Constitution, he said. Talk of "sources and methods" only obscured the real issue. "They always use the phrase sources and methods and the phrase national security," Pike said. "But in the final analysis the issue is, 'Shall Congress be a coequal branch of the Government?' "[47]

In Pike's view, he and his committee were finally assuming the constitutional responsibilities that their colleagues had shirked for years. When Lee suggested that previous committees had not insisted on this right of unilateral declassification, Pike lectured the bureaucrat in stentorian tones that resounded throughout the committee room: "That is exactly what is wrong, Mr. Lee. For decades, other committees of Congress have not done their job, and you have loved it in the executive branch. You tell us that Congress has been advised of this. What does that mean? It means the executive branch comes up and whispers in one friendly Congressman's ear or another friendly Congressman's ear, and that is exactly what you want to continue, and that is exactly what I think has led us into the mess we are in."[48]

Pike's eloquent outrage inspired several other committee members to defend the "people's right to know." Moderate Democrat Morgan Murphy compared the situation to Watergate. "I hear the same argument I heard in the defense of President Nixon," he told Lee. "He has a right to keep things secret, he has a right not to turn over tapes, and he has a right not to turn over documents. But I thought the Supreme Court settled that matter."[49]

Pike dramatically presented the issue as a fight between secrecy and democracy. Apparently, he said, the CIA "would simply prefer that we operated in a dictatorship where only one branch of the Government has any power over secrecy. I simply submit to you that that is not the way I read the Constitution of the United States."[50]

The battle had begun. On one side, angry congressmen believed that the executive was just "looking for excuses" to attack an assertive committee, in Otis Pike's words.[51] Disgusted by their colleagues' failures during the Johnson and Nixon presidencies, these House members were determined to reestablish a proper balance between the branches of government and to tame the imperial presidency. On the other side, an appointed president was equally determined not to allow any weakening of what he viewed as the chief executive's constitutional prerogatives. As Rogovin says, "Pike challenged the president's men, and they weren't going to be challenged."[52]

Over the next ten days, the situation escalated into "the most serious constitutional confrontation between the legislative and executive branches since the Watergate scandal," according to the *New York Times*.[53] The committee issued subpoenas for more secret documents; Ford said he would defy the subpoenas unless the committee promised not to release the documents; in that case, Pike announced, he would take the president to court. In Rogovin's view, both sides were behaving "like children playing." At one point, Rogovin recalls, he told his clients, "The only thing we've got left to do is to send a Marine battalion up to get the documents from Pike. This is silly; are we going to go to war against our own Congress?"[54]

Both the Ford administration and the committee members attempted to win public opinion to their side. In the first salvo of a massive public relations offensive against the committee, President Ford proclaimed at a press conference that the release of the four words would have been a crime if a private citizen had disclosed them.[55] In a speech in San Francisco, Ford attacked the Pike committee and promised not to compromise "our intelligence sources and the higher national secrets" by giving it further information.[56] William Colby broke twenty-eight years of precedent by holding the first-ever press conference by a CIA director, saying that the release of the four words was a grave breach of national security. Faced with a crisis of legitimacy, the CIA's leaders decided that the secret agency could not afford to continue to ignore the press; it must actively woo the media and the public.

Pike eagerly met the White House challenge and heightened the war of words between the two branches. Appearing on *Face the Nation*, he declared that the CIA was too incompetent to anticipate a Soviet attack on the United States.[57] Not content with enraging the CIA, he also tried to humiliate the highest-ranking White House liaison with the committee. A few months before, White House counsel Rod Hills—the husband of trade representative Carla Hills—had accidentally left his notebook in Pike's office. Now that open warfare had broken out between the committee and the executive branch, Pike returned the notebook to the president with a tongue-in-cheek cover letter. "It is my understanding that because of an alleged breach of security you would like me to provide you with all secret documents in my possession," Pike wrote. "I have only one such document." It was, of course, the notebook, which contained some copies of letters from Colby to Pike marked "Secret Sensitive" and some newspaper clippings "which do not appear to be classified." Pike expressed his relief at ridding himself of the notebook, "for it does in my judgment represent a grave breach of security, and I am delighted to be able to present it to you and make a clean breast of the whole sorry affair." He suggested that Ford fire the staff member who had lost the documents, but he did not name Hills directly. "While I detest informers, the gravity of the situation and the seriousness of the offense compel me to give you a hint with which I suspect the F.B.I. will be able to track him down. He is the husband of a member of your Cabinet." Pike then added a postscript: "If he loses it again, it's O.K., I have a copy."[58]

In Pike's view, the notebook issue highlighted the hypocrisy and inconsistency of the executive branch's policies on secrecy. Even as they accused him of acting irresponsibly, White House aides were overzealously classifying documents and then losing them. Pike gleefully inserted a copy of the letter into the *Congressional Record*. But his joke caused his primary White House contact to despise him and convinced other administration officials that he was childish and spiteful.[59]

At this early stage, Pike seemed to be winning the battle for press support. Liberal columnists Tom Wicker and Anthony Lewis lauded the chairman, with Lewis proclaiming that the country's true national security depended on such congressional boldness. "In the deepest sense, the safety of liberty in this country rests on respect for the separation of powers—on Congress as a balance to the growth of presidential power," Lewis wrote.[60] Most important, the committee received an unqualified endorsement from the *New York Times* editorial board. Under the headline "Son of Watergate," the *Times* praised Congress for finally exercising its essential oversight functions. Rather than protecting national security, the Ford administration was trying "to keep the House probers from delving as deeply as they should into the shadowland of intelligence activities."[61]

Then, unexpectedly, the committee encountered a new, even more difficult problem—and a more wily adversary than President Ford. The Pike committee fortunes began to sour as soon as its members decided to take on Henry Kissinger.

As the Pike staff members gathered information on the intelligence agencies' performance during the Turkish invasion of Cyprus, they learned of a crucial document. Thomas Boyatt, the head of the State Department's Cyprus desk, had written a memo criticizing the quality of the intelligence he received during the crisis. Boyatt had then been removed from his post. The foreign service officer wanted to discuss his memo with committee members and allow them to read it for themselves.

But his superiors would not let the committee see the memo. On 25 September, in the midst of the crisis over the committee's right to declassify documents, Lawrence Eagleburger, a high-ranking State Department official, appeared before the committee to announce that relinquishing the Boyatt memo would be tantamount to surrendering to McCarthyism. Under the orders of Secretary of State Kissinger, foreign service officers would not be allowed to testify to Congress about policy recommendations they had made to their superiors. Similarly, no documents concerning those recommendations would be given to Congress.

This policy went far beyond the president's earlier decision to restrict the flow of documents to the committee. Ford had always agreed that the committee had the right to examine documents, just not the right to release them unilaterally. By contrast, Kissinger informed the committee that it had no right at all to certain documents or testimony, regardless of its plans for release. He maintained that this was necessary to protect officials from McCarthyite inquisitions and to ensure that policy disputes within the department were frank and candid. Not all executive branch officials agreed with this hard-line position—especially in cases where lower-ranking employees wanted to testify. Attorney General Edward Levi, for example, suggested at a White House meeting that the administration should consider a compromise "before Henry gets too intoxicated with the principle involved."[62] But Kissinger refused to compromise on this issue.

Kissinger's State Department was a much more dangerous adversary for the committee than Colby's CIA. At the time, Kissinger wore two hats as secretary of state and national security adviser. He was highly regarded by a large proportion of the public: he had been the diplomatic wizard behind Nixon's rapprochement with China, the first Strategic Arms Limitation Treaty (SALT), and the secret Paris peace talks. Many Americans viewed Kissinger as an indispensable holdover from the Nixon administration whose presence ensured continuity in American foreign policy.

Kissinger also enjoyed the best press relations of any post–World War II American policymaker. His talent for cultivating the Washington press corps was legendary; he spent as much as half of each working day in conversation with reporters. He rewarded those reporters who made him look good and exploded in rage at those who did not.[63] His flattery of influential reporters and columnists, along with his willingness to share insights and return phone calls, helped to project an image that was envied by the presidents he served. In one week in 1972, for example, after Nixon revealed Kissinger's secret trips to Paris, *Time* called the secretary a "brilliant" policymaker with "diverse talents, energy and intellect," while *Newsweek* glorified the "skilled and cool negotiator" who was also an "intellectual par excellence."[64]

Pike, by contrast, was far from adept at generating favorable press coverage. Neither he nor any of his committee members could rival Kissinger's access to key columnists and editorial writers. Nor did Pike share Senator Church's talent for grabbing the press's attention with concrete, sensational examples of abuses. The House committee did not even have a press secretary; the overworked and inexperienced chief of staff handled all queries from reporters. In this battle for media opinion with one of the biggest media stars of the postwar period, Otis Pike and his committee were seriously overmatched.

Kissinger quickly began to rally his friends in the press. Aaron Donner, the chief counsel of the Pike committee, received a phone call from *Times* columnist James "Scotty" Reston shortly after the committee challenged Kissinger. "This is Scotty Reston of the *Times*," the celebrated journalist bellowed into the phone. "What the hell are you guys doing down there? Are you reviving McCarthyism?" Kissinger, a close friend of Reston's, had apparently convinced the columnist and others in the press that the committee was unfairly attacking the State Department. "It was obvious [Reston] started out with a full head of steam, and someone had stoked the fires," Donner says.[65]

Someone had stoked the fires at the editorial boards as well. The prestige newspapers were unanimous in condemning the committee. On

28 September, the *New York Times* editorial board turned against the Pike committee permanently. Charging that Pike was "hip-shooting toward some high noon in a federal courtroom," the *Times* lectured the chairman that a "less emotional and more patient approach to the administration's recalcitrance" was needed.[66] The *Washington Post*, the celebrated antagonist of presidential secrecy, supported Ford and Kissinger against the committee.[67] The *Washington Star* started a trend with its headline accompanying a critical editorial; "Pike's Pique" captured the media's increasingly predominant image of the chairman as overly zealous, impatient, irrational, and even childish.[68]

At first, the committee remained undeterred by Kissinger's popularity. In fact, Eagleburger's pronouncement on State Department witnesses seemed to unite the members more than ever before. Robert McClory said he did not know how the committee could fulfill its mandate "with the kind of lack of cooperation which I think we are getting from the State Department."[69] Republican Jim Johnson said he resented the implication that State Department employees would be "bullied or beaten with a rubber hose" by the committee; Boyatt, after all, *wanted* to testify to them.[70] Several committee members charged that the State Department was more concerned with protecting its public image than protecting one dissenting employee.

As the confrontation continued, however, the Republicans on the committee began to feel uncomfortable about opposing the Republican White House. McClory, the ranking minority member, had been in a similarly delicate position on the House Judiciary Committee during the 1974 impeachment hearings. Although he was intensely loyal to his party, McClory had been gravely disturbed by the abuses of power of the Nixon White House. He had ultimately voted to impeach Nixon on two articles and had introduced the only Republican-sponsored article.[71]

Now, once again, he found himself torn between his loyalty to his party and his faithfulness to the House as an institution. A respected, moderately conservative Illinois Republican, McClory did not want to confront the president, a close friend whom he described as "open, forthright, and cooperative."[72] He had many common interests with the White House Republicans, and he frequently briefed them on the committee's plans and strategy.[73] But he sincerely believed that the executive branch did not have the exclusive right to declassify and release information. Such an assumption was insulting to Congress.[74] Furthermore, he and the other three Republicans believed that the White House had orchestrated a false crisis and attacked the committee unfairly when it protested the release of the "four words."[75]

McClory's ambivalence alarmed the Ford administration. Max Friedersdorf, congressional relations director, nervously informed Chief of Staff Don Rumsfeld that "McClory is clearly lined up with Chairman Pike and the Democrats against the White House." Friedersdorf concluded that "we have absolutely no base of support in the entire committee."[76]

Although McClory refused to support the White House, however, he did not want this battle to reach the courts, where either his president or his committee might be humiliated. He worked energetically to forge a compromise, at least on the declassification issue.[77]

On 26 September, McClory finally persuaded his president and his chairman to meet face-to-face to resolve their differences. The two sides were still far apart on the issue of access to State Department memos and witnesses. But McClory expressed hope that the committee and the president were close to an agreement on the issue of the release of classified documents. Committee staff members and White House aides worked through the weekend to produce an accord. The committee members appeared ready to surrender an important principle and let the president or the courts have some say on declassification. In return, they expected unfettered access to CIA documents.

The White House did not meet their expectations. On Monday morning, the committee received a box full of documents it had subpoenaed from the CIA, the first such delivery since the committee had released the four words. But the CIA had heavily censored the documents; moreover, it announced that it would censor all documents it handed over in the future as well. "In essence," Pike said, "what they are saying is, they are not going to give to this committee anything they don't want to have made public."[78]

The committee was not at all satisfied. Robert Giaimo protested that the executive branch had somehow made the committee, not the CIA, seem the villain. "The fact of the matter is, we didn't commit errors of judgment, or mistakes in intelligence, or improper and illegal acts in this committee."[79] The committee might as well quit if it could not get the necessary information, Giaimo said. "Let's not delude ourselves. Let's say, 'Let's hang it up and let them run rampant, as they have these past 25 years, and hopefully the executive will purify its own agencies because Congress doesn't want to take that responsibility.' "[80] Enraged by the

President Ford meets with members of the Pike committee on 26 September 1975 to devise an agreement on the release of classified documents. *Clockwise from President Ford:* John Marsh, counselor to the president; Secretary of State Henry Kissinger; Philip Buchen, counselor to the president; William Colby, CIA director; Representative Robert McClory; Representative Otis Pike; Representative John Rhodes; and Speaker Carl Albert. (Courtesy Gerald R. Ford Library)

administration's bad faith, the committee voted 10–3 to ask the House to cite Colby for contempt. The committee had reached the precipice.

In this case, the threat seemed to work. The next morning, on the last day of September, Colby delivered a package of documents to the committee with only fifty words deleted. Pike personally verified that the fifty words were not significant. The newspapers trumpeted the committee's apparent triumph: "CIA Bows to Pike, Yields Documents," read the huge, four-column headline of the lead story in the *Washington Post*.[81]

But in reality, as Pike admitted in public session, the committee had not won a great victory. Colby had surrendered the absolute minimum necessary to avoid being cited for contempt. In return for the documents, the committee had made a crucial concession: it promised not to reveal classified material without the approval of the president or, failing that, the courts. Pressured by time constraints and dwindling support, the committee quietly conceded the issue of unilateral congressional disclosure of classified documents.

By agreeing to the so-called "Colby compromise," Pike ran into opposition on his left for the first time. His main opponent, unexpectedly, was Les Aspin. The congressman from Wisconsin astutely pointed out that the agreement was rather vague. Did the restrictions on release apply only to the newest batch of papers? Did the agreement establish a precedent for other committees in Congress?[82] Ultimately, however, only Giaimo and Dellums joined Aspin in voting against the compromise that, for all its problems, had restored the flow of secret documents to the committee.

Aspin did not point out the biggest potential problem of this compromise: whether it applied to the committee's final report. Nor did any other committee member address the issue. This failure to clarify the compromise would later prove to be a fateful omission.

The Colby compromise solved only half of the problems dividing the committee and the Ford administration. The committee had agreed not to cite William Colby for contempt, but what about Henry Kissinger? The troublesome issue of committee access to State Department witnesses—and more specifically the Boyatt memorandum—remained unresolved.

Undeterred by an increasingly negative press, the committee voted on 2 October to subpoena the Boyatt memorandum. Kissinger and his defenders responded by intensifying the public relations campaign against the committee. The dean of U.S. foreign policy during the Cold War, George Kennan, wrote the *Washington Post* that Kissinger had "no choice" but to refuse the committee's demands.[83] More than 200 middle-ranking foreign service officers signed a letter supporting the secretary and his contention that the committee was indulging in McCarthyism. "The Foreign Service is just now—after 20 years—overcoming the legacy of that bitter question: 'Who lost China?' " the letter said. "Some of us recall the fate of those of our colleagues who were swept up—and away—in the debate."[84]

This allusion to an earlier, now discredited period of congressional assertiveness proved to be a powerful weapon against Pike. Kissinger had not pioneered the use of the McCarthy analogy against the investigators. Since the start of the inquiry, journalists had accused Seymour Hersh of using "McCarthyite" tactics, compared Daniel Schorr to the reporters who had disseminated McCarthy's allegations, and charged the two committees with destroying the CIA as McCarthy had wrecked the State Department.[85] These attacks had been isolated and infrequent, however.

Now, with Kissinger's encouragement, pundits on the op-ed pages frequently compared the Pike committee members to the reckless and destructive late senator from Wisconsin.

A few parallels did exist between the Pike committee investigation and the anticommunist crusades of the 1950s. The Pike committee members, like Joseph McCarthy, were demanding secret documents from the executive branch. Moreover, the committee was attacking the CIA, as McCarthy did in the last days before his fall.

But the two inquiries had many more differences than similarities. The Pike committee was not forcing anyone to testify. The members wanted to understand the connection between intelligence and policymaking in the State Department, not ruin the careers of low- and middle-ranking foreign service officers. Furthermore, the committee majority's ideology could not have been more different from the red-baiters of twenty years before. Indeed, in many cases the critics who compared the Pike inquiry to McCarthyism were the very people who had supported McCarthy, at least for a while, in the 1950s. One could even say that McCarthy had helped to create the practices that the committee was now condemning; the McCarthyite hysteria, after all, had encouraged the FBI and the CIA to use any methods necessary to fight the Communists. But these distinctions were lost in the press coverage.

Kissinger's friends in the press, such as *New York Times* columnist James Reston, applauded the secretary for standing firm against congressional attempts to usurp executive prerogatives. The current secretary of state would never follow "John Foster Dulles's example of throwing staff officers to his critics," Reston wrote.[86] This particular staff officer's desire to be thrown to Congress was lost in the hyperbole.

The editorial page of the *New York Times*, which had once lauded the investigators, now joined the chorus of voices comparing the investigation to a witch-hunt. In an editorial headlined "Neo-McCarthyism?," the paper declared that the committee's insistence on seeing the Boyatt memorandum was "clearly contrary to the national interest." In refusing to let Boyatt testify, Kissinger was upholding the "responsible" principle that policymakers, not lower-level assistants, should be held accountable for their decisions.[87]

The confrontation between Kissinger and the committee reached a climax on 31 October when the secretary appeared in person before the committee. Kissinger repeated a compromise offer he had made previously: the committee members could examine a summary of Boyatt's memorandum, amalgamated with other documents, but they could not examine the memo itself. Pike was disgusted. "The best evidence of what Mr. Boyatt said is not your summary of it, or anybody else's summary of it," he told Kissinger. "It is what Mr. Boyatt said."[88] Pike declared that the committee had a legal and moral right to review the document and that, at any rate, Boyatt himself had no objections. McClory lent the minority's support to Pike's demands. But Kissinger retorted that he could not allow the committee to set a precedent that future committees might abuse.

During the hearing, Kissinger dueled with committee members to win public relations points. Congressman Dellums, seeking to explain the committee's reasons for targeting the secretary, launched into a long harangue:

> You occupy practically every position of importance in the 40 Committee structure. You are Special Assistant to the President for National Security Affairs. You are also Secretary of State. We have testimony that you have participated in directing operations which were not fully discussed, analyzed, or evaluated by those authorized to do so. In fact, sometimes they were purposefully hidden. You have been involved in wiretaps of employees. . . . You now refuse information to Congress on a rather specious basis. Frankly, Mr. Secretary, and I mean this very sincerely, I am concerned with your power, and the method of your operation, and I am afraid of the result on American policy, and I believe the direction of operations outside the National Security Council and the full 40 Committee may indeed be contrary to law. Would you please comment, sir?

Kissinger paused artfully. "Except for that," he asked Dellums with a wry smile, "there is nothing wrong with my operation?"[89]

The room broke up in laughter. Television audiences that evening saw the image of the clever cabinet official besting the humorless, abrasive congressman.[90] Once again, the Pike committee members had lost an opportunity to communicate their side of the story to the public. Even though Republican committee members and some presidential advisers did not support Kissinger's crusade to keep the Boyatt memo from the committee, the master of the media knew how to impress a more influential audience: the press. The politically savvy Frank Church might have been able to blunt Kissinger's attack, but Otis Pike and his members were overwhelmed by the secretary's superior skills in media manipulation.

The Pike committee's powerful nemesis seemed to suffer a temporary setback a few days later when Ford unexpectedly stripped Kissinger of one of his government posts. The president announced that Kissinger's deputy, Brent Scowcroft, would become national security adviser as part of an extensive executive branch shake-up. But it quickly became obvious that Kissinger had still come out ahead in the affair: one of his longtime rivals, Secretary of Defense James Schlesinger, was fired by the president. Ford also fired another Kissinger foe, William Colby. The White House had been considering replacing Colby since early summer, and now his role in the Church committee's dart gun hearings ensured his departure. George Bush, former head of the Republican Party, current U.S. ambassador to China, and a good friend of Ford's, became head of central intelligence in Colby's place.[91]

Ford's decision to fire Colby infuriated the two intelligence chairmen. "Concealment is now the order of the day," Frank Church declared on national television.[92] Pike disputed the media's conclusion that Colby had been fired because he had disclosed too much to Congress. "It has been my own experience and judgment that if you are asked precisely the right question, you will give an honest answer," he told Colby at the next hearing. "You do not make it easy for us to ask the right question."[93] Although Colby and Schlesinger, the two CIA reformers, had lost their jobs, their predecessor—who was at the center of so many of the press allegations—remained comfortably ensconced as ambassador in Tehran. "It looks like Dick Helms outlasted both of us," Schlesinger told Colby the night they were fired.[94]

Two days after the White House reorganization, the Pike committee met to consider Kissinger's compromise offer of an "amalgamated" memo. Finally persuaded by the White House, McClory and the Republicans now argued in favor of compromise. Pike, however, insisted that any amalgamation would be an affront to Congress and an obstacle to the investigation. Both sides sought to win the allegiance of the Democrats in the middle.

Les Aspin once again took a position opposed to the chairman. In the Colby compromise, he had advised against accommodation; now that Kissinger was involved, he argued in favor of agreement. He contended that the House as a whole would consider the committee's crusade ridiculous and refuse to find Kissinger in contempt. "To go to the floor of the House, telling our colleagues on the House floor that we have all the information, but we don't have Thomas Boyatt's name associated with the particular paragraphs that he is talking about, I think will puzzle our colleagues," he said.[95] Pike in turn was contemptuous of an "amalgamated" document; he asked sarcastically if a dictionary would comply with the subpoena. "I suspect the Boyatt memorandum was in today's *Washington Post*, also, if you can find the words," he said snidely to Aspin.[96]

In Aspin's view, one trivial memorandum was hardly worth a confrontation with a man as powerful as Kissinger. To Pike, however, as with the four words, the document symbolized something far greater: Congress's status as a coequal branch of government. "I would submit," he said, "that the issue is the right of Congress to get information."[97] The Colby compromise had involved the release of information; by contrast, the proposed compromise with Kissinger involved the committee's right to access to information at all. The issue of access, in his view, was even more important than disclosure. In refusing to support him, the members were kowtowing to Kissinger's power and influence. He feared that "the conclusion has been reached by a lot of our Members that this is not the right man to go after—not that this isn't the right issue. There wasn't any reluctance to go after William Colby on a subpoena."[98]

In the end, however, Pike could not convince most of his colleagues. Only Giaimo, Dellums, and Stanton joined Pike in voting against the Kissinger compromise to defend congressional access; conservative Democrat Milford also voted against it because he did not believe the committee should have the Boyatt memorandum at all, in any form. The final vote was 8–5 against the chairman.

After Kissinger's victory, the Pike committee lost whatever unity it had ever possessed. The righteous—and self-righteous—members who had voted against compromising with the secretary were furious with their erstwhile allies from their own party. Pike began the next public session by declaring that he would not vote for any more subpoenas if the committee did not plan to uphold them. "I take a rather dim view of posturing—of charading and pretending that we are going after information—without some assurance from the committee that we are really going after the information," he said.[99] Dellums agreed that "it is tragic for us to assume the responsibility to investigate, issue subpoenas all over hell and back, and then when they say 'no' back away routinely."[100]

The members who had voted for the compromise were deeply offended by the attacks. Aspin responded that he would not vote for any subpoenas if he could not compromise on them. "I don't want to be in the position of having voted for a subpoena, and then voting for substantial compliance and being accused of selling out when I am trying to do the job."[101] The Wisconsin representative proceeded to vote "present" for each subpoena vote. Giaimo responded by voting "present" himself "because I don't think this committee is serious about enforcing its sub-poenas." To underline the point, he explained, "I am not voting 'Present' for the same reasons the gentleman from Wisconsin is."[102]

The deep divisions among the committee members were illustrated by an exchange between Hayes and Dellums. Hayes was angered when Dellums praised the staff for being more aggressive than the committee members:

> Hayes: I don't really feel I am down here to be aggressive, and I don't feel, quite frankly, that the entire matter is getting adequate debate.
> Dellums: I am in total, absolute, unequivocal disagreement with my colleague. I think we are here to be assertive.
> Hayes: I wouldn't have guessed otherwise what you thought.
> Dellums: If you are going to yield, yield. If not, I won't try to take the time because I won't be combative with my colleague.[103]

Dellums angrily concluded that "maybe the honeymoon is over" for the committee, "and that is fine, too. The truth will get out anyway."[104] The House committee's reservoir of goodwill and collegiality had been exhausted. The difference in style between Otis Pike's squabbling band of truth-seekers and Frank Church's respected panel of experienced statesmen had never been more obvious.

In between the nasty exchanges, the Pike committee still managed to approve seven subpoenas requesting documents from the CIA, the National Security Agency, the Defense Intelligence Agency, the State Department, and the National Security Council. These documents could provide unprecedented insight into the workings of the intelligence community. They showed the approval process for covert action and the connection between intelligence and policymaking. They could tell the committee whether the CIA initiated covert actions on its own or whether it was directed by the president—in effect, whether it was a rogue elephant. Unfortunately, however, the subpoenas once again brought the committee into personal combat with Henry Kissinger.

The CIA, the National Security Agency, and the Defense Intelligence Agency all agreed to supply the documents. But the executive branch at first refused to comply fully with the three subpoenas directed to the State Department and the National Security Council—in other words, those addressed to Kissinger. The committee could respond by negotiating with Kissinger, or, alternatively, it could first ask the House to cite Kissinger for contempt, then negotiate from a position of strength. The committee had taken the latter approach successfully with William Colby, but a majority had refused to take a hard-line approach with Kissinger over the Boyatt memorandum.

This time, however, Kissinger was refusing to provide a different type of document: the recommendations of policymakers, not just those of a lower-level analyst like Boyatt. Moreover, the administration had not offered the committee any alternative. At least with the Boyatt memo, the State Department had promised to deliver an "amalgamated" document containing Boyatt's words. Given these differences, an overwhelming majority of the committee now decided to recommend that the House initiate contempt proceedings against the secretary.

Two of the proposed contempt citations, which the committee passed by a 10–2 vote, concerned Kissinger's refusal to provide documents necessary for determining who had proposed and approved covert operations. One subpoena, addressed to the national security adviser, requested the records of the special National Security Council group charged with approving covert actions (called the 40 Committee in the Nixon administration). The other, addressed to the secretary of state, asked for State Department requests for covert operations.

The final contempt citation condemned Kissinger in his role as national security adviser for failing to furnish documents on arms control verification. A former member of the Joint Chiefs of Staff, Admiral Elmo Zumwalt, had charged Kissinger with ignoring evidence of Soviet cheating on the SALT agreement to protect détente. These were serious accusations—essentially charges of treason—and the committee voted 10–1, with only McClory in opposition, to cite Kissinger for contempt for his refusal to respond.

The administration appeared stunned by the committee's swift action and moved quickly to compromise on the two subpoenas addressed to the national security adviser. The White House claimed that the subpoenas had been imprecisely worded and, even more important, improperly addressed to Kissinger. After all, Ford advisers argued, Kissinger had been removed as national security adviser two weeks before, and his successor had not yet been sworn in. It was unclear whether White House aides had suffered from genuine bureaucratic confusion during the transition, or whether they had deliberately exploited the situation to delay responding.[105] Now that they were faced with contempt citations, the president's advisers scrambled to find the remaining SALT compliance documents and to invite the committee members to the

White House to examine the subpoenaed 40 Committee records (without surrendering them to the committee's custody). Pike and his committee agreed that these White House actions amounted to "substantial compliance" with the two subpoenas.

But on the third subpoena, President Ford made the surprising decision to invoke executive privilege for the first time since Richard Nixon had occupied the Oval Office. The State Department documents on covert action, Ford declared, "revealed to an unacceptable degree the consultation process involving advice and recommendations to Presidents Kennedy, Johnson and Nixon."[106]

Memos from the president's aides suggest, however, that Ford was more concerned with the abstract principle of defending executive privilege than with protecting these particular documents. Jack Marsh advised the president that a battle with Congress over executive privilege was inevitable; therefore, the president should aim to provoke a confrontation in a dispute the White House was sure to win. The Pike committee subpoena, in Marsh's view, provided just such an opportunity.[107]

The administration hoped to humiliate the committee on the House floor, thus upholding executive privilege without resorting to the courts. Administration officials began their campaign by working to turn public opinion against the investigators. Kissinger declared that the committee's action would "raise serious questions all over the world of what this country is doing to itself and what the necessity is to torment ourselves like this month after month."[108] In a major speech in Detroit, he called on Americans to end "the self-flagellation that has done so much harm to this nation's capacity to conduct foreign policy."[109] Other officials spread the message that an attack on Kissinger was an attack on America's international image. One Kissinger assistant told the press it was "unbelievable" that the committee would cite the secretary "on the eve of an important summit meeting, two weeks before a Presidential visit to China and less than a month before a major NATO meeting."[110] The globe-trotting secretary, the man who represented the United States in Moscow and Beijing, was too important to bother with what he called the "frivolous" requests of Congress.[111]

Kissinger's friends in the press once again leaped to his defense. The Los Angeles Times invoked the popular image of McCarthyism; the Tulsa Daily World called Pike a "spoiled child" and "small-minded egotist" who was recklessly encouraging the worst tendencies of the "power-happy and irresponsible Legislative Branch."[112] William Safire declared that Pike was assaulting the constitutional balance of powers.[113]

One of the most fervent defenses of executive privilege came from the newspaper partly responsible for Congress's newly acquired confidence: the *Washington Post*. Nixon's onetime nemesis declared that the committee had acted with "abandon" and called the contempt citation "unnecessary and unwise." The newspaper chastised the committee for its attempt to "invade the President's prerogative to conduct foreign policy" and intrude upon "the legitimate powers of the office of the Presidency." The committee, in the *Post*'s view, was irresponsible. "In its zeal, the Pike committee—unlike its Senate counterpart—has brushed by the time-tested 'political' ways in which *responsible* standing committees can and do gain access discreetly to material which would not be forthcoming in the context of a hostile political confrontation."[114]

The *Post* editorial amazed liberal columnist Anthony Lewis. The newspaper had "fought the Presidential mystique so bravely in Watergate," he wrote. Why did it now defend presidential secrecy? The only way to understand the *Post*'s inconsistency, Lewis said, is to "conclude that Henry Kissinger operates much more effectively among the Washington press than either of his presidents."[115]

This conclusion was certainly true, but the editorial denunciations of the Pike committee went beyond a personal defense of Henry Kissinger. Many editors and publishers seemed most concerned that a congressional committee was "intruding on the prerogatives of the presidency." As the *Worcester Telegram* asked its readers: "Should the concept of presidential privilege be entirely discarded just because it was abused during the Watergate crisis?"[116]

The majority of House members appeared to be as reluctant as the press to support the committee's assertion of congressional power. Pike tried hard to persuade the House to support his committee. In a "dear colleague" letter, he told House members that "contrary to widely published rumors," citing the secretary for contempt would not "cause the earth to tremble nor the sun to stop in its tracks. No one is seeking to place Mr. Kissinger in jail, and the worst that can happen to him is that he might have to provide the documents subpoenaed to Congress."[117] Pike protested that a Kissinger victory on this issue, following on the heels of the Boyatt memo fiasco, would imply that the State Department was immune from oversight. He wrote: "If the recommendations of lower level officers in the State Department are to be denied to Congress on the grounds of 'McCarthyism' and those of top level officers in the State Department on the grounds of 'executive privilege' then the State Department has arrogated unto itself total non-accountability."[118] In a meeting with the House leadership, Pike defiantly refused to be dissuaded from pursuing the contempt charges.[119]

Conservative Democrats surveyed by the White House congressional relations office were not moved by Pike's arguments. One of these conservatives, George Mahon of Texas, told the White House that he deplored "the continual confrontation between the Committee and the executive branch" and believed that "we are in the process of tearing our country apart."[120] His views were shared by another southern Democrat, Dale Milford, who warned the House that his colleagues' proposed contempt citation could "force this nation into a full-fledged Constitutional confrontation . . . which could result in a disastrous loss of public confidence in both branches of government."[121]

Indeed, public confidence in both the investigators and the targets of the investigation had already begun to erode. Disgusted and confused by the committees' revelations, the American public gave contradictory and ambivalent responses to pollsters measuring opinion on the intelligence investigations. On the one hand, confidence in the secret agencies had fallen to an all-time low. Only 32 percent of the public viewed the CIA favorably, while 49 percent gave positive ratings to the FBI.[122] Large majorities disapproved of the FBI's suggestion to Martin Luther King, Jr., that he commit suicide (80 percent), the CIA's deals with the Mafia to kill Castro (74 percent), and the CIA's domestic spying (61 percent). A substantial plurality, 41 percent, doubted that "the CIA and FBI have learned their lessons and now will run things properly."[123]

On the other hand, much of the public disapproved of the two committees. The Church committee was viewed unfavorably by 40 percent of those polled, while only 38 percent approved of the committee. The Pike committee received positive ratings from only 36 percent of the public, while 40 percent disapproved of its work.[124] A majority of those polled feared that the investigations prevented the agencies from doing their jobs properly, and a plurality agreed that Congress should not tighten controls on the agencies.[125] The investigators, it seemed, faced a catch-22 situation: their mission required that they publicize their discoveries, but the very act of publicizing the deeds of secret agencies seemed to alienate many citizens. Moreover, these revelations were very unpleasant ("not the kind of truths we most need now," as Senator J. William Fulbright had said).[126] Americans were not inclined to applaud those who delivered the bad news.

The investigators' battles with the executive had failed to generate strong public support for reform. Moreover, they had helped to erode

Americans' faith in government. Given this public mood, most congress-men and mainstream journalists believed that now was not the time to force a showdown with the imperial presidency. They did not want the anguish of "another executive-legislative confrontation so soon after the last experience," as Congressman John Anderson said.[127] They wanted the Pike committee to be "responsible" and back away from the fight.

Unexpectedly, at the same time, President Ford's advisers reconsidered their earlier decision and chose to retreat from confrontation as well. The president and his men thought they might win on the floor of the House and were certain they would win in court. They decided, however, that the protracted battle might not be worth the costs after all. Kissinger would be humiliated if even a sizable minority of House members voted against him; the courts might duck the issue and rule on a technicality, thus depriving Ford of the validation of executive privilege he so eagerly sought; and presidential intransigence might provide a unifying cause to the badly divided Democrats in the House.[128] Moreover, the Ford admin-istration, like the congressional leadership, was aware that an epic battle between the two branches might cause the public to despise *both* the confrontational Congress and the secretive executive.

The president offered Pike a compromise: a State Department official would read aloud from the recommendations but would not allow the committee to see the actual documents. In this way, the committee would receive its information, but the president could maintain that he had upheld "executive privilege" by prohibiting the committee members from seeing the documents themselves. Pike, who realized the long odds he faced in the House and in the courts, quickly agreed to Ford's terms.

The White House had decided to forgo its legally sound but potentially divisive crusade. This partial victory for the committee members had come at great cost, however. The editorial boards of the *New York Times* and the *Washington Post* had turned against them. Of the major colum-nists, only Anthony Lewis consistently defended them. The congressio-nal leadership, too, had abandoned them. As they headed into their final month and what would become their greatest crisis, the committee mem-bers found themselves in a dangerously isolated and weakened position.

By focusing on the Pike committee's confrontations with Kissinger and the president, the press slighted the House investigators' substantive accomplishments. Beyond the headlines, the committee had made some remarkable discoveries. The critical issue in the intelligence investigations was the extent of the president's control over the CIA. Was it a rogue elephant, as Senator Church maintained, or merely a tool of the presidency? Was the solution to give the president more power over the runaway CIA or to find some way to rein in the runaway presidency?

After the last fight with Kissinger, the Pike committee members were finally allowed to examine the documents that would help resolve this question. In an inquiry unprecedented in Congress and the executive branch, the committee asked: Who originally proposed covert actions? What types of covert action were used the most? And who ultimately approved those actions?

The 40 Committee was formally charged with discussing and approving covert actions. But the Pike committee discovered that the 40 Committee approval process was often "relatively informal, extraordinarily secretive, and pro forma." The group did not even meet during 1973 and 1974; all approvals were done "telephonically." This allowed the CIA chief and Kissinger, who served as chairman of the 40 Committee, to dominate the process.[129]

Ironically, the most significant revelation about covert action approval came from Kissinger himself. In his appearance before the Pike committee, pressed by the toughest questioning he had ever faced on Capitol Hill, Kissinger demolished the doctrine of "plausible denial." For years, presidents had insulated themselves from the negative repercussions of U.S. covert actions by denying responsibility for them. But, in an apparent attempt to minimize his own role, Kissinger told the Pike committee that every covert action undertaken in recent years had been approved by the president himself. To save his own skin, the powerful secretary had given the first authoritative confirmation of the president's true power over the CIA.[130] As Pike told his committee, "One of the things that we have learned as we have progressed down this road is that the CIA does not go galloping off conducting operations by itself."[131] The CIA, he concluded at another hearing, "was no rogue elephant."[132] The committee's final report was even more damning: "All evidence in hand suggests that the CIA, far from being out of control, has been utterly responsive to the instructions of the President and the Assistant to the President for National Security Affairs."[133]

This indictment of the presidency was potentially more alarming than any of the abuses uncovered by the Church committee. If the CIA truly acted on its own, then reforms, though difficult, would be relatively straightforward: the president would simply need more control over the agency. But the Pike committee concluded that the presidency, rather than the CIA, needed to be reformed. And an imperial presidency is much more difficult to change than a rogue elephant.

By finding "the presidency" rather than "the president" at fault, the Pike committee resurrected the problems that Congress had tried to bury after Nixon resigned. The Pike committee concluded that many abuses were not merely the fault of Richard Nixon or certain individuals at the CIA; instead, all presidents could abuse their power by using the secret tools at their disposal. Otis Pike realized that this conclusion threatened some of the deepest beliefs of the American public. In Watergate, he said, the American people were asked to believe that "their President had been a bad person. In this situation they are asked much more; they are asked to believe that their country has been evil. And nobody wants to believe that."[134]

Loch Johnson, a Church committee staff member and scholar, has disputed the conclusion that Pike was "tougher" than Church. "Both committees were tough at different times on different issues," he says, contending that the Church investigations into assassinations, covert actions, and COINTELPRO were as threatening to the intelligence community as any of Pike's inquiries.[135] These Church committee probes were aggressive and significant. But they focused on CIA and FBI abuses, which could be—and were—dismissed as aberrations. Unlike Church, Pike examined the agencies' daily operations and asked whether they were successful, accountable, and congruent with national ideals. He did not ask what the intelligence agencies had done wrong but evaluated what they had done right—which was little or nothing, in his view. Potentially, this moderate from Long Island, this longtime supporter of the Vietnam War, posed more of a threat to the intelligence community than the dove from Idaho.

Despite their vulnerable position after the confrontations with the president and Kissinger, Pike and his colleagues still had one more chance to make a difference through their final report. They could not know that the report itself would be their undoing.

Drowning in red tape, incomprehensible data, and
daily tons of paper, burdened with so much trivia
that no forest was visible among the trees,
constantly prejudiced by political judgments and
wishful thinking, our intelligence community is
repeatedly, consistently, unchangingly, and
dangerously weak. That is the thrust of our report,
but that is a secret.

Otis Pike, in *Congressional Record* (9 March 1976),
94th Cong., 2d sess.

Counterattack

The Investigators under Siege

As Otis Pike and his committee headed into the final phase of the intelligence investigations, they were bruised and weakened by their repeated confrontations with the White House. The controversies over the release of the four classified words, the charges of McCarthyism during the battles with Henry Kissinger, and the disputes over access to documents had cost the committee valuable time and support from the press. The war, however, was still far from over; despite its setbacks, the committee was determined to discover the truth about the intelligence community and recommend some basic reforms. The Church committee, too, was on the defensive after the president's attempt to squelch its assassination report. But the senators looked forward to the opportunity to write an influential final report. Both sets of reformers, in short, still had the chance to regain their momentum and propose far-reaching recommendations.

The committees did not, however, anticipate the speed or force of the coming backlash. The investigators had been delayed by internal squabbles, unexpected additions to their agendas, and executive hostility to their task. Now, as they struggled to wrap up their investigations, they discovered that the lost time had cost them dearly. The targets of their probes had taken advantage of the long months of investigation to mobilize their forces.

The intelligence community had many defenders during the first months of the investigations, but they did not coordinate their efforts. Then, in the spring of 1975, four months after Seymour Hersh's domestic spying revelations and two months after the start of the congressional investigations, one CIA official skilled in molding public opinion in foreign countries decided to use his talents to help the agency resolve its troubles at home.

David Atlee Phillips was one of a new breed of spies who realized that the post-Watergate CIA would have to abandon its aversion to publicity and work actively to attract public support. A high-ranking CIA official who had specialized in propaganda, Phillips believed that the intelligence agencies were severely handicapped in the battle for American public opinion. Whereas CIA critics seemed to have easy access to the media, agency supporters—accustomed to a lifetime of protecting the CIA from public scrutiny—had no experience with public relations.

In March, Phillips quit his job at the CIA and devoted his time to organizing retired officers into an effective, pro-intelligence lobby. In ten months, he had mobilized 600 like-minded former spies in the Association of Retired Intelligence Officers (ARIO).

Phillips's campaign was thorough and sophisticated. Not only did he speak, write, and lobby on behalf of the CIA, but also he encouraged the hundreds of ARIO members to do the same. He helped to organize national and regional committees in charge of training speakers, conducting research, and writing op-ed articles. ARIO members were guided in their quest to shape public opinion by "background material" distributed to them by the national organization. Phillips's forty-eight-page packet included samples of effective speeches and op-ed pieces, possible questions and answers on intelligence, useful quotes, and tips for the reclusive spy now forced to defend his profession at Rotary Club luncheons. "There are three P's that must exist or be observed to be effective: the speaker must be *principled*, he must be *prepared* and he must be *pleasant*," the packet's introduction said.[1]

The organization satisfied a pressing need of the modern, "objective" journalist. Accustomed to printing both sides of elite opinion on an issue, reporters sought sources on the "other side" of the intelligence debate to balance against the congressional committee sources. But the CIA had not always been readily accessible. Phillips changed that situation: he guaranteed reporters that pithy, pro-CIA quotes were just a phone call away. By early 1976, his organization was so powerful that its officials were pressuring news organizations into making retractions and appearing before Congress to give their views on intelligence oversight.[2] In the months to come, Phillips and the ARIO would help to promote the view that CIA officers were physically endangered by the investigations.

Like the intelligence professionals, the Ford administration was also slow to organize a response to the investigations. The president had, of course, consistently voiced his opposition to aggressive investigations. In April, for example, Ford had signaled his support for the intelligence community by highlighting the issue in his "State of the World" speech to Congress. Sounding a theme that he would not abandon for the next thirteen months, Ford charged that a "sensationalized public debate over legitimate intelligence activities" endangered the nation. "It ties our hands while our potential enemies operate with secrecy, with skill, and with vast resources. Any investigation must be conducted with maximum discretion and dispatch to avoid *crippling* a national institution."[3] In the months to come, Ford spoke of the "crippling" or "dismantling" of the CIA whenever he mentioned the intelligence investigations. The president's endorsement of this argument ensured that it would receive prominent and respectful treatment from the press.

Aside from the occasional passage in Ford's speeches, however, the administration had no "coordinated political strategy" to protect the intelligence community. As key advisers told the president in September, the administration had no plan to explain the issues to the public, to "provide leadership to those in Congress who are sympathetic to your position," or to "deter unwise legislation" in Congress.[4]

Impressed by this argument, the president quickly agreed to reorganize the executive branch's response to the investigations. On 19 September, in the midst of the crisis with the Pike committee over the disclosure of classified information, he created a special high-level group to deal with the investigators. From that day forward, all executive responses to the congressional committees were handled by the Intelligence Coordinating Group (ICG). This body met every day and included National Security Adviser and Secretary of State Henry Kissinger, Defense Secretary James Schlesinger, Attorney General Edward Levi, Budget Director James Lynn, Director of Central Intelligence William Colby, Chief of Staff Donald Rumsfeld, and presidential counsels Philip Buchen and Jack Marsh.

Many of these men had personal and political differences with one another. Kissinger, with his great ego and enormous influence on national security policy, often feuded with several other Ford advisers, notably Schlesinger. Moreover, Kissinger maintained that several of his colleagues on the ICG had not handled the investigations correctly: William Colby, he believed, had been too open with congressional investigators, while Jack Marsh had not tried hard enough to protect Kissinger from the investigators.[5] In fact, partly in response to these feuds, President Ford would soon decide to fire Colby and Schlesinger, demote Kissinger, and move Rumsfeld to the Defense Department. Yet despite these rifts and changes in personnel, the ICG was still remarkably successful in accomplishing its goals.

The *New York Times* reported that the ICG was "drawing up the 'order of battle' for the coming confrontation with Congress."[6] Certainly a primary goal of the group, as memos regarding its establishment make clear, was to "counter the build-up of momentum" behind the congressional effort for drastic reforms.[7] Beyond this short-term goal, however, these top aides wanted to ensure that the president would not face an unpalatable choice, as he had with the Hughes-Ryan amendment—that of either signing a bill he disliked or killing all chances for reform.[8] The way to avoid this dilemma was to devise an alternative reform plan within the executive branch. As the main staff member for the group wrote, "We should not view this simply as a 'damage control' operation but, rather, we should seize the initiative and attempt to make something positive out of this."[9] To arrange support for this presidential initiative, a subcommittee of the ICG drew up a schedule for presidential speeches and administration op-ed pieces. In addition, the group identified "outside experts" and groups who supported the president's position and gave them "assignments" to write op-eds based on a "master plan" to organize public support.[10]

As the Pike and Church committees began their public hearings in the fall of 1975, they faced a much better organized opposition. The retired intelligence operatives were mobilized and ready; the White House had abandoned its reactive stance and was preparing for future battles.

In the coming public relations war with the investigators, the defenders of secrecy had one main advantage: they had a monopoly on the authorized disclosure of information. If the president wanted information disclosed, he could simply reveal it. The executive branch could declassify at will.

The congressional investigators, however, often faced a catch-22 situation. Sometimes the only way a congressman could inform the public of an intelligence failure or abuse was to leak the information to the press. Yet at the same time, Congress was trying to prove itself a "responsible" recipient of classified information. One leak might destroy the credibility of the investigations as a whole—especially if the executive branch could exploit that leak.

A congressman first faced this dilemma in 1974. Michael Harrington, who suspected CIA involvement in the coup against Chile's Salvador Allende, asked the House oversight subcommittee to question Colby about the coup. When Harrington read the transcript of the inquiry, he discovered that the CIA director had been "comparatively candid" in revealing some agency involvement in Chile.[11] Harrington was not sure how to proceed. He now knew that the executive had deceived the public, but he had signed an oath not to disclose this classified information. After he discussed Colby's testimony with colleagues and friends, the story leaked to the *Times*.

Harrington's role in the Chile revelations did not provoke an official response from the House at the time. But several months later, after Harrington turned against Lucien Nedzi and lobbied for an aggressive intelligence investigation, the defenders of secrecy in the House suddenly revived the moribund Chile issue. The Armed Services Committee abruptly denied him access to secret files; the Ethics Committee, which had existed for eight years, voted to make Harrington the target of its first formal investigation. Many congressmen speculated that the probe was directed by the executive branch in an attempt to discredit the continuing House investigation.[12] Ultimately, the Ethics Committee dropped its inquiry because of a technical error in the way the secret meeting with Colby had been conducted.[13]

Even though the Harrington inquiry was abandoned, it helped to create and sustain the public image of Congress as an untrustworthy, undisciplined institution. Other unauthorized disclosures throughout the investigations bolstered this image. Some of these leaks came from the Pike committee. On 1 November, Daniel Schorr reported on CBS that the Nixon administration had cynically urged the Kurds to revolt against the Iraqi government and then had abandoned them when the movement no longer suited the shah of Iran, an American ally. Many observers believed that one of the committee members or staff members had leaked the report to Schorr rather than going through the cumbersome process the committee had devised with the executive branch for releasing information.[14]

More leaks came from other congressional committees. The Hughes-Ryan amendment required the administration to brief eight congressional committees on continuing covert actions but provided no means for committee members to object to these operations. Faced with this problem, Senator Dick Clark of Iowa decided to seek publicly a congressional ban on aid to Angola, thus exposing U.S. involvement there without disclosing the details of that covert action.[15] In another prominent case of congressional disclosure, members of an oversight committee or their staff leaked the news that the United States planned to give $6 million to Italian anticommunist parties in the upcoming election.[16] The congressmen responsible for these leaks contended that they were serving the public interest, but they were also providing evidence for the president's argument that Congress could not be trusted with national secrets.

Even when congressmen did not leak national security information, the executive branch sometimes tried to imply that they had. William Colby's public criticism of the Church committee's decision to publish twelve names in its assassination report is an example. All of the names had been previously reported in news stories; one man had identified himself in a letter to the editor. Even Barry Goldwater agreed with the rest of the committee that the names should be included. But Colby used this incident to suggest that the committee was putting agents' lives in jeopardy. "This does pose the potential for retaliation," he told the press, "either against the physical safety or the livelihood or the families of some of the individuals involved." He conceded that many of the names were widely known but insisted that there was "a vast difference in my mind between their appearance in press stories and their official confirmation in a committee report."[17] Although Church dismissed Colby's protest as "absurd," the CIA director had succeeded in suggesting to the public that reckless congressmen were endangering human lives.[18]

This implication was potentially damaging to the investigators, especially since some individuals—who were not affiliated with the committees—*were* trying to endanger these agents. During these months of investigations and exposés, a few disaffected CIA employees decided that the only way to change the agency was to expose its agents. Philip Agee's 1975 book, *Inside the Company*, included an appendix that listed all of the officers and agents he could remember from his days in the agency.[19] "The most effective and important systematic efforts to counter the CIA that can be undertaken right now," Agee wrote in a magazine article, "are . . . the identification, exposure and neutralization of its people working abroad."[20]

Even before Agee published his book in England, former foreign service officer John Marks had written an article for the *Washington Monthly* explaining how to use government publications to identify CIA officers.[21] Both Agee and Marks served as advisers to the Fifth Estate, a Washington organization founded by author Norman Mailer that was dedicated to the exposure of the CIA. The Fifth Estate's magazine, *Counterspy*, published lists of CIA agents around the world. Frequently, foreign publications would print *Counterspy*'s lists or devise their own. These activists hoped that exposure would force the CIA to bring its officers home and cease its interventionist activities abroad.

The exposure of CIA employees had more deadly effects, however. In its winter 1975 issue, *Counterspy* revealed the identity of the CIA station chief in Lima, Peru. The revelation was not an investigative coup: the officer, Richard Welch, had previously been identified by the Peruvian press. The magazine did not even give Welch's assignment correctly, for he had since moved to Athens. Even though he had been identified in Peru, Welch chose to occupy a house in Athens that had been used by many of his CIA predecessors. The agency had, in fact, warned him not to move into this house, but he had rejected the advice.[22]

Given this transparent cover, an Athens newspaper easily identified Welch as the station chief and printed his name, address, and phone number. A short time later, on 23 December 1975, as Welch was returning from a Christmas party, he was ambushed by masked men outside his home and shot to death. The CIA now had an official martyr.

"Never before," Daniel Schorr commented on the evening news, "has a fallen secret agent come home as such a public hero."[23] The executive branch found Welch's death very useful in its public relations campaign

Army pallbearers carry the casket of assassinated CIA officer Richard Welch out of the Fort Meyer Memorial Chapel following funeral services on 6 January 1976. (Courtesy Gerald R. Ford Library)

against the congressional and journalistic investigators. Over the protests of the Veterans of Foreign Wars, the president waived restrictions and authorized Welch's body to be buried in Arlington National Cemetery, an honor usually reserved for those who had served in the armed forces. When his casket arrived at Andrews Air Force Base, it was greeted by an air force honor guard, William Colby, several high-ranking presidential aides, dozens of reporters and cameramen, and ARIO founder David Phillips.[24] The plane carrying the hero's body had circled the airport for fifteen minutes so that it could land live on the morning news.[25] In short, the executive branch "danced with joy on his grave," Church committee counsel F. A. O. Schwarz, Jr., says. "Not that they were glad he was dead. They just exploited it in an utterly inappropriate way."[26] Some investigators even speculated darkly that the CIA itself had been behind the assassination, though a Greek terrorist group later took responsibility for this and other killings.[27]

The elaborate publicity surrounding the body's arrival in the United States was merely a prelude to the pomp of the funeral. The Arlington ceremony featured honor guards, dozens of fluttering flags, and the horse-drawn caisson that had carried President Kennedy, as well as a

President Ford escorts the widow of Richard Welch, Maria Cristina Welch, to her motorcade following funeral services for her husband. (Courtesy Gerald R. Ford Library)

guest list that included the president and "a rare and glittering tableau of the American national security establishment."[28] The executive branch handled the death "magnificently, in a malevolent sort of way," in the view of Pike committee chief counsel Aaron Donner. "I don't think a president could be buried with more pomp and circumstance," he says.[29]

Live coverage on breakfast television was only part of the favorable publicity the CIA reaped from the Welch killing. Welch was eulogized as a "scholar, wit, athlete, spy" on news and editorial pages across the nation.[30] He seemed to fit perfectly the Cold War image of the heroic American secret agent. One of his most fervent admirers was the *Washington Post*, which ran thirteen stories on Welch during the week after his death. In a mournful editorial, the *Post* called the murder "the entirely predictable result of the disclosure tactics chosen by certain American critics of the agency."[31]

But just who were these critics, these people responsible for Richard Welch's death? The president and his spokesmen were careful not to blame the investigating committees.[32] But CIA counsel Mitchell Rogovin later conceded that the executive branch "waved it around like a bloody shirt." Although the administration did not say " 'Senator Church, you've got blood on your hands,' " Rogovin has commented, that implication was "unsaid—and loudly unsaid."[33]

Critics outside the administration did not bother to leave the implication unsaid. Some opponents of the investigations tried to link Church's disclosure of names in the assassination report to Welch's death. For example, General Daniel Graham wrote that Church insisted on publishing the names "despite the strong and cogent pleas of William Colby that the naming of large numbers of CIA men and their contacts would put their lives and well-being in jeopardy—a warning that came tragically true in Greece, where a CIA man was assassinated."[34] This statement, though literally true, unfairly implied that Church had identified Welch. Church tried to clear up this confusion by issuing press releases stating that his committee had never received Welch's name—or that of any field operator—and calling for criminal sanctions for people who identified such agents.[35] But that did not stop the press from occasionally equating the committee disclosures with those of *Counterspy*, nor did it stop many citizens from wrongly concluding that the investigations had led to murder.[36]

The other villain frequently accused of causing Welch's death was "the press." Welch's admirers often attributed his assassination to his exposure by this monolithic "press," without distinguishing *Counterspy* from mainstream publications. In fact, almost all of the journalists queried by *MORE* magazine after Welch's death said they would not have published his name.[37] But the media, with their live television coverage and their front-page pictures of Welch's grieving widow, served as willing conduits for the administration's propaganda campaign. Ironically, as *Washington Post* ombudsman Charles Seib pointed out, "the press was used to publicize what in its broad effect was an attack on itself."[38]

Frank Church later said that he believed the administration tried to use the Welch death to "close down the investigation as soon as possible and to try to keep control of whatever remedies were sought."[39] The executive branch's exploitation of the murder was so successful that one outraged writer called it a "cold war coup d'etat."[40]

Many congressmen were more sympathetic to the CIA—and hostile to the investigators—after the Welch assassination. Even if most congressmen understood that their colleagues should not be blamed for *Counterspy*'s sins, they also knew that their constituents might not make such a distinction. To erase the image of congressional responsibility for the death of a patriot, these congressmen wanted to appear strongly opposed to the disclosure of *any* secrets.

Thanks to the executive's shrewd decision to publicly mourn a secret agent's murder, the investigators were already on the defensive as they began drafting their final reports and recommendations.

The Pike committee staff director, Searle Field, and his chief investigator, Jack Boos, spent the first few weeks of January squirreled away in the committee offices, frantically writing the committee's final report. They worked day and night to complete a draft in time for the members' return from the winter break on 19 January. Field, a protégé of the maverick, sharp-tongued Senator Lowell Weicker and a veteran of the Watergate committee staff, tried to craft a report that was direct and accessible. He did not want to write "a boring and dry recitation," he later commented. "We believed that what we had come across was of sufficient concern to state it in a way that people could understand."[41]

The final report was indeed easy to understand. It condemned the FBI, the CIA, and the secretary of state in words that could not be misinterpreted. For example, it noted that Kissinger had a "passion for secrecy" and that his statements were "at variance with the facts."[42] After a seventy-page initial section of complaints about the executive's lack of cooperation, the report discussed in much greater detail than the public hearings the committee's findings on the intelligence community's spending practices, its failure to predict crises, and the risks that it posed to the American public.

In a controversial passage, the report also described and passed judgment on recent American covert actions abroad. In September, after the dispute over the committee's release of the four classified words, Pike had agreed to consult the president before disclosing secret information. Accordingly, the committee had asked the president in December to approve the release of special reports on covert actions in Angola and Italy. (On a tie vote, the committee had decided not to further publicize the Kurdish operation.)[43] After Ford prohibited the committee from issuing these extra reports, however, the final report indulged in the transparent artifice of describing—and condemning—the operations in Iraq and Italy without naming the countries involved. For example, after describing a covert action in a country that was obviously Iraq, the report said: "Even in the context of covert action, ours was a cynical enterprise."[44]

Many Pike committee staff members were proud of the report, maintaining that such egregious abuses and errors by the intelligence community deserved blunt condemnation. They believed that a direct, hard-hitting report was necessary to awaken the public to the seriousness of the CIA's problems.

But to CIA officials, the "slanted, generally slanderous, misleading and petty" report was proof of their doubts about the fairness of Pike and his staff. "Being cynical and disillusioned, my response to this nasty paper is that there is not much we can say to which the Committee will pay any attention," the CIA's deputy general counsel wrote in an internal memo.[45]

CIA officials disagreed about whether the report's blunt language would generate support for reform. "It's easy to understand, easy to read and it can be easily distorted," one official wrote. "This is a very damaging report to the intelligence profession."[46] But the associate deputy director for intelligence, Paul Walsh, suggested that the report's "extreme shrillness" and its "obvious bias" would actually hurt the committee's cause. "I believe the tilt and the tone of the report are so extreme that we would be better off letting it stand as it is so that it will be its own best witness against itself," he wrote.[47]

As executive branch officials pondered their response to the report, copies of the final draft circulated among the committee members, their staff, and the executive branch. At this time, committee members knew that giving the report to the press would be a violation of committee rules. The draft was not marked "classified," however, because the chairman did not believe that it contained legitimate secrets.

Since the report was not classified and was scheduled for public release within a week, it would not have been uncommon—and it certainly would not have been a crime—for a committee or staff member to guarantee big headlines for the report by leaking it early to the media. As I. F. Stone later noted, it also would have been possible for someone in the executive branch to leak it. Even though the report condemned the CIA, Stone argued, shrewd intelligence agents might have realized that the leak would discredit the committee more than the agency.[48] This argument, however, supposed a more prescient CIA than the one described in the report.[49]

In any event, bits of the report began appearing in the New York Times on 20 January—the day after the staff distributed it to the members and to the executive branch. For the next week, the Times reported several committee charges, sometimes supported by direct quotes from "portions" of the draft "made available to the New York Times." According to these stories, the CIA had systematically undervalued the military assistance it had given the Angolans, thus hiding the extent of the aid; the

CIA and the State Department possibly permitted the 1974 Greek coup in Cyprus that provoked a Turkish invasion; eleven full-time CIA agents had posed as reporters overseas; and the CIA had spied on dissidents at U.S. colleges.[50]

As their supposedly secret draft was splashed across the front pages, the frustrated and angry committee members met to approve a final version of the report. The CIA disagreed sharply with Pike's contention that the report did not contain legitimate secrets. As the last days of January flew by, representatives of the secret agencies held marathon negotiating sessions with the staff in an attempt to persuade the committee to delete parts of the report. "We compressed into a forty-eight-hour period something that should have taken two weeks," Rogovin later said bitterly.[51] The committee did agree to some changes of tone and substance, but Pike and the majority refused to compromise on many issues.

Before it could release the report, the committee also had to solve two procedural problems. The first seemed easy to remedy. The committee's deadline for submitting the report was 31 January, but it seemed impossible to finish the final draft, allow the minority members the customary five days for comment, and propose final recommendations by that time. The chairman had always been reluctant to request an extension of the deadline, fearing that not meeting the original deadline would cause public opinion to turn against the investigation.[52] At this point, however, he agreed to request a ten-day continuation solely for the purpose of adding minority views and making recommendations. He needed unanimous consent from the House for an extension or, failing that, a special rule from the Rules Committee. Pike seemed certain that the Rules Committee would readily agree to his request.[53]

The second problem was more complex and potentially dangerous for the committee. Pike had agreed in September to let the president approve the release of secret documents. In December, the committee had sought presidential approval of reports on Angola and Italy. But now, in the last weeks of the investigation, the chairman made a startling claim: the agreement, he said, did not apply to the committee's *final* report. Submitting the final report to the president for approval would amount to prior censorship and a violation of the separation of powers, he maintained.

Pike and the president's men apparently had never discussed whether the disclosure agreement applied to the final report. The executive branch maintained that the report was covered by the agreement and that to claim otherwise was pure sophistry. For his part, Pike may have genuinely believed that the report was in a different category from interim releases of information. He later explained that the final report was a committee creation, entirely different from the executive documents covered under the September agreement, and that the members never would have approved the agreement if they thought it applied to the final report.[54] On the other hand, Pike may have regretted the compromise and decided to find a way out of it. Whatever their true motives, the chairman and a majority of committee members now insisted that they had a right to decide what should and should not be published in their final report.[55]

The committee minority was outraged by this "preposterous and outrageous interpretation of the agreement," as David Treen said.[56] Robert McClory agreed that the unilateral release of secret information in the report would "do a great disservice to the reputation and to the important work of this committee."[57] But the Democrats argued that surrendering the principle of congressional declassification would be a disservice to the House.

In its penultimate act before turning to recommendations, the committee voted 8–4 to include classified information in its report. The next day, 23 January, the members voted 9–4 to issue the report at last.[58] The Government Printing Office began to prepare the most important document about the U.S. intelligence community yet to be published.

Now that the report's release and distribution seemed imminent, the river of leaks became a flood. On Monday morning, 26 January, the *New York Times* announced that it now had a complete copy—not just "portions"—of the report and printed several new charges over the next five days. The most sensational revelations concerned covert actions, including the information that an Italian neofascist general had recently received $800,000 from a reluctant CIA at the direction of the U.S. ambassador.[59]

This time, however, the *Times* did not have exclusive possession of the Pike report. Daniel Schorr also obtained a copy of the report after the committee formally approved it and began to broadcast a number of stories on its contents. At one point, he even showed a copy of what appeared to be the first page of the report on the air.[60] In his most significant story, Schorr disclosed that Democratic senator Henry Jackson had secretly advised the CIA on how to protect itself from a congressional investigation.[61]

The contents of the report were potentially devastating to the executive branch. Its unauthorized release, however, enabled the CIA and the White House to divert attention from what it contained to the way it had been disclosed. White House spokesman Ron Nessen charged that the leaks raised "serious questions about how classified material can be handled by Congress when national security is at stake." Once again, William Colby held a press conference at CIA headquarters to condemn the committee.[62]

Most of the committee members were enraged and demoralized by the leaks. Robert Kasten urged Pike to find the leaker. "What do you recommend precisely? Lie detector tests for Members of Congress?" Pike asked in exasperation.[63]

Meanwhile, defenders of the intelligence community—galvanized by outrage over the leaks—began mobilizing to block the formal release of the report. In ordinary circumstances, this would not have been possible. House committees have the power to issue reports on their own authority. But there was one glitch in the committee's plan: Pike needed to ask the House for a short extension. As he expected, the 435 members would not give unanimous consent for the extension. This forced him to ask the Rules Committee for a special rule, an effort the chairman clearly considered to be pro forma.

In a shocking setback, however, Pike encountered a hostile and deeply divided Rules Committee. Many of its members were incensed by the leaks and by Pike's interpretation of his agreement with the president. Although Pike pleaded with them to uphold Congress's power and autonomy, most members were more impressed by McClory's argument that the committee had no right to include classified information in its report without presidential approval. After a stormy session, and apparently without the prior knowledge of the House leadership, the committee voted 9–7 across party lines to give Pike his extension—*but only on the condition that the president approve the report.* Stunned and furious, Pike charged that his report was being held hostage. "The White House and the CIA have jointly engineered the biggest cover-up since Watergate," he told the press.[64]

The chairman still had one last chance to save his report: the House as a whole had to approve the Rules Committee recommendation. The next day, Pike and a majority of committee members tried desperately to persuade their colleagues—most of whom had not yet read the report—to support them. Pike angrily told the House that his agreement with the executive did not apply to the final report. In any case, he said, it was absurd to give the president unlimited power to keep secret anything he found inconvenient. "A secret is a fact or an opinion to which some bureaucrat has applied a rubber stamp," Pike argued.[65] Jim Johnson, the one Republican on the committee who supported the report's release, said he could not understand why Congress wanted to cover up "despicable, detestable" acts. "We are being castigated by those who perpetrated the acts and then classified them," he said.[66] Moderate Democrat Morgan Murphy argued that once again the issue was the constitutional responsibility of the House. "If we are not a coequal branch of this Government, if we are not equal to the President and to the Supreme Court, then let the CIA write this report; let the President write this report; and we ought to fold our tent and go home."[67]

In response, the opponents of release claimed that further revelations would endanger individual agents and the national security. The ghost of Richard Welch was invoked several times, even though the report had nothing to do with him personally. The committee's critics argued that a skilled intelligence analyst could use the report to identify the agency's vital "sources and methods."

But above all, the representatives were moved by the argument that the committee had given its word to the president that it would not publish classified information without his approval. "That is the question that is involved here today," McClory told the House. "Can a committee of Congress be trusted to fulfill an agreement it makes with the executive branch?"[68] David Treen astutely asked why the committee had bothered to ask the president to approve its covert action reports if he had, in fact, no right to "censor" its reports.[69]

In the end, a variety of factors influenced the House members: lack of confidence in the Pike committee's rushed and confrontational investigation; anger and frustration over the leaks; suspicion about the report itself, which they had not had time to read; concern that the public might blame Congress for Richard Welch's death; and the conviction that the House was "honor-bound," because of Pike's compromise with the White House in September, to submit the report to the president first. Most important, however, was the unwillingness of many House members to take responsibility for intelligence oversight. They preferred to let the president decide what could safely be released to the public. Political scientist J. Leiper Freeman has shown that 215 members of Congress who voted to suppress the Pike report had voted three months earlier to keep the CIA's budget secret.[70] These congressmen, largely conservative and disproportionately southern, did not want Congress to dispute executive claims of "national security." Less than two years after Nixon's resignation, despite all of the talk about the "fighting" post-Watergate Congress and the resurgence of congressional power, a surprising proportion of the House voted to let the president have the last word on classification.

And so came the final irony: the House of Representatives, after spending one year and several hundred thousand dollars on an intelligence investigation, voted more than 2 to 1 not to let the public learn what the committee had discovered.[71] Pike complained that the vote made a "travesty of the whole doctrine of separation of powers" and that his committee's work had been "entirely an exercise in futility."[72] He, and a majority of his committee, agreed that they would rather let their "late lamented" report die than submit it to the White House for censorship.[73]

Thus the Pike report seemed destined to remain unread and unpublished in its entirety—that is, until Daniel Schorr began contemplating his duty to history.

Schorr had covered the Pike investigation so closely and so successfully that the chairman had once complained that he "share[d] membership on this committee from time to time."[74] Schorr's excellent sources enabled him to be one of only two reporters who gained access to the entire Pike report. In fact, as he soon discovered, he alone possessed a copy of the report, for *New York Times* reporter John Crewdson had only taken notes from it rather than photocopying it. Now he faced a difficult decision: What was his journalistic responsibility as the sole owner of a classified, suppressed report?[75]

Schorr did not waste much time agonizing over his options. "If Congress could be manipulated into deciding to suppress information," he later wrote, "I could not help to implement that decision." His responsibilities as a journalist were to put information before the public, he believed; "*not* to publish was to me the unacceptable decision; to try to arrange publication was the natural duty of a reporter."[76] It was also the natural inclination of a reporter to publicize—indeed, flaunt—an impressive scoop.

Schorr first approached his bosses at CBS. Could he broadcast a half-hour television special on the contents of the report? If not, what about publishing the report in book form? "We owe it to history to publish it," he told them.[77] But CBS officials were unenthusiastic. Schorr began to realize that a regulated corporation "constantly worried about the good will of Congress" was unlikely to defy the House.[78] He also wondered whether CBS's previous connections to the CIA contributed to the network's reluctance to publish the damaging document. Even as he was trying to arrange publication of the report, Schorr broadcast a story on charges by Sig Mickelson, former president of CBS News, that two former CBS stringers had worked for the CIA with CBS chairman Bill Paley's approval. Paley called the charges "absolutely untrue." Network executives then intervened to cancel Schorr's live interview with Mickelson scheduled for the next morning.[79] After he was not invited to a meeting between Paley and new CIA head George Bush, Schorr began to wonder: "If CBS was not, at this point, part of the answer to suppression of CIA secrets, was CBS perhaps part of the problem?"[80]

Meanwhile, Schorr began to search for another sponsor. He turned to a natural source: the Reporters' Committee for the Freedom of the Press, a First Amendment group. Realizing the potential financial rewards of publication, and not wanting to seem to profit from national secrets, Schorr offered to donate all of the money he might make from the venture to the committee. In return, the committee's board members tried to help him find a publisher. They referred him to Peter Tufo, a New York City lawyer with publishing contacts. Schorr did not know that Tufo was also the counsel for Clay Felker, the publisher of *New York* magazine and New York's alternative newspaper, the *Village Voice*.

Tufo quickly informed Schorr that he could not find a paperback publisher willing to take the report. He could, however, arrange publication with Felker. "Oh, Christ, not that!" Schorr exclaimed.[81] He had no love for Felker's publications, which had printed unflattering profiles of him after Richard Helms had inadvertently made him a celebrity by exploding at him on national television. Moreover, he wanted the report to appear as a paperback, not in a newspaper or magazine. But Tufo, who did not disclose his connection to Felker, told him there were no other options. Schorr reluctantly agreed.

He did not agree to write a signed introduction, however. Now that the report would appear in an alternative publication, rather than a CBS-endorsed paperback, he decided to keep his role in the affair secret. Schorr contended that these secretive methods were necessary to protect his source; critics would later maintain that he knew publication would anger his employer. In any event, Schorr made the crucial decision to turn "an act of disclosure into a covert action." He later admitted that this was a "terrible mistake."[82]

As Schorr was conducting his frantic negotiations to publish the report, the Pike committee members, happily unaware of the disaster about to befall them, tried to salvage something from their long effort through their recommendations. Over the course of several days in early February, the committee devised an ambitious wish list: abolishing the Defense Intelligence Agency and the Internal Security Division of the FBI, writing a legislative charter for the National Security Agency, creating an "intelligence czar" separate from the CIA, requiring court orders for FBI infiltration of American organizations, and requiring the agencies to disclose their total budgets.

The committee also recommended several ways to make those who authorized U.S. covert actions more accountable. Only Ron Dellums, Jim Johnson, and William Lehman voted to abolish all covert operations. But the committee as a whole recommended enlarging the 40 Committee, which approved covert operations; requiring the president to put his covert action findings in writing; prohibiting assassinations and paramilitary operations; and requiring the executive to notify congressional overseers within forty-eight hours after the start of covert actions. Finally, the Pike committee recommended that the House establish a nine- to thirteen-member permanent oversight committee, which would have the right to declassify information on a majority vote.

As the Pike committee finished its work on 10 February, the members congratulated each other for their impressive—albeit controversial—contribution to an understanding of the nation's secret government. "Given the circumstances, problems, and lack of support, I think we did our best," Dellums told his colleagues. "I hope what we have done will have some impact on the course of history in this country."[83] The next day, the *Village Voice* published the text of their secret report.

The publication was the last in a series of disasters for the Pike committee. It was also the first episode in a continuing drama that would destroy Daniel Schorr's career, at least temporarily. Schorr quickly realized that he would pay a price for trying to keep his role secret. On the morning of 11 February, a colleague whom Schorr considered a friend, Laurence Stern of the *Washington Post*, called to inform him that the *Village Voice* had published the Pike report that morning in a twenty-four-page supplement. Far from reflecting Schorr's high-minded concerns about First Amendment rights, the tabloid trumpeted its scoop in red capital letters: "THE CIA REPORT THE PRESIDENT DOESN'T WANT YOU TO READ."

Stern wanted to know if Schorr was the source, but Schorr was reluctant to reveal his role. The two journalists had a long conversation that wandered on and off the record. Despite Schorr's "sophistic evasions," the *Post* reporter eventually learned enough to identify the correspondent as the source of the report.[84]

The next morning, the *Post* identified Schorr not only as the purveyor of secret documents but also as the lead actor in what it suggested was "a journalistic morality play."[85] Over the subsequent weeks and months, media coverage of the report leak repeatedly emphasized this "morality play"—Schorr's decision to publish a secret report, his clandestine actions in arranging publication, his decision to give the profits to the Reporters' Committee—rather than the contents of the report. The Schorr drama, after all, was a simple, easily communicated story, while the report's substance was more difficult to understand and translate. Moreover, journalists, driven by the routines of their profession to report only "news," saw the Schorr leak as the new element in an otherwise old story.

The leak also gave the prestige newspapers' editorial boards the chance to distance themselves from "irresponsible" journalists like Schorr. The *Washington Post*, for example, never editorialized on the report's revelations, only on the leaks. The *New York Times* self-righteously condemned the "counterproductive rash of leaked reports and premature disclosures"—disclosures that its reporters had eagerly sought and its editors had prominently published.[86]

The media's shift in attention from the report's charges to their premature disclosure was skillfully encouraged by the executive branch. President Ford offered Congress the FBI's help in finding Schorr's source, while Secretary Kissinger again declared that "we are facing here a new version of McCarthyism."[87] Rogovin, the CIA's counsel, later admitted that the executive branch's "concern" over the report's damage to national security was less than genuine. "No one really felt that Western Civilization was at risk," he says.[88] But at the time, the administration had no qualms about implying otherwise.

The House swiftly joined in the counterattack on Schorr. Within days, the House Ethics Committee voted to investigate the leak, requested $350,000 to conduct the investigation, and threatened Schorr with contempt of Congress if he refused to disclose his source. Having learned its lesson from the recent Harrington inquest, the Ethics Committee made sure that no technical errors impeded its first full, formal investigation.[89] Schorr could face jail time or, at the least, suspension of his credentials to cover Congress.

As the legislative and executive branches of government rushed to condemn Schorr, the institution that liked to call itself the "fourth branch of government" failed to defend him. Schorr's employer quickly distanced itself from the controversial correspondent. The network was feeling pressure from nervous affiliates who were worried about the response of government regulators and from viewers who began to question the network's credibility.[90] As one citizen wrote the CBS president, "So long as Daniel Schorr is functioning as a news source for CBS, the public has the obligation to question the truth of any CBS report and to suspect an ulterior motive behind any CBS release."[91] Under these circumstances, CBS was so anxious to be rid of Schorr that network officials offered him severance pay in addition to the two years of salary remaining on his contract in return for his resignation. Before he agreed, however, Schorr insisted that the forced resignation be kept secret; he did not want the Ethics Committee to realize the extent of his vulnerability. Publicly, the network announced that Schorr had been temporarily "relieved" of all reporting duties because of his "adversary position" in the pending investigation.[92]

Many other reporters and producers seemed just as eager as CBS to dissociate themselves from Schorr. Some of the editorials condemning him were so vitriolic, a rare Schorr supporter noted, that they "read as if they had been written by former Vice President Agnew."[93] The worst blow came from an unexpected source. The *New York Times*, Seymour Hersh's employer and the one voice Schorr must have hoped would be raised in his defense, charged that Schorr was engaged in "selling secrets."[94] The *Washington Post's* ombudsman Charles Seib also chided Schorr for not realizing that "the dollar sign is a danger sign in journalism."[95] As I. F. Stone observed, this criticism of Schorr could only be described as "insufferably hypocritical."[96] After all, Schorr had arranged to donate his profits, while the *Post* and the *Times* had profited from publishing the Pentagon Papers.

The attacks on Schorr were not limited to the editorial pages. Once again, as had happened after Richard Helms had verbally attacked him the year before, a series of unflattering profiles of Schorr appeared. *Newsweek*, for example, discussed the "questions of his ethics" and his reputation "for egoism and overly aggressive reporting."[97] The prominent journalists on the Reporters' Committee, far from defending their decision to accept the profits from Schorr's enterprise, charged that he was trying to make them a "partner in his calumny."[98] The worst attacks came from Laurence Stern of the *Washington Post*, whose article in the

Columbia Journalism Review criticized the Pike committee and its report as well as Schorr's judgment in this "morality play for the Fourth Estate." Schorr, who was particularly angered by this piece because he had considered Stern his friend, wrote a nasty rejoinder in the next issue, to which Stern wrote an even nastier reply.[99]

A few journalists did defend Schorr. After he had been "relieved of duties" by CBS and threatened with contempt, three *New York Times* columnists opposed the editorial position of their newspaper by supporting the veteran correspondent. Tom Wicker disputed that he was "selling secrets," while Russell Baker wondered whether Congress was showing "symptoms of Nixon envy" in setting up its own plumber squad.[100] William Safire suggested that CBS had been looking for an excuse to fire Schorr ever since his report on the network's connections to the CIA.[101]

But these friendly columns were unusual. Rather than defending a respected if unpopular colleague from government persecution, most members of the Fourth Estate rushed to reassure the public and the government that they were not as irresponsible as Dan Schorr. When the investigator became the target of investigation, he was left to face the coming ordeal nearly alone.

Daniel Schorr thought he was upholding the First Amendment by publishing the Pike committee's final report; in return, he was fired by his boss, investigated by the government, and scorned by his colleagues. And Schorr was only the most visible victim of a larger phenomenon: the backlash against all of the congressional and journalistic investigators. After the triumphs and high expectations of the year before, the investigations had collapsed in embarrassment, frustration, and despair.

Why were the media so reluctant to defend Schorr? Many observers at the time blamed Schorr's gift for making enemies as well as the pressures of competitive journalism.[102] As with Seymour Hersh, it was easy for rivals who had missed the story to denigrate their more successful colleague's accomplishments.

But the number and scale of the attacks on Schorr indicate that something more was happening than simple revenge on an unpopular colleague. In leaking the report, Schorr had defied not only Congress and the president but also the public mood. As David Ignatius said in a perceptive piece in the *Washington Monthly*, Schorr had "misjudged the public temper. This was *not* the Pentagon Papers and he was *not* Daniel Ellsberg, and this was not even the same *country*, anymore, that had needed the press to batter its corrupted institutions, force a lying President out of office, strip the cover of national security from the CIA."[103] A December 1975 Harris poll had shown that slightly more respondents disapproved of the investigators than approved of them—and this poll was taken before Welch's death and the leak.[104] Much of the public was tired of the Daniel Schorrs and Seymour Hershes and Otis Pikes who seemed to be threatening the security of the nation and its secret agents. Anthony Lewis reported that congressmen were hearing from their constituents that they did not want to know about any more American crimes or embarrassments.[105] Watergate was over; the "necessary demolition," as Ignatius said, had been accomplished. "But Dan Schorr—ever the reporter—was still battering away."[106]

Schorr partly understood this at the time. In his first major speech after his suspension, he used the metaphor of a pendulum to explain how the public mood in the United States had alternately shifted from valuing liberty to prizing security. "I got hit by a swinging pendulum," he said.[107]

But Schorr was not the only one hit by that pendulum. After the executive counterattack, after the murder of Richard Welch, after the Pike report debacle, all of the investigators were stunned, wounded, and unsure how to proceed.

I was fighting for (a) survival of the agency, (b)

survival of the covert action mission. We won both.

William Colby, interview, 30 March 1992

Unwelcome Truths

The End of the Investigations

The secret agencies clearly emerged the winners of their long battle with the investigators. The Pike committee collapsed in frustration and mutual recriminations. The Church committee issued a massive, detailed final report, but some of its sections on foreign intelligence struck many critics as vague and timid. Meanwhile, the executive branch proposed new "reforms" that would effectively legalize some of the past abuses and punish those who exposed them. The only immediate reform to emerge from the investigations—the creation of a permanent oversight committee—almost failed.

And how effective was that reform? Critics have questioned whether the permanent committee has exercised adequate oversight. In many ways, Congress has continued its reluctance to challenge the secret agencies. Despite its post-Watergate reputation for skepticism, the press has also hesitated to question and expose the secret government.

Why, given the early high expectations for great reform, did the investigations achieve so little? Why did these extensive, far-reaching inquiries result only in restoring the CIA's credibility? The answer can be found in the attitudes toward the secret government held by the press, the Congress, and the public. Despite the rising distrust of governmental secrecy after Vietnam and Watergate, many journalists, congressmen, and other Americans were not sure how much they wanted to know about the nation's dirty secrets.

The leak of the House committee final report was not the final act of the investigations, though the Pike committee members undoubtedly wished it had been. After they issued their recommendations, the members hoped to put the investigation—and all of its frustrations—behind them. But their opponents would not let them escape so easily. The next month, the CIA accused the committee of losing 232 secret and top secret documents, including sensitive discussions of U.S.-Soviet arms talks. Pike, calling the controversy a "fine covert domestic operation," charged that the CIA had orchestrated the dispute to further discredit his committee.[1] After a few days of sensational publicity, the committee staff found nearly all of the missing documents in the CIA's own files.

The committee was not so lucky with its other major ordeal—the inquiry into the leak of the report. Over the next six months, the House Ethics Committee staff, headed by a former FBI agent, directed a massive probe to discover Daniel Schorr's source. The investigation, which included interviews with almost 400 people, did produce some surprises. Les Aspin confessed that he had leaked a copy of the report not to Schorr but to the CIA. After Pike had decreed that the agency could not receive a final draft before the rest of the public, CIA counsel Mitchell Rogovin had urged some friendly members to give him a copy anyway. The Republican members refused, but Aspin proved more obliging. In addition, Aspin's legislative assistant admitted that he had leaked three pages of the report concerning the Reuters News Agency to a Reuters employee.[2]

But this startling news, while it appalled other members and staff members, did not bring the investigators any closer to finding Schorr's source. Many copies of the report that had been circulated to committee members and the executive branch had been shredded. As a result, the investigators could not locate a draft that matched the *Village Voice* text exactly. Unlucky with the physical evidence, they tried to find the culprit through cross-examination. During two months of hearings, the Ethics Committee interrogated all of the Pike committee members and staff members, as well as many executive officials. The testimony frequently became hostile or theatrical. Robert Kasten attacked Aspin's breach of security; Morgan Murphy blasted Democratic leaders for appointing committee members to fill a "quota" (an obvious swipe at Ron Dellums, the only black member); and James Stanton astonished observers by claiming that the whole fiasco was a CIA plot. Schorr had told him, Stanton claimed, that his source was in the CIA.[3]

The climax of the hearings was the dramatic appearance of Schorr himself. With his measured diction, familiar to millions of television viewers, Schorr read an eloquent opening statement defending his right to shield his source. "To betray a source would be for me to betray myself, my career, and my life," he concluded, "and to say that I refuse to do it isn't quite saying it right. I cannot do it."[4] Despite eight warnings from the chairman that he would be prosecuted, Schorr refused to answer questions.

The Ethics Committee members were clearly emboldened by the earlier media attacks on Schorr. "There have been literally hundreds of editorials in newspapers throughout the country," James Quillen of Tennessee told Schorr, "who do not agree with what you did."[5] *Editor and Publisher*, the bible of newspaper management, had also denounced the correspondent, Quillen noted.

Schorr's actual appearance before the inquisition, however, finally persuaded many editorial boards to reverse their stands. It was one thing to condemn Schorr for "selling secrets"; it was another to stand by and let Congress jail him for protecting his source—and thereby upholding a cardinal rule of journalism. For example, *Washington Post* ombudsman Charles Seib, who had earlier criticized Schorr for not realizing that "the dollar sign is a danger sign in journalism," now wrote that the "confidentiality [of sources] is essential to an effective free press, and a free press is vital to our system."[6] More than 5,000 journalists signed a petition protesting the inquiry. At last, Daniel Schorr found himself on the popular side of journalistic ethics.

Intimidated by this sudden shift of media opinion, and embarrassed that they were reduced to harassing a newsman to accomplish their task, the Ethics Committee finally voted 6–5 against starting contempt proceedings. The majority did, however, condemn Schorr's actions as "reprehensible."[7]

Several Ethics Committee members believed that they knew who was responsible for leaking the report. Toward the end of the probe, the congressmen questioned two Pike committee staff members and one legislative assistant for ten hours in closed session. The investigators sought to pit the witnesses against one another to trap their suspect.

But the tactic did not work. According to the committee's final report, the source was "someone on or very close to the Select Committee staff," but the members could not be more definite.[8] One member, Thomas Foley of Washington, dissented from the majority's conclusions, saying that the committee could not definitively rule out the executive branch as the source of the leak.[9] Years later, staff and committee members have called the leak inquiry "frustrating," "tragic," and "horrible." "They went after some of our staff people as if they were Communist spies, as if they were traitors," Robert Giaimo says.[10]

Beyond the personal cost to the targets of the probe, the prolonged report debacle also confirmed House members' fear that aggressive intelligence oversight was politically dangerous. Congressman Dellums expressed the feelings of many of the frustrated reformers when he called the inquiry "an absurd exercise in futility, where the investigator has now become the investigatee, and the intelligence community is no longer being looked at and the press is no longer writing about the abuses."[11] It would be many years before the House would begin to exercise aggressive oversight again.

Meanwhile, the Senate investigation, though it had adopted an entirely different agenda and style than the Pike panel, was also seriously wounded by the disaster in the House. From the beginning, many Americans had equated the two investigations. A December 1975 Harris poll showed only a 2 percentage point difference in approval ratings for the two committees, with 38 percent of the public approving of Church's work and 36 percent approving of the Pike committee.[12] "To see ourselves rated virtually neck-and-neck with the House committee, even though we had avoided most of its pitfalls, was truly disheartening," wrote Church committee staff member Loch Johnson.[13]

The poll was taken before Richard Welch's assassination and the Pike report leak; presumably, the committees fared even worse after those events.[14] After the leak, the Senate investigators tried to redirect the attention of the press to the substance of the abuses they had uncovered, while prudently redoubling their own security. But the backlash against the House investigators affected the Senate committee as well. As Johnson wrote, "We fully realized we might join our House brothers in the same boiling caldron, with the CIA adding the salt, the White House bellowing the flames afresh, and the intelligence officials dancing around the fire in delight."[15]

As enthusiasm for the congressional and journalistic investigations cooled, President Ford seized the opportunity to announce his own intelligence recommendations. These reforms had been planned for months, but the president had not been sure when to propose them. Now, after the Welch death and the Pike leak, the investigators suspected that he had decided to "turn retreat into rout on Capitol Hill," as Loch Johnson put it.[16]

In a speech broadcast live by the three television networks, Ford proposed a minor reorganization of the intelligence community, including creating a new executive branch oversight board, strengthening the office of the director of central intelligence, and establishing new procedures and a new name for the executive committee responsible for approving covert actions. He prohibited assassination by executive order and later released some new guidelines for the FBI.

But the thrust of his proposals was to *strengthen* the agencies and the laws protecting their secrecy. The president's response, in many cases, to the revelations of domestic spying by the CIA was to make that spying legal. For example, he asked Congress to give the agencies authority to open Americans' mail and listen to their conversations in cases of suspected foreign espionage. The intelligence agencies had justified many of the CIA and FBI excesses of the 1960s on the grounds of just such "suspected" espionage.[17] Both Pike and Church denounced the proposed changes; Church commented that they gave the CIA "a bigger shield and a longer sword with which to stab about."[18]

In addition, the president wanted to make it a criminal offense for government employees to disclose intelligence "sources and methods" to unauthorized persons, including journalists. The Espionage Act only covered leaks to foreign agents. Many journalists were astounded by Ford's audacity in proposing to silence the whistle-blowers who had started the investigations by alerting Seymour Hersh. "My immediate reaction is that these proposals would have emanated from the Nixon Administration," said the president of the Associated Press managing editors.[19] Tom Wicker called the proposals "Kafkaesque 'reforms' that would largely prevent further disclosure while doing little about what was actually exposed—not vital secrets but the blunders, abuses and crimes of the CIA."[20] The *Washington Post*, however, proved its "responsibility" by agreeing that the president needed to take "stringent steps" to protect government secrets.[21]

Fourteen months after Hersh exposed illegal CIA domestic spying, twelve months after an outraged Congress voted to investigate these charges, the president proposed measures that would make domestic spying legal in broadly defined cases and would have put Hersh's sources in jail. It remained to be seen whether the Church committee could achieve real reforms in this new atmosphere.

In April 1976, the Church committee staff released its magnum opus: six volumes and several thousand pages of final reports. These volumes were quite different in tone and substance from the Pike committee's final report. The three core volumes covered foreign and military intelligence, domestic operations, and selected case studies. Three supplementary volumes summarized the history of the CIA, the performance of the intelligence agencies in investigating John Kennedy's assassination, and the evolution and organization of U.S. intelligence.[22]

Although the committee strongly condemned the FBI's abuses, its assessment of foreign intelligence was much more equivocal. Three liberal committee members complained that the CIA had persuaded the committee to alter the report "to the point where some of its most important implications are either lost, or obscured in vague language."[23] George Lardner, Jr., who covered the investigations for the *Washington Post*, charged that the committee was "almost sycophantic" in some of its assessments of the CIA. The most obvious example was the committee's "limp" condemnation of Operation CHAOS, the CIA domestic spying program that the Rockefeller Commission had called illegal and improper.[24]

The tone of the report—another major difference from the Pike report—was also very reserved. The six-volume set seemed "designed more as a resource document for those who will frame the new intelligence law than an indictment of abuse or misbehavior by the intelligence community," commented a *New York Times* reporter.[25] Church committee chief counsel F. A. O. Schwarz, Jr., later noted that the foreign intelligence reports were "less detailed" and "more wary" than they would have been if they had been released before Richard Welch's death.[26] On the agency side, William Colby confessed that he gave a "sigh of relief" when he compared the report with what he had initially feared it might say.[27]

However, though generally reserved in language and tone, the report did compile a massive record of the secret government that would be useful to scholars for years to come. The committee documented the CIA's "excessive" use of covert action, including 900 major projects and several thousand minor ones since 1961.[28] The report disclosed other alarming numbers. The CIA had placed the names of 1.5 million potentially "subversive" Americans in a computer database as the result of its mail-opening program; the agency had also opened files on more than 7,000 Americans during its domestic spying operation. The CIA and FBI together had opened 380,000 letters, while the FBI had undertaken 500,000 investigations of dissidents without winning any convictions.[29] In one strongly worded passage, the report put the "rogue elephant" metaphor to rest, concluding that the CIA, "in broad terms, is not 'out of control.'"[30]

Moreover, though the Church committee's report was milder than the Pike report, the senators' eighty-seven recommendations for foreign intelligence and ninety-six recommendations for domestic intelligence were more far-reaching. Frank Church's moralistic influence was apparent in the committee's suggested restrictions on covert actions. No covert operations should subvert democratic governments or support "internal security forces which engage in the systematic violation of human rights," the committee advised. In any case, the Senate oversight committee should be notified of covert actions in advance.[31]

But would there be an oversight committee? After the Pike leak and the Welch death, even that mild reform seemed in jeopardy. In the early months of 1976, the Church committee's proposal for a new oversight committee moved through the Senate "with about the same ease and confidence as pioneers once passed through Comanche territory," Loch Johnson wrote.[32]

On 27 and 28 April, as the Church committee's final report was being released to the public, the Senate Rules Committee shocked the partisans of reform by replacing Church's amended oversight bill with a new bill calling for a "temporary" oversight committee that would "study" the issue for another fifteen months. "Fifteen months studying the intelligence agencies? I couldn't believe my ears. I thought we had just done that!" Loch Johnson later commented.[33] In a popular cartoon drawn by Tony Auth, a man labeled "Congressional Oversight" shouted "I give up!" even as he trained a gun on the intelligence agencies.[34]

A majority of Rules Committee members had decided not to antagonize other committees by stealing their oversight duties and giving them to a new committee. In addition, most senators no longer felt pressure from their constituents for reform. "Hysteria has subsided. Congress is taking a more objective view," said Rules Committee member James B. Allen.[35]

Over the next two weeks, the Church committee majority negotiated frantically with their recalcitrant colleagues in the Senate to work out a compromise. They seemed to attain bipartisan support by promising to share some jurisdiction with the standing committees. That compromise threatened to fall apart, however, when Church committee members Barry Goldwater and John Tower, along with longtime overseer Senator John Stennis, actively opposed it.

During the five debates on the issue, Church and Walter Mondale argued that secret power endangered democracy, while Tower and his supporters responded that sharing too much information with Congress endangered national security.[36] Ultimately, the Senate voted more than 2 to 1 to reject a crippling amendment sponsored by Tower. The final vote to establish the new oversight committee was 72–22.[37] The investigators had achieved one reform.

A new day of congressional oversight was dawning—or so it seemed. The Senate's permanent oversight committee began meeting immediately after the end of the Church investigation. In July 1977, partly to make the two houses of Congress consistent, the House finally voted to create its own intelligence committee.[38] The House intelligence committee, however, was not the lineal descendant of the Pike committee. In fact, Pike and most of the liberal Democrats who had served on his committee voted against the permanent committee because they thought it was, as Michael Harrington put it, a "sham" reform.[39] The establishment of the permanent committee laid the foundation for reducing the number of House committees receiving intelligence information. One scholar has called its creation "a victory for executive secrecy."[40]

Congress reorganized its oversight system again in 1980, when it passed the Intelligence Oversight Act. The new law, which superseded the Hughes-Ryan amendment of 1974, drastically reduced the number of congressional overseers. Although it required the CIA to inform Congress of broader categories of intelligence activities, access to this information was now restricted to the two permanent select committees. The

House and Senate Appropriations, Foreign Affairs, and Armed Services Committees would no longer receive intelligence briefings.

The investigations resulted in remarkably few legal changes for the intelligence community. In the executive branch, the next president, Jimmy Carter, imposed stricter controls on the secret agencies through an executive order. Vice President Mondale worked hard to ensure the agencies' accountability.[41] But Carter's executive order was not permanent, and the next administration quickly changed it. Meanwhile, in Congress, both oversight committees spent years considering new charters for the intelligence community to replace the vague clauses in the National Security Act of 1947. Ultimately, however, Congress abandoned these legislative blueprints because of opposition from the intelligence community and a lack of enthusiasm from the Carter administration. Advocates for stricter accountability did achieve one reform in 1978 with the passage of the Foreign Intelligence Surveillance Act, which required the FBI and NSA to obtain court orders for wiretaps in the United States.

When Ronald Reagan came into office in 1981, he swiftly loosened the regulations hindering the CIA and the FBI.[42] He allowed CIA domestic spying in certain cases, permitted physical surveillance of Americans abroad, and authorized some covert actions in the United States. Most important, he appointed his campaign manager and former OSS agent William Casey to be director of central intelligence. Casey was determined to free the CIA from the fetters imposed after Watergate—and he was willing to evade and subvert the law to do so.[43]

Still, as agency directors and executive orders came and went, the permanent intelligence committees continued to oversee the intelligence community. The question remains: Did they improve congressional oversight?

Some Church committee staff members are particularly proud of their work on the FBI. According to F. A. O. Schwarz, Jr., the Church committee's chief counsel, there is now much less danger of the United States becoming a "totalitarian police state" because of FBI reform.[44] The FBI did become more accountable during the Carter administration. Carter's Justice Department even won convictions of two former top FBI officials who had violated Americans' constitutional rights by authorizing break-ins.[45]

But after taking office, Ronald Reagan swiftly pardoned the convicted officials and relaxed the guidelines constraining the FBI. As a result, the bureau again infiltrated groups that were politically opposed to the administration. In the early 1980s, the FBI spied on the Committee in Solidarity with the People of El Salvador, the sanctuary movement for Central American refugees, and the Physicians for Social Responsibility, which later won a Nobel Peace Prize.[46]

The verdict on congressional oversight of the CIA since 1976 is mixed. Political scientist and Church committee staff member Loch Johnson contends that the investigations prompted a "new vigilance" by congressional overseers, thus enhancing American freedom.[47] In Johnson's view, the two permanent intelligence committees have complemented one another and have ensured the constant exercise of tough oversight. Another political scientist, Frank Smist, Jr., argues that the permanent committees have grown supportive of the intelligence community and practice "institutional" rather than "investigative" oversight. Institutional overseers defer to the executive branch and tend to become advocates for the agencies they oversee, while investigative overseers are aggressive and suspicious. Still, Smist thinks that the permanent committees, despite their decreasing aggressiveness, have "developed and strengthened congressional power and authority in intelligence."[48] Ron Dellums, a tough congressional investigator and a member of the permanent intelligence committee from 1991 to 1993, also believes that the investigations have helped to improve oversight.[49]

Other investigators and scholars argue that the investigations had limited effects. Michael Harrington, who led the effort to launch the House investigation and was later removed from the committee because of his alleged leaks the year before, believes that Congress's message to the agencies has been consistent, both before and after the investigations: "Engage in mischief but do it discreetly."[50] Some members of the Ford administration are also skeptical of the long-term effects of the investigations. "After seeing some of the things that went on in the Reagan administration," says Phil Buchen, President Ford's counsel, "I'm not sure the reform was lasting."[51] Richard Helms, the man at the center of many of the investigations' revelations, agrees that the inquiries did not result in many changes. And that, he thinks, is a good thing for the country. "After all, if you want these things done, they have to get done somehow. And the more strictures and pressures and so forth that are put on the people doing it, the harder it is to do it," he says.[52] Several scholars of the intelligence community maintain that the congressional oversight committees have had "very limited impact," as John Prados has written.[53]

The journalists who played crucial roles in the probes are also unimpressed by the results. Seymour Hersh, whose domestic spying stories prompted the entire inquiry, does not believe that the committees accomplished much. "They had a chance to put a crimp in [covert operations], but they didn't have the stomach for it," he says.[54] George Lardner, Jr., of the *Washington Post* has condemned what he calls Congress's "pallid" response to the investigations.[55] "All that seems left," he wrote in 1978, "is the steady tattoo of suggestions that the scandals were somehow imagined."[56]

Scholars and former investigators also disagree about the connections between the investigations and the Iran-contra affair. In 1986, Congress and the American people discovered that the executive branch, despite the reforms of the 1970s, was still evading congressional oversight of intelligence. This time, executive officials had sold arms to Iran and diverted the profits to a counterrevolutionary army that Congress had refused to fund. Once again, executive agencies had lied to Congress; once again, the role of the president in these illegal activities was obscured by the doctrine of "plausible denial."

Did Iran-contra prove the inquiries' failure, or did it demonstrate their success? On the one hand, those who believe that the investigations were successful contend that it is impossible for lawmakers to force the executive branch to obey the law. "We have a lot of laws against murder in this country," says former senator and Church committee member Charles Mathias. "Just passing a law doesn't prevent something from happening."[57] The Iran-contra investigating committee agreed that the scandal "resulted from the failure of individuals to observe the law, not from deficiencies in existing law or in our system of governance."[58] Some former investigators even suggest that the inquiries were responsible for the laws that made Iran-contra a crime. "Probably, absent our work, the procedural and substantive rules that caused there to be an [Iran-contra] investigation in the first place wouldn't have existed," says Church committee counsel F. A. O. Schwarz, Jr.[59]

This contention is only partly true. The requirement that the president provide congressional overseers with written presidential "findings" on covert operations—a requirement substantially ignored by the Reagan administration—actually originated in the Hughes-Ryan amendment of 1974.[60] The Boland amendment, which prohibited the use of U.S. government funds to support the contras in Nicaragua, was inspired by the Clark amendment's cutoff of funds for Angola. And although the Clark amendment was passed in 1975, it had little to do with the Church and Pike investigations. Finally, the idea that Congress should be notified of covert actions in a "timely" manner also originated in the Hughes-Ryan amendment. However, the Intelligence Oversight Act of 1980, which was based loosely on the reform proposals of the Church committee and its successor, did strengthen these reporting requirements, although it also reduced the number of committees receiving the information.

One could argue that the oversight reforms of the post-Watergate era, including the Hughes-Ryan amendment, the Clark amendment, and the 1980 Intelligence Oversight Act, created the statutory requirements that transformed Iran-contra from a secret executive operation into a series of crimes. The implication, then, would be that the reforms enabled the culprits to be punished, even if they did not solve the underlying problems. The system worked, once again.

But one expert on relations among the three branches of government contends that Iran-contra shows just how *unreformed* the foreign policymaking system remains. Vietnam, Watergate, and the intelligence investigations exposed "deeper systemic flaws" in the foreign policymaking process, says Harold Hongju Koh, and these flaws were never remedied.[61] Until Congress devises a new national security charter that includes real foreign affairs accountability for the president, Koh argues, the country will continue to suffer through agonizing scandals—scandals that are anything but "aberrational."

Indeed, what was aberrational about the investigations of 1975 was not the abuses they exposed but Congress's great passion for uncovering those abuses. Before Iran-contra became public, for example, the successors to the Church and Pike committees did not energetically investigate charges that the Reagan administration was violating the law. Unlike the hard-nosed investigative committees of 1975, the permanent intelligence committees trusted executive branch officials; often, they did not seem to want to know that officials were lying to them.[62]

Just months before the Iran-contra scandal was exposed, reporter Leslie Gelb of the *New York Times* concluded that congressional oversight of the CIA had produced a "decade of support" for the agency by Congress. Senator Daniel Patrick Moynihan, a former vice chairman of the intelligence committee, told Gelb: "Like other legislative committees, ours came to be an advocate for the agency it was overseeing." In contrast to the brash, skeptical young staff members of the Pike committee, the House intelligence committee of ten years later was staffed largely by former CIA officers.[63]

Ultimately, the very existence of the new oversight committees helped reassure Congress and the public that the CIA was under control. As I. F. Stone said at the end of the investigations, their net effect "has been to accustom the public mind to the evils exposed and to institutionalize and legalize them by systems of congressional 'oversight.'"[64] Coming to a similar conclusion from a different ideological perspective, historian Rhodri Jeffreys-Jones has written that the investigations laid the foundation for "a new legitimacy" for the CIA, which he believes was a positive development.[65]

William Colby also believes that the new oversight has helped to restore the legitimacy of the CIA. The oversight system "works well now," he says. "The agency's stronger for it; the Congress is supportive to a degree that it would not be if it didn't have that kind of responsibility."[66] Many of the new overseers agree that Congress should see the CIA as a partner, not an adversary. As David Durenberger, chair of the Senate intelligence committee during Iran-contra, explained, "The purpose [of oversight] is to help intelligence, not to have an audit team sitting on the back of the [CIA] operations department."[67] Otis Pike had a very different view of his job.

In Colby's opinion, this unanticipated outcome of the investigations was much better than the "slew of crippling legislation" he once feared.[68] Others agree—or at least believe that the establishment of permanent committees was the best that could reasonably be achieved. But this new partnership between Congress and the CIA is hardly what most investigators had hoped to accomplish, at least in the beginning. When Seymour Hersh exposed the CIA's domestic spying, when Michael Harrington demanded that the House investigate the charges, when Otis Pike confronted Henry Kissinger, when Frank Church issued his assassination report, and when Daniel Schorr arranged to publish the Pike report, they never expected that the end result of their efforts would be to legitimize the secret government. After Vietnam and Watergate, many reformers had hoped to attain a new democratic accountability for the secret agencies. They had wanted to restructure the intelligence community, enact restrictive laws, write new charters, even abolish covert action. In the end, though, many were happy to settle for a new congressional committee.

Most participants in the investigations have strong opinions about the committees' tactical mistakes—mistakes they believe cost them the support necessary for real reforms. Otis Pike was too confrontational; Frank Church was not confrontational enough. The Pike committee was too harsh in its assessments of the CIA; the Church committee was too vague. The participants also like to point to pivotal developments that transformed the investigations. If only the Pike committee had not sprung so many leaks, if only Richard Welch had not been killed, if only the CIA and the White House had not exploited these events so cleverly, then things would have turned out very differently.

These postmortem assessments are valuable, especially for political scientists interested in learning lessons for the future. But from a historical perspective, these tactical considerations seem relatively minor. The most intriguing aspect of the intelligence investigations is not the "mistakes" made by the committee chairmen. Instead, it is the way public opinion turned against them—a shift, it seems, that would have happened even if the investigators had avoided their worst mistakes. If Otis Pike, with impressive foresight, had decided to compromise more and demand less, one doubts whether much would have changed. The House committee might have released a tamer report, and the House might have established a permanent committee a year earlier. But these are relatively minor differences. The final outcome—with Congress on the defensive and the secret agencies on the rebound—would have been the same.

Ultimately, the foremost problem faced by both committees was the change in the political climate. As Nicholas Horrock of the *New York Times* described it, Watergate had driven a "fortuitous wedge into the secret workings of government, like an opening in an overcast sky." The investigators could not accomplish their long and messy task before "the sky closed again"[69]—or, to use Daniel Schorr's metaphor, before the pendulum swung.

Why did that pendulum swing? At the start of the inquiries, the timing seemed perfect for thorough investigations. After Vietnam and Watergate, public skepticism of the imperial presidency and the secret government was at its height.

This was the only time in post–World War II American history, in fact, when such investigations could have occurred. Vietnam and Watergate had so transformed the cautious *New York Times* that it hired a famous muckraker, gave him months to investigate a Cold War institution, then splashed his stories across the front page. The new Congress, in turn, was so shocked by these revelations that it finally voted to investigate the secret government, after more than 400 previous such proposals had died.

But even in 1975, as we have seen, Congress, the press, and the public were uneasy about going too far—about examining too closely all of the dark secrets in the nation's musty corners. Ultimately, many Americans were tired of the controversy and the constant battering of the nation's institutions.

One institution that was consistently reluctant to challenge the nation's foreign intelligence agencies was the American press. Few observers, however, realized this at the time. Defenders of the intelligence community charged that the press was endangering the nation's security, while supporters of reform applauded the media's fearlessness. They believed that the media's triumph in Watergate had transformed the press corps into a battalion of daring, independent investigators—the "myth" of post-Watergate journalism, as Michael Schudson has called it.[70]

Many journalists were indeed willing to question the open operations of the government, seeking out stories on corruption, incompetence, or personal immorality. These reporters tried to emulate Woodward and Bernstein, or at least pop culture's mythic image of Woodward and Bernstein. But only a very few reporters dared to challenge the secret government. Those who did so won no prizes for their efforts. Seymour Hersh's domestic spying stories were underplayed by all but his own newspaper. A whispering campaign in Washington questioned the veracity of his stories and prevented him from winning a Pulitzer Prize. Daniel Schorr was also attacked by his colleagues, first for his mistake on the spy-in-the-White-House story, then for his role in the publication of the Pike report.

Even the *New York Times,* the most aggressive news organization throughout the year of investigations, proved receptive to government pleas for secrecy. The *Times* refused to publicize President Ford's unintentional disclosure of assassination plots. It joined many other papers in suppressing the *Glomar Explorer* story and led the editorial attacks on the Pike committee and on Schorr. The real question, as Tom Wicker wrote in 1978, is not *"whether* the press has lacked aggressiveness in challenging the national-security mystique, but *why?"*[71] Why, indeed, did most journalists decide to defer to the administration instead of pursuing sensational stories?

In part, this deference was a defensive reaction. Intellectuals and columnists like Max Kampelman, Irving Kristol, and Joseph Kraft would continue to condemn the "imperial media" for years to come.[72] Many journalists were intimidated by these attacks. In these first post-Watergate years, journalists' greatest fear was that the government would restrict press freedom. One Columbia University journalism professor wrote in 1978: "The equivalent of an Official Secrets Act is being forged in this country today, link by link. The inevitable result is a weakening of the First Amendment."[73] John B. Oakes, editorial page editor of the *New York Times*, worried at the end of the investigations that freedom of the press "today is under more serious attack than at any time since the Sedition Act nearly two centuries ago." Oakes concluded—as did many of his colleagues throughout the year of intelligence—that the press needed to exercise more "responsible self-restraint" and reassure the public that it would not "defy the national interest."[74] Daniel Schorr provided a case study in what could happen to the "irresponsible" journalist.

For many journalists, even more important than their fear of public anger or government repression was their concern that their critics might, in fact, be right. Maybe they *had* gone too far. Most journalists, despite their talk of serving as the "Fourth Estate," were not happy being adversaries. They wanted to appear responsible. Tom Wicker maintained that the greatest threat to press freedom did not come from the government: "At least as great a threat, I believe, comes from the press itself—in its longing for a respectable place in the established political and economic order, in its fear of the reaction that boldness and independence will always evoke."[75] Those who criticized Cold War institutions risked losing their status among their elite friends and sources.

The media wanted to appear particularly responsible in their coverage of foreign policy. The FBI of J. Edgar Hoover, guilty of domestic abuses, received unsparing criticism from the press. But the CIA's assassination plots, the raising of the Russian submarine, and the Pike report prompted a more ambiguous response. These stories involved foreign policy—the bipartisan Cold War foreign policy that the media had endorsed for years.

Other scholars have demonstrated that the supposedly adversarial press of the late 1960s and early 1970s was actually rather timid. Daniel Hallin has shown that reporters were not nearly as aggressive in covering Vietnam as conventional wisdom might suggest.[76] Similarly, Ben Bagdikian has demonstrated that in 1972—the year of the Watergate break-in—the press was so intimidated by the Nixon administration's attacks that it tried to avoid angering or embarrassing the president.[77]

The media also lacked investigative zeal *after* Watergate—indeed, throughout the most celebrated case of post-Watergate investigative reporting. The press during the year of intelligence was nervous about its newfound power, fearful of a public and governmental backlash, and receptive to government requests for self-censorship. Vietnam and Watergate may have transformed the way the press covered domestic political scandals, but most journalists still shied away from questioning the national security state.

The "fighting Ninety-fourth" Congress also disappointed those on the left who had expected it to challenge the secret agencies. "Has Congress forgotten Watergate so soon?" Anthony Lewis lamented after the House suppressed the Pike report. "Has it forgotten that exercise of its own power is the constitutional answer to the imperial presidency?"[78]

Powerful forces in Congress had opposed intelligence reform from the start. As Harry Howe Ransom has noted, many leaders of Congress shared responsibility for the CIA abuses. Before the investigations, Congress had not lacked oversight committees; it had simply lacked *zealous* oversight committees. Many senior members like Senator John Stennis and Representative Edward Hébert had preferred to overlook the intelligence agencies' excesses. They formed a strong, self-interested lobby against revelation and reform.[79]

Even those members who had not known about the abuses had supported the expansion of the imperial presidency and the secret government. Many Cold War liberals in the 1950s and 1960s had tacitly endorsed the policies that seemed so repugnant when they were exposed just a few years later, as Garry Wills has written. They "believed in their own version of a higher code, of an 'enlightened' internationalism that had to evade, by benign deception, popular tendencies toward isolationism on the one hand and a crude anticommunism on the other."[80] Cold War liberals wanted the secret agencies to have complete freedom to fight communism. If, at times, this freedom encouraged them to abandon "long-standing American concepts of 'fair play,'" in the words of the Doolittle report, then that was the price that had to be paid.

Presidents and congressmen of both parties had shared this "fundamentally repugnant" philosophy, as General Doolittle had labeled it. As a result, the problems raised by the intelligence inquiries were more complex and intractable than those of Watergate. The Watergate horrors, after all, had ended with Nixon's resignation. Now it appeared that Roosevelt, Eisenhower, Kennedy, and Johnson had also been guilty of sanctioning abuses, at least implicitly.

Given these conclusions, there seemed to be only one solution: to reduce the foreign policy powers of the presidency. But Congress, even after Vietnam and Watergate, had proved willing to do this only in rare, well-defined cases. During Nixon's impeachment inquiry, for example, the House Judiciary Committee decided not to recommend an article of impeachment for Nixon's secret bombing of Cambodia. Although they were not afraid to challenge the president on domestic abuses, a majority of the committee members were reluctant to question the president's foreign policy powers.[81] Throughout the intelligence investigations, most members of Congress preferred to defer to the executive branch on national security matters. This reluctance is an example of what Aaron Wildavsky has called the "two presidencies" and Theodore Draper has termed the "bifurcated presidency": a presidency tightly controlled on the domestic front but allowed great latitude in foreign affairs.[82] By giving the president responsibility for the secret agencies, congressmen avoided potentially unpopular decisions about covert actions at home and abroad.

Under certain circumstances, however, Congress might have marshaled the courage to challenge the president over the secret government. If the public had lobbied legislators for real reforms, if the polls had shown strong public support for changes, Congress might have responded. That support, however, never materialized.

At first, most investigators assumed that the post-Watergate public would applaud efforts to expose more government abuses. Frank Church clearly hoped that his chairmanship of the Senate investigation would boost his campaign for the presidency. Other liberals also believed that the inquiries would help the careers of those who led them. Columnist Mary McGrory, for example, praised Church in late 1975 as "this year's messenger with the bad news." And, she continued, "if the country is ready to face the facts about itself, Church could become our next president."[83]

But the investigations never truly aroused the public the way Church had hoped. This apathetic response might have been a product of what sociologists call the "issue-attention cycle." According to Anthony Downs, American public attention does not remain focused on any one issue for long, "even if it involves a continuing problem of crucial importance to society."[84] Typically, Downs says, a new problem will vault into the center of public attention, stay there a short time, then quickly fade from public view as people realize how difficult, threatening, or costly the solutions would be—or simply after they get bored with hearing about the problem. During the investigations, congressmen frequently commented that their constituents did not seem interested in intelligence abuses after the initial flurry of revelations. "This is not the Watergate investigation," one member of Congress told the *New York Times* as early as May 1975. "Nobody ever talks to me about it on home trips, and I hear very little about it here."[85]

Some commentators argued that Americans could not sustain their outrage because they had become jaded by scandal. The public had already learned about the My Lai massacre, the secret bombing of Cambodia, the secret war in Laos, and the Watergate scandals. As a result, Americans had experienced "a kind of deadening of moral nerve-ends, a near-inability to be surprised, let alone disturbed," by new revelations, the *Washington Post* editorialized.[86] The "years of revelation and shock," as columnist Meg Greenfield put it, had produced an "anesthetizing effect" on many Americans.[87]

Americans also may have doubted that they or their representatives had the power to change the secret agencies. A December 1975 poll showed that only 30 percent believed that the investigations would produce real reforms, while 41 percent were more skeptical. Moreover, with public confidence in all governmental institutions at a historic low, most Americans did not trust the Congress to devise solutions.

Finally, many Americans resisted believing the news that their government had committed crimes. During the years of the liberal consensus, there had been no dialogue in American political culture about CIA or FBI activities. Most Americans' knowledge of these agencies came from popular culture, which portrayed U.S. agents as heroes. Once Vietnam and Watergate had shattered the liberal consensus, suddenly the American people learned about the murder plots, drug testing, and harassment of dissidents that had been carried out in their name. They had been taught a "child's history" of the world, as Richard Helms's biographer Thomas Powers has explained, and they did not want to learn about the real history written by Helms and his colleagues. "To discover oneself the victim of so many illusions, all at once, is disorienting," Powers has noted.[88]

It is painful for any nation to learn about its government's dirty tricks, but it is perhaps most painful for Americans, who hold their government to a high moral standard. As Michael Schudson has commented, "That is not to say that other peoples expect their governments to be immoral, but there may be an unusual American spirit that the government is expressive of and representative of its people and that we cannot think well of ourselves if we cannot think well of our leaders."[89] America is, after all, supposed to be the "city on a hill," admired and emulated by the rest of the world. Subverting foreign governments and plotting to assassinate foreign leaders does not fit well with this image.

Nor does secrecy in general. American government is based on the diffusion of power and on democratic accountability. A secret agency undercuts these checks and balances. For this reason, the establishment of the CIA would seem to contradict American ideals. Yet after World War II, most Americans came to believe that they needed a CIA to match the Soviets' worldwide intelligence network.

The country has never resolved this contradiction between its ideals and its acceptance of Cold War secrecy and subversion. Most policymakers decided to maintain American illusions by keeping the public ignorant of secret operations. They concluded—perhaps correctly—that many Americans wanted to be kept in ignorance. Russell Baker commented ironically on this ignorance in a column on U.S. intervention in Chile. He noted that some in Congress wanted to punish Michael Harrington for telling others about this secret action. "If we are becoming the enemy we set out to thwart," Baker wrote, "the least Congress can do is punish anybody who threatens to let us know about it."[90]

Richard Helms contends that this attitude reveals that "we're basically a rather hypocritical nation; we like things to be done, but we don't want to have the blood on our own hands."[91] Some American opponents of covert action agree with him. The *Dayton Daily News* editorial board was annoyed that Americans would "pretend" to be shocked by the Church committee assassination report. "We have never before known the details—and they are sordid and ludicrous in the extreme—but we have known that American policy has at times meant interfering in the internal affairs of other countries and trying to bring down their governments," the paper scolded.[92] A *Washington Post* reader urged Americans to admit that they supported "covert subversive activities" in other countries or take responsibility for attempting to limit them.[93] Most Americans refused to make that choice, however. They preferred to leave the CIA's undemocratic actions in the "attic of the implicit," as columnist Rod MacLeish said, rather than bringing them down to the more painful level of explicit endorsement.[94]

The intelligence investigations forced Americans to face difficult questions concerning the competence of their intelligence agencies, the moral basis of American foreign policy, the health of the constitutional system of checks and balances, and the tensions between secrecy and democracy.

The inquiries asked them to doubt the morality of J. Edgar Hoover and John F. Kennedy—men they had regarded as true American heroes—and to question whether their nation truly adhered to its professed ideals.

One year earlier, Americans had faced equally difficult questions during the Watergate scandal. But not even Watergate had shaken most Americans' support for "the system," political scientists have shown.[95] Having survived that shock, most Americans were reluctant to challenge the system's legitimacy now. As one American wrote to the president in 1975, "Let's not turn the CIA probe into another Watergate. Just try to take steps to prevent the recurrence of alleged illegal activities."[96] It was much easier to assume that the investigations had taken care of past problems—and that the system had worked—than to challenge American illusions.

Given the power of these illusions, perhaps it is more surprising that the investigations occurred at all than that they failed to achieve their goals. For twenty-five years, Congress and the press had allowed the executive branch to conduct secret operations with little accountability. Then, for a moment, a determined group of investigators in the press and Congress decided to challenge that secret government. Before their challenge faded, they uncovered information vital to all Americans struggling to understand the events of the Cold War. For a brief moment, they forced the nation to debate the perils of secrecy in a democracy.

Epilogue

Throughout the year of intelligence, critics charged that the investigators were trying to exploit the inquiries for their own gain: Seymour Hersh wanted another Pulitzer Prize; Frank Church wanted to become president. Ultimately, however, none of the investigators benefited professionally from the investigations—and Church, at least, wondered if they might have wrecked his career.

Senator Church had clearly hoped that the investigations would boost his presidential campaign, but he quickly faded as a candidate. His biographers contend that the inquiries damaged his candidacy by delaying his entry into the race and alienating some voters.[1] After conceding to Jimmy Carter in June 1976, Church was cheered by a pollster's finding that he was the most popular, viable candidate to be Carter's running mate.[2] Then, when Carter did not choose him, he speculated that his reputation as a CIA foe might have destroyed his chances for higher office. Perhaps, he told his son, the agency had covertly ruined his chances for the vice presidency by passing along unfounded rumors of KGB infiltration of his staff.[3]

Church also must have wondered whether his role as investigator of the secret government contributed to his reelection defeat in conservative Idaho in 1980. His opponents circulated flyers highlighting his "anti-CIA witch-hunt."[4] Edward Korry, a former U.S. ambassador to Chile and a noted Church antagonist during the investigations, came to Idaho to campaign against him. Polls, however, showed that his support of the Panama Canal treaty disturbed far more of his constituents than the intelligence inquiries.[5] In 1984, Church died of pancreatic cancer at age fifty-nine.

Unlike Church, Otis Pike did not toss his hat into the ring for higher office during the investigations. Many observers at the time, though, speculated that he hoped a Senate seat—or possibly an important chairmanship—might come his way if the inquiry proceeded smoothly. In the end, of course, the investigation proved anything but helpful to his public image, and he had to settle for reelection to the House. After one more term in Congress, he decided to retire voluntarily. Switching easily to a new career, he began writing a syndicated political column.

Daniel Schorr also rebounded from his greatest professional crisis. After his forced retirement from journalism, Schorr spent his time writing a book about his experiences and rebuilding his reputation. Besides defending himself on the lecture circuit, he fired off indignant letters to magazines that continued to malign him for "stealing" and "selling" public documents.[6] After the Justice Department concluded its investigation of him in April 1977 without charging him, he began to put his career back together. He taught for a year at the University of California at Berkeley, then returned to broadcasting in 1980 as the Cable News Network's senior Washington correspondent. In 1985, he began his current job as a news analyst for National Public Radio.

Seymour Hersh continued his illustrious investigative career with the *New York Times*, but the iconoclastic reporter soon began to fall out of favor with newly promoted executive editor Abe Rosenthal. Years later, Rosenthal declared that if Hersh had submitted some of his famous mid-1970s stories five years later, he would not have published them.[7] Hersh ended his permanent association with the *Times* in 1979 when

Rosenthal refused to give him a leave of absence to write his award-winning, highly critical biography of Henry Kissinger, *The Price of Power*.[8] Hersh has since authored several best-selling nonfiction books, frequently drawing upon his knowledge of the intelligence community.

Unlike these two unusual practitioners of investigative journalism, the press as a whole after 1975 continued to retreat from the aggressive journalism associated with Watergate—a retreat first shown in the intelligence investigations. In 1982, for example, the retiring president of the Society of American Newspaper Editors told his colleagues: "We should make peace with the government. We should not be its enemy. . . . We should cure ourselves of the adversarial mindset. The adversarial culture is a disease attacking the nation's vital organs."[9] One journalism historian has even called the late 1970s and 1980s a "new age of deference" for the press.[10] Reporters covering domestic issues were not always deferential, of course, but most journalists continued to avoid questioning foreign policy and the national security state.

Congress began a new era of oversight in 1976. The "newness" of this era, however, became the subject of much controversy, as discussed in the previous chapter. In 1986, the two successors to the Church and Pike committees discovered that the Reagan administration had evaded and ignored the intelligence reforms enacted since the 1970s and had lied to the overseers. In 1987, former Church committee member John Tower, who headed the presidential commission that investigated the scandal, pronounced the Iran-contra affair to be an "aberration." In 1988, the joint congressional investigating committee concluded that the existing oversight laws were adequate and that the system had worked. This view was widely shared by opinion leaders. In the 1990s, there seems little prospect that lawmakers or journalists will again question the fundamental soundness of the existing oversight system.

Notes

Abbreviations

The following abbreviations are used throughout the notes.

BSUL   Boise State University Library, Boise, Idaho

CIA doc.   Central Intelligence Agency document obtained under Freedom of Information Act

GRFL   Gerald R. Ford Library, Ann Arbor, Michigan

LC   Library of Congress, Washington, D.C.

TNA   Television News Archive, Vanderbilt University, Nashville, Tennessee

Introduction

1. The focus of this book reflects the journalistic and congressional investigators' emphasis on the CIA. Although the Church committee investigated all of the intelligence agencies, the Pike committee made only a cursory examination of the FBI. With the notable exception of the *Washington Post* series discussed in Chapter 2, most of the press revelations concerned the CIA.

2. For examples of calls for major reform, see Tom Wicker, "The Truth Is Needed," *New York Times*, 24 December 1974, 19; Tom Braden, "What's Wrong with the CIA?," *Saturday Review*, 5 April 1975, 14–18; Tom Braden, "CIA: Power and Arrogance," *Washington Post*, 27 April 1975, C2; Seymour Hersh, "At Its Best, How Good Is CIA in a Democracy?," *New York Times*, 15 June 1975, sec. 4, p. 1; Tom Wicker, "Destroy the Monster," *New York Times*, 12 September 1975, 33; press release, Senator Walter Mondale, October 1975, ser. 10.6, box 1, folder 21, Frank Church Collection, BSUL; Laurence Stern, "Intelligence Network Overhaul Suggested," *Washington Post*, 6 December 1975, A3; Harry Rositzke, "Revamping the CIA: Easier Said Than Done," *Washington Post*, 18 January 1976, F3; and Garry Wills, "Controlling the Rogue Presidency," *Washington Post*, 25 January 1976, F1. All *New York Times* citations are to section 1 of the newspaper unless otherwise noted.

3. Seymour Hersh, "Democrats Vote Wide CIA Study by Senate Panel," *New York Times*, 21 January 1975, 1.

4. Alan Wolfe, "The Emergence of the Dual State," *The Nation*, 29 March 1975, 369.

5. A year and a half after the Pike committee had been discredited, the House finally voted to establish a permanent intelligence committee, largely because the Carter administration and the Senate intelligence committee wanted one. But there was no direct line from the Pike committee to the later permanent committee. In fact, most of the Democrats who had served on the Pike committee and its predecessor, the Nedzi committee, attacked the creation of the permanent committee as a "sham" reform. For more information on this topic, see Chapter 8.

6. Columnist John D. Lofton quoted in Anthony Lewis, "The Teller of Truth," *New York Times*, 10 July 1975, 29.

7. F. Forrester Church, *Father and Son: A Personal Biography of Senator Frank*

Church of Idaho (New York: Harper and Row, 1985), 121–23. Church believed that the CIA, angry with him over the investigation, had spread a rumor that the Soviets had infiltrated his committee staff. The agency may have informed Democratic presidential candidate Jimmy Carter of this rumor, Church thought, thus persuading Carter to choose Walter Mondale over Church as his running mate in 1976.

8. Richard Helms quoted in PBS documentary, *Secret Intelligence*, pt. 3, *Learning to Say No* (1988). Helms expressed similar opinions in an interview with the author, 23 March 1992.

9. Interview, Seymour Hersh, 23 March 1992.

10. Loch Johnson, *A Season of Inquiry: Congress and Intelligence* (Chicago: Dorsey Press, 1988). Other participants in the "year of intelligence" who have written about the investigations at varying length include William Colby with Peter Forbath, *Honorable Men: My Life in the CIA* (New York: Simon and Schuster, 1978); David Atlee Phillips, *The Night Watch* (New York: Atheneum, 1977); Ray Cline, *The CIA under Reagan, Bush, and Casey* (Washington, D.C.: Acropolis Books, 1981); Daniel Schorr, *Clearing the Air* (Boston: Houghton Mifflin, 1977); Daniel Schorr, "My 17 Months on the CIA Watch," *Rolling Stone*, 8 April 1976, 32; John Tower, *Consequences* (Boston: Little, Brown, 1991); Barry Goldwater, *Goldwater* (New York: Doubleday, 1988); Gregory F. Treverton, *Covert Action: The Limits of Intervention in the Postwar World* (New York: Basic Books, 1987); Gregory Rushford, "Making Enemies: The Pike Committee's Struggle to Get the Facts," *Washington Monthly*, July/August 1976, 42–52; F. A. O. Schwarz, Jr., "Intelligence Activities and the Rights of Americans," speech to the American Bar Association, 16 November 1976; and John T. Elliff, "Congress and the Intelligence Community," in *Congress Reconsidered*, edited by Laurence C. Dodd and Bruce I. Oppenheimer (New York: Praeger, 1977), 193–206.

11. Frank J. Smist, Jr., *Congress Oversees the United States Intelligence Community, 1947–1989* (Knoxville: University of Tennessee Press, 1990); Rhodri Jeffreys-Jones, *The CIA and American Democracy* (New Haven: Yale University Press, 1989). In addition, several other scholars have written more briefly about the investigations. See John Ranelagh, *The Agency: The Rise and Decline of the CIA* (London: Weidenfeld and Nicolson, 1986); John M. Oseth, *Regulating U.S. Intelligence Operations* (Lexington: University Press of Kentucky, 1985); Morton H. Halperin, Jerry J. Berman, Robert L. Borosage, and Christine M. Marwick, *The Lawless State: The Crimes of the U.S. Intelligence Agencies* (New York: Penguin, 1981); Athan Theoharis, *Spying on Americans: Political Surveillance from Hoover to the Huston Plan* (Philadelphia: Temple University Press, 1978); David Wise, *The American Police State* (New York: Random House, 1976); J. Leiper Freeman, "Investigating the Executive Intelligence: The Fate of the Pike Committee," *Capitol Studies* 5 (Fall 1977): 103–18; and Harry Howe Ransom, "Congress and Reform of the CIA," *Policy Studies Journal* 5 (Summer 1977): 476–80.

12. See Godfrey Hodgson, *America in Our Time* (New York: Vintage Books, 1978).

13. James L. Sundquist, *The Decline and Resurgence of Congress* (Washington, D.C.: Brookings Institution, 1981); Thomas M. Franck, ed., *The Tethered Presidency: Congressional Restraints on Executive Power* (New York: New York University

Press, 1981); Marvin Stone, "Presidency: Imperial or Imperiled?," *U.S. News and World Report*, 15 January 1979, 88. See also Cecil V. Crabb, Jr., and Pat M. Holt, *Invitation to Struggle: Congress, the President, and Foreign Policy* (Washington, D.C.: Congressional Quarterly Press, 1989); Thomas M. Franck and Edward Weisband, *Foreign Policy by Congress* (New York: Oxford University Press, 1979); Gordon S. Jones and John A. Marini, eds., *The Imperial Congress: Crisis in the Separation of Powers* (New York: Pharos Books, 1988); and John Robert Greene, *The Limits of Power: The Nixon and Ford Administrations* (Bloomington: Indiana University Press, 1992).

14. Louis Koenig, "Historical Perspective: The Swings and Roundabouts of Presidential Power," in Franck, *Tethered Presidency*, 57 (emphasis added).

15. Daniel Hallin, "The Media, the War in Vietnam, and Political Support: A Critique of the Thesis of an Oppositional Media," *Journal of Politics* 46 (February 1984): 2–24.

16. The phrase "imperial media" was the title of Joseph Kraft's essay in *Commentary* 71 (May 1981): 36–47 and of Robert Entman's essay in *Politics and the Oval Office: Towards Presidential Governance*, edited by Arnold J. Meltsner (San Francisco: Institute for Contemporary Studies, 1981), 79–101. Other examples of this thesis include Samuel P. Huntington, "The Democratic Distemper," *Public Interest* 41 (Fall 1975): 9–38; Samuel P. Huntington, *American Politics: The Promise of Disharmony* (Cambridge: Harvard University Press, 1981); Stanley Rothman, "The Mass Media in Post-Industrial America," in *The Third Century*, edited by Seymour Martin Lipset (Stanford: Hoover Institution Press, 1979); and Peter B. Clark, "The Opinion Machine: Intellectuals, the Mass Media, and American Government," in *Mass Media and Modern Democracy*, edited by Harry M. Clor (Chicago: Rand McNally, 1974).

17. Suzanne Garment, *Scandal: The Culture of Mistrust in American Politics* (New York: Times Books, 1991); Larry J. Sabato, *Feeding Frenzy: How Attack Journalism Has Transformed American Politics* (New York: Free Press, 1991).

18. For examples of this view of the press coverage of the investigations, see Phillips, *Night Watch*, 291–92; Colby, *Honorable Men*, 12; Cline, *The CIA under Reagan, Bush, and Casey*; Jeffreys-Jones, *The CIA and American Democracy*, 199; and Ernest W. Lefever and Roy Godson, *The CIA and the American Ethic: An Unfinished Debate* (Washington, D.C.: Ethics and Public Policy Center of Georgetown University, 1979), chap. 4.

19. Michael Schudson, *Watergate in American Memory* (New York: Basic Books, 1992), chap. 6.

20. William W. Keller, *The Liberals and J. Edgar Hoover* (Princeton: Princeton University Press, 1989). Keller is primarily concerned with the FBI, but his argument applies equally well to the CIA.

21. Taylor Branch, "The Trial of the CIA," *New York Times Magazine*, 12 September 1976, 126.

22. In this book, I have not made a distinction between print and broadcast reports because the two media did not take substantially different approaches to this subject. Because the vast majority of CBS reports were filed by Daniel Schorr, who was trained as a print reporter and thus had unusually sharp investigative skills for a

television journalist, the content and tone of those reports were not qualitatively different from the content and tone of the printed stories. Much more difference in reporting existed between *Time* magazine and the *New York Times*, for example, than between CBS and the *Times*.

Chapter One

1. Seymour Hersh, "Huge CIA Operation Reported in U.S. against Antiwar Forces, Other Dissidents in Nixon Years," *New York Times*, 22 December 1974, 1.

2. The figures are cited in a snide *Time* magazine story, "Congratulations," 20 January 1975, 63.

3. William Colby with Peter Forbath, *Honorable Men: My Life in the CIA* (New York: Simon and Schuster, 1978), 391.

4. "Year of Intelligence," *New York Times*, 8 February 1975, 24.

5. Walter Pincus, "Covering Intelligence," *New Republic*, 1 February 1975, 12.

6. Harry Howe Ransom, "Congress and the Intelligence Agencies," in *Congress against the President*, edited by Harvey C. Mansfield (New York: Praeger, 1975), 155–56.

7. Congress had charged the Hoover Commission, headed by former president Herbert Hoover, with surveying the organization of the executive branch. The commission then delegated the examination of the intelligence agencies to a task force chaired by General Mark Clark. But President Eisenhower, to avoid a public examination of the CIA's covert operations, requested a separate, secret investigation of the agency's Directorate for Plans. Neither the Hoover Commission nor Congress objected.

8. U.S. Senate Select Committee to Study Governmental Operations with Respect to Intelligence Activities, *Final Reports*, Book IV, *Supplementary Detailed Staff Reports on Foreign and Military Intelligence*, 94th Cong., 2d sess., 1976, 52–53n. For a good history and analysis of the Doolittle committee, see ibid., pp. 52–55. For other discussions of the Doolittle report, see William R. Corson, *Armies of Ignorance: The Rise of the American Intelligence Establishment* (New York: Dial Press/ James Wade, 1977), 347–48, and John Ranelagh, *The Agency: The Rise and Decline of the CIA* (London: Weidenfeld and Nicolson, 1986), 276–79.

9. For more on the congressional attempts to improve oversight in the 1950s and 1960s, see Chapter 3.

10. For general discussions of Cold War culture, see Stephen J. Whitfield, *The Culture of the Cold War* (Baltimore: Johns Hopkins University Press, 1991); Paul Boyer, *By the Bomb's Early Light: American Thought and Culture at the Dawn of the Atomic Age* (New York: Pantheon, 1985; reprint, with a new preface by the author, Chapel Hill: University of North Carolina Press, 1994); Elaine May, *Homeward Bound* (New York: Basic Books, 1988); Michael Paul Rogin, *Ronald Reagan, the Movie, and Other Episodes in Political Demonology* (Berkeley: University of California Press, 1987); Nora Sayre, *Running Time: Films of the Cold War* (New York: Dial Press, 1982); and Peter Biskind, *Seeing Is Believing: How Hollywood Taught Us to Stop Worrying and Love the Fifties* (New York: Pantheon, 1983). For discussions of Cold War spy novels, see John G. Cawelti and Bruce A. Rosenberg, *The*

Spy Story (Chicago: University of Chicago Press, 1987); David Stafford, *The Silent Game: The Real World of Imaginary Spies* (Athens: University of Georgia Press, 1991); and Wesley K. Wark, ed., *Spy Fiction, Spy Films, and Real Intelligence* (London: Frank Cass, 1991).

11. For a discussion of spy shows on television, see Erik Barnouw, *Tube of Plenty: The Evolution of American Television* (New York: Oxford University Press, 1975), 366–73. For an example of a pro-CIA movie from this era, see *Operation CIA* (1965).

12. Richard Gid Powers, *G-Men: Hoover's FBI in American Popular Culture* (Carbondale: Southern Illinois University Press, 1983), 95.

13. For more on the relationship between the FBI and the press, see Sanford J. Ungar, "Among the Piranhas: A Journalist and the FBI," *Columbia Journalism Review*, September/October 1976, 19–26, and "The Forgotten Case of Sam Jaffe," *Columbia Journalism Review*, November/December 1976, 54–55; and "The CIA, the FBI, and the Media: Excerpts from the Senate Report on Intelligence Activities," *Columbia Journalism Review*, July/August 1976, 37–42.

14. Curt Gentry, *J. Edgar Hoover: The Man and the Secrets* (New York: Norton, 1991), 586–88.

15. Thomas Powers, *The Man Who Kept the Secrets: Richard Helms and the CIA* (New York: Alfred A. Knopf, 1979), 258.

16. The exceptions were Gordon Liddy, a former FBI agent, and Virgilio Gonzales, a locksmith.

17. Quoted in Stanley Kutler, *The Wars of Watergate* (New York: Alfred A. Knopf, 1990), 218.

18. In testimony to the Church committee, Nixon said he was referring to the Marchetti case, in which the CIA sued to stop former employee Victor Marchetti from publishing information he had learned while at the agency. The White House, according to Nixon, had helped the CIA suppress parts of the Marchetti book. John Crewdson, "Nixon Explains His Taped Cryptic Remark about Helms," *New York Times*, 12 March 1976, 15. Others have speculated that Nixon was referring to the CIA's assassination plots, its domestic spying, or some other, as yet undisclosed, secrets.

19. For an intriguing examination of CIA connections to Watergate, see Jim Hougan, *Secret Agenda: Watergate, Deep Throat, and the CIA* (New York: Random House, 1984).

20. David Atlee Phillips, *The Night Watch* (New York: Atheneum, 1977), 255.

21. George Gallup, *The Gallup Poll: Public Opinion, 1972–1977* (Wilmington, Del.: Scholarly Resources, 1978), 1:347, 369. Three percent disapproved of the way he handled his job, and 26 percent had no opinion. Ford's approval ratings in his "honeymoon" period were roughly comparable to those of his recent predecessors: Richard Nixon (59 percent), Lyndon Johnson (79 percent), John Kennedy (72 percent), and Dwight Eisenhower (68 percent).

22. Seymour Martin Lipset and William Schneider, *The Confidence Gap: Business, Labor, and Government in the Public Mind* (Baltimore: Johns Hopkins University Press, 1987), 17.

23. Anthony Lewis, "Lying in State: I," *New York Times*, 14 July 1975, 25.

24. Gallup, *Public Opinion, 1972–1977*, 1:146–47, 498, 596–97; George Gallup,

The Gallup Poll: Public Opinion, 1935–1971 (New York: Random House, 1972), 3:1977, 2259.

25. Harrington had discussed the secret testimony earlier with reporter Laurence Stern of the *Washington Post*, but he had made Stern promise not to write about it. When Harrington learned that Hersh had independently obtained a copy of his summary of the testimony, he alerted Stern and freed him to write his own story about the testimony. Hersh's detailed exposé and Stern's somewhat more rushed story both appeared on 8 September.

26. Seymour Hersh, "CIA Chief Tells House of $8-Million Campaign against Allende in '70–'73," *New York Times*, 8 September 1974, 1. Colby contends that he never used the word "destabilize" and that Harrington's letter summarizing his testimony (and thus Hersh's story) was exaggerated. Harrington admitted writing the letter, which was sent to other congressmen, but insisted he was not responsible for leaking it to the press.

27. Michael Schudson, *Discovering the News: A Social History of American Newspapers* (New York: Basic Books, 1978), 71.

28. Ibid., 141.

29. Ibid., 121–59. For a perceptive discussion of objectivity, see also Ben Bagdikian, *The Media Monopoly* (Boston: Beacon Press, 1987), 130–31.

30. James Reston, *The Artillery of the Press: Its Influence on American Foreign Policy* (New York: Harper and Row, 1967), ix.

31. Quoted in Daniel Hallin, *The "Uncensored War": The Media and Vietnam* (New York: Oxford University Press, 1986), 71.

32. Ibid., 8, 25.

33. Quoted in Howard Bray, *The Pillars of the Post* (New York: Norton, 1980), 30.

34. On *The Nation*, see Carey McWilliams, *The Education of Carey McWilliams* (New York: Simon and Schuster, 1978). On Stone, see Robert C. Cottrell, *Izzy: A Biography of I. F. Stone* (New Brunswick: Rutgers University Press, 1992).

35. William A. Dorman and Mansour Fahrang, *The U.S. Press and Iran: Foreign Policy and the Journalism of Deference* (Berkeley: University of California Press, 1987), 31–62.

36. Richard H. Immerman, *The CIA in Guatemala: The Foreign Policy of Intervention* (Austin: University of Texas Press, 1982), 111–14.

37. "New York Times Covers and Aids 1953 CIA Coup in Iran," *Counterspy* 4 (September/October 1980): 1. Journalist Jonathan Kwitny repeated *Counterspy's* accusations in his book *Endless Enemies: The Making of an Unfriendly World* (New York: Congdon and Weed, 1984). Dorman and Fahrang, however, conclude that Love was not consciously an agent of the CIA (*The U.S. Press and Iran*, 56–62).

38. Dorman and Fahrang, *The U.S. Press and Iran*, 50–62.

39. Immerman, *The CIA in Guatemala*, 113–14, 235 (n. 47); Harrison E. Salisbury, *Without Fear or Favor: The New York Times and Its Times* (New York: Times Books, 1980), 478–82.

40. Salisbury, *Without Fear or Favor*, 512–13; Bray, *Pillars of the Post*, 34; Reston, *Artillery of the Press*, 20.

41. James Aronson, *The Press and the Cold War* (New York: Monthly Review Press, 1990), 153–69.

42. Reston, *Artillery of the Press*, ix.

43. Aronson, *Press and the Cold War*, 162.

44. Ibid., 163.

45. In one case, a mainstream reporter decided to publish old CIA secrets, but the rest of the press did not follow up on the revelations. In 1967, columnist Drew Pearson wrote that the CIA had tried to kill Fidel Castro. But because the information was classified, several years old, and could not be confirmed by official sources, Pearson's colleagues let the story die. Pearson's willingness to challenge governmental secrecy would later be emulated by his partner and successor, Jack Anderson. See Chapter 4.

46. U.S. Senate Select Committee to Study Governmental Operations with Respect to Intelligence Activities, *Final Reports*, Book I, *Foreign and Military Intelligence*, 191–201. For more on the CIA and the media, see Loch Johnson, *America's Secret Power: The CIA in a Democratic Society* (New York: Oxford University Press, 1989), 183–203, and Stuart Loory, "The CIA's Use of the Press: A 'Mighty Wurlitzer,'" *Columbia Journalism Review*, September/October 1974, 9–18.

47. Carl Bernstein, "The CIA and the Media," *Rolling Stone*, 20 October 1977, 55–67.

48. See articles by John Crewdson and Joseph Treaster in the *New York Times*, 25–28 December 1977. *Times* reporter Harrison Salisbury later did his own investigation of the *Times*-CIA links and concluded that it was unlikely that there was any formal arrangement between the two institutions. Salisbury, *Without Fear or Favor*, 496.

49. Bernstein, "The CIA and the Media," 59–60, 63.

50. Quoted in Dorman and Fahrang, *The U.S. Press and Iran*, 56.

51. Quoted in Loch Johnson, *A Season of Inquiry: Congress and Intelligence* (Chicago: Dorsey Press, 1988), 8 (emphasis added).

52. David Halberstam, *The Powers That Be* (New York: Alfred A. Knopf, 1979), 449.

53. Ibid., 568.

54. "Newspapers," *Time*, 21 October 1966, 87.

55. Hallin, *"Uncensored War,"* 161–62.

56. Halberstam, *Powers That Be*, 512.

57. Salisbury, *Without Fear or Favor*, 13.

58. "Has the Press Done a Job on Nixon?," *Columbia Journalism Review*, January/February 1974, 58.

59. Ibid.

60. Colby, *Honorable Men*, 12.

61. Daniel Patrick Moynihan, "The Presidency and the Press," *Commentary* 51 (March 1971): 43, 52.

62. Paul H. Weaver, "The New Journalism and the Old: Thoughts after Watergate," *Public Interest* 35 (Spring 1974): 84–85.

63. Louis Harris, *The Harris Survey Yearbook of Public Opinion, 1973* (New York: Louis Harris and Associates, 1976), 146.

64. Quoted in Leonard Downie, Jr., *The New Muckrakers* (Washington, D.C.: New Republic Book Company, 1976), 234.

65. "Covering Watergate: Success and Backlash," *Time*, 8 July 1974, 68.

66. Quoted in Chalmers Roberts, *In the Shadow of Power: The Story of the Washington Post* (Cabin John, Md.: Seven Locks Press, 1989), 443.

67. Tom Wicker, *On Press* (New York: Viking Press, 1978), 240.

68. Katharine Graham, "The Press after Watergate: Getting Down to New Business," *New York Magazine*, 4 November 1974, 69, 71.

69. "Passing Comment," *Columbia Journalism Review*, September/October 1974, 1.

70. Daniel Schorr, *Clearing the Air* (Boston: Houghton Mifflin, 1977), 113–15.

71. Interview, Ben Bradlee, 30 March 1992.

72. William Greider, *Who Will Tell the People?: The Betrayal of American Democracy* (New York: Simon and Schuster, 1992), 297.

73. William Greider, "Aftergate," *Esquire*, September 1975, 101, 133.

Chapter Two

1. William Colby with Peter Forbath, *Honorable Men: My Life in the CIA* (New York: Simon and Schuster, 1978), 12.

2. See Loch Johnson, *A Season of Inquiry: Congress and Intelligence* (Chicago: Dorsey Press, 1988), 11; Frank J. Smist, Jr., *Congress Oversees the United States Intelligence Community, 1947–1989* (Knoxville: University of Tennessee Press, 1990), 65–68, 187–90; and Rhodri Jeffreys-Jones, *The CIA and American Democracy* (New Haven: Yale University Press, 1989), 202–3. All three accounts emphasize the initial aggressiveness of the press.

3. Colby, *Honorable Men*, 332, 338.

4. Seymour Hersh, *The Reporter's Obligation: An Address* (Tucson: University of Arizona Press, 1975), 12.

5. Joe Eszterhas, "The Toughest Reporter in America," *Rolling Stone*, 24 April 1975, 72. See also Harrison Salisbury, *Without Fear or Favor: The New York Times and Its Times* (New York: Times Books, 1980), 426.

6. Alan Wolfe, "Henry's Nemesis," *The Nation*, 23–30 July 1983, 86.

7. Quoted in Leonard Downie, Jr., *The New Muckrakers* (Washington, D.C.: New Republic Book Company, 1976), 87.

8. Salisbury, *Without Fear or Favor*, 529.

9. Editorial, *New York Times*, 8 June 1954, 26. Mansfield introduced his first intelligence reform bill in 1953 and his last in 1958. For more on Mansfield's efforts, see Chapter 3.

10. Salisbury, *Without Fear or Favor*, 514–15.

11. Ibid., 515.

12. Tom Wicker, *On Press* (New York: Viking Press, 1978), 234.

13. "CIA: Maker of Policy or Tool?," *New York Times*, 25 April 1966, 1. The series ran through 29 April 1966.

14. Salisbury, *Without Fear or Favor*, 527.

15. David Halberstam, *The Powers That Be* (New York: Alfred A. Knopf, 1979), 568.

16. Salisbury, *Without Fear or Favor*, 530.

17. Ibid., 443; Joseph C. Goulden, *Fit to Print: A. M. Rosenthal and His Times* (Secaucus, N.J.: Lyle Stuart, 1988), 19.

18. Goulden, *Fit to Print*, 20–21.

19. Ibid., 193.

20. Hersh, *The Reporter's Obligation*, 10.

21. Seymour Hersh, "Huge CIA Operation Reported in U.S. against Antiwar Forces, Other Dissidents in Nixon Years," *New York Times*, 22 December 1974, 1.

22. Seymour Hersh, "Underground for the CIA in New York: An Ex-Agent Tells of Spying on Students," *New York Times*, 29 December 1974, 1.

23. Interview, Seymour Hersh, 23 March 1992.

24. Salisbury, *Without Fear or Favor*, 534. Bradlee heatedly denies that he made this comment, saying that he always regarded Hersh's exposé as a "hell of a story." Interview, Ben Bradlee, 30 March 1992.

25. Laurence Stern, "Exposing the CIA (Again)," *Columbia Journalism Review*, March/April 1975, 55.

26. "The CIA's 'Illegal Domestic Spying,'" *Washington Post*, 5 January 1975, B6.

27. "A New CIA Furor," *Newsweek*, 6 January 1975, 10.

28. "Supersnoop," *Time*, 6 January 1975, 65.

29. James Kilpatrick, "Cool Off the CIA Stew," *Twin Falls (Idaho) Times News*, 13 January 1975, clipping in ser. 2.6, box 1, folder 1, Frank Church Collection, BSUL.

30. Ronald Kessler, "Accused CIA Aide Disclaims Spy Role," *Washington Post*, 25 December 1974, A1. Angleton's jibe about Hersh's speech may have been intended to slur the reporter's lack of Eastern Establishment credentials or may have been anti-Semitic. Hersh came from a middle-class, midwestern Jewish family and had attended the University of Chicago. The *Post* writer who reported Angleton's comments did not attempt to interpret them.

31. Laurence Stern, "Justice Department Gave the CIA Names of 9,000 Americans," *Washington Post*, 9 January 1976, A1; Jack Anderson, "CIA's Files Said to Support Denials," *Washington Post*, 9 January 1976, B7. Hersh was amazed and disgusted by this angle. Interview, Seymour Hersh, 23 March 1992.

32. "The CIA's 'Illegal Domestic Spying.'"

33. Quoted in Anthony Lewis's column, "The Teller of Truth," *New York Times*, 10 July 1975, 29.

34. *CBS Evening News*, 24 December 1974, TNA.

35. *CBS Evening News*, 6 January 1975, TNA.

36. Seymour Hersh, "CIA Admits Domestic Acts, Denies 'Massive' Illegality," *New York Times*, 16 January 1975, 1.

37. William Greider and Spencer Rich, "Colby Admits CIA Spying in U.S.," *Washington Post*, 16 January 1975, A1; "A Peek in the CIA's Closet," *Newsweek*, 27 January 1975, 28.

38. William Safire, "The Thrill Is Gone," *New York Times*, 30 January 1975, 35.

39. Ronald Kessler, "FBI Had Files on Congress, Ex-Aides Say," *Washington Post*, 19 January 1975, A1.

40. Ronald Kessler, "FBI Tapped King at 1964 Convention," *Washington Post*, 26 January 1975, A1.

41. Arthur M. Schlesinger, Jr., *Robert Kennedy and His Times* (Boston: Houghton Mifflin, 1978), 250.

42. Howard Bray, *The Pillars of the Post* (New York: Norton, 1980), 107.

43. Taylor Branch, "The Trial of the CIA," *New York Times Magazine*, 12 September 1976, 125.

44. Joe Eszterhas, "The Reporter Who Broke the My Lai Massacre, the Secret Bombing of Cambodia, and the CIA Domestic Spying Stories," *Rolling Stone*, 10 April 1975, 49.

45. Charles B. Seib, "Games Newspapers Play," *Washington Post*, 23 January 1976, A15. Hersh himself believes that competition was the most important factor influencing the *Post*. Interview, Seymour Hersh, 23 March 1992.

46. Leslie Gelb, "The CIA and the Press," *New Republic*, 22 March 1975, 15.

47. J. William Fulbright, "Fulbright on the Press," *Columbia Journalism Review*, November/December 1975, 41, 45.

48. Gelb, "The CIA and the Press," 15.

Chapter Three

1. Morris Ogul, *Congress Oversees the Bureaucracy* (Pittsburgh: University of Pittsburgh Press, 1976), 3–4.

2. Harry Howe Ransom, "Congress and the Intelligence Agencies," in *Congress against the President*, edited by Harvey C. Mansfield (New York: Praeger, 1975), 159.

3. Quoted in Loch Johnson, *A Season of Inquiry: Congress and Intelligence* (Chicago: Dorsey Press, 1988), 6.

4. Quoted in Harry Howe Ransom, *The Intelligence Establishment* (Cambridge: Harvard University Press, 1970), 169.

5. Ransom, "Congress and the Intelligence Agencies," 159, 160.

6. Ransom, *The Intelligence Establishment*, 172.

7. Stephen Ambrose, *Ike's Spies: Eisenhower and the Espionage Establishment* (Garden City, N.Y.: Doubleday, 1981), 187.

8. For a detailed discussion of the Mansfield resolution, see Ransom, *The Intelligence Establishment*, 163–72.

9. Ibid., 172–79.

10. Arthur M. Schlesinger, Jr., *The Imperial Presidency* (Boston: Houghton Mifflin, 1973).

11. James L. Sundquist, *The Decline and Resurgence of Congress* (Washington, D.C.: Brookings Institution, 1981), 155–95.

12. David R. Mayhew, *Divided We Govern: Party Control, Lawmaking, and Investigations, 1946–1990* (New Haven: Yale University Press, 1991), 28. Mayhew studied investigations that generated twenty or more *New York Times* front-page articles. It should be noted that his findings do not necessarily mean that congressional oversight as a whole declined but that one aspect of oversight declined: dramatic investigations that produced more than twenty stories on the front page of the *Times*.

13. Ibid., 30.

14. Ogul, *Congress Oversees the Bureaucracy*, 16.

15. John Prados, *Presidents' Secret Wars: CIA and Pentagon Covert Operations since World War II* (New York: William Morrow and Company, 1986), 331–32.

16. Interview, Howard Baker, 27 March 1992.

17. Baker scored a perfect 100 on the conservative American Security Council's index of crucial national security votes in 1974. Michael Barone, Grant Ujifasa, and Douglas Matthews, *The Almanac of American Politics, 1976* (New York: E. P. Dutton, 1975), 795.

18. U.S. Senate, *Congressional Record* (2 October 1974), 93d Cong., 2d sess., 120, pt. 25:33480.

19. U.S. House, *Congressional Record* (24 September 1974), 93d Cong., 2d sess., 120, pt. 24:32441–43.

20. Unnamed congressman quoted in Rowland Evans and Robert Novak, "Congressional Straitjacket for the CIA," *Washington Post*, 22 January 1975, A21.

21. Memo, Henry Kissinger to Gerald Ford, "Foreign Aid Bill," 19 December 1974, and letter, William Colby to Gerald Ford, 18 December 1974, both in folder "FO 3-2 12/1/74–12/31/74," box 15, White House Central Files Subject File, GRFL.

22. William Colby with Peter Forbath, *Honorable Men: My Life in the CIA* (New York: Simon and Schuster, 1978), 397, 398.

23. Ibid., 398.

24. Gerald R. Ford, *A Time to Heal* (New York: Harper and Row, 1979), 265.

25. Curt Gentry, *J. Edgar Hoover: The Man and the Secrets* (New York: Norton, 1991), 384, 557, 628–30.

26. Letter, Gerald Ford to Al Wiersma, 31 May 1967, folder "B54-12," box B54, Gerald Ford Congressional Papers, GRFL.

27. Newsletter, Congressman Jerry Ford to constituents, 1 March 1967, folder "Newsletter 1967," box D3, Gerald Ford Congressional Papers, GRFL.

28. Speech, Gerald R. Ford to Congress, 17 April 1962, folder "Defense Department Appropriations for FY 1963 (3)," box H3, Gerald Ford Congressional Papers, GRFL, reprinted in U.S. House, *Congressional Record* (17 April 1962), 87th Cong., 2d sess., 108, pt. 5:6838–40.

29. "Goldwater Calls 94th 'Dangerous,'" *Washington Post*, 2 February 1975, A14.

30. Colby, *Honorable Men*, 403.

31. Ford, *A Time to Heal*, 230.

32. Telephone interview, Gerald R. Ford, 4 April 1994.

33. Richard Cheney, "The Ford Presidency in Perspective," and Donald H. Rumsfeld, "The Ford Presidency: Some Personal Reflections," in *Gerald R. Ford and the Politics of Post-Watergate America*, edited by Bernard J. Firestone and Alexej Ugrinsky (Westport, Conn.: Greenwood Press, 1993), 3–11.

34. Memo, Jack Marsh to the president, 24 December 1974, folder "Intelligence—Rockefeller Commission: General," box 7, Richard B. Cheney Files, GRFL.

35. Draft memo, Richard Cheney to Gerald Ford, "CIA—The Colby Report," 27 December 1974, folder "Intelligence—The Colby Report," box 5, Richard B. Cheney Files, GRFL.

36. Untitled draft memo, 26 December 1974, folder "Intelligence—Rockefeller Commission: General," box 7, Richard B. Cheney Files, GRFL.

37. "A True-Blue-Ribbon Panel," *Newsweek*, 20 January 1975, 20.

38. Joseph Kraft, "A Sad Commission," *Washington Post*, 7 January 1975, A15.

39. Louis Harris, "35% Support Ford-Named CIA Panel," *Washington Post*, 17 February 1975, A3.

40. "Investigating the CIA," *New York Times*, 7 January 1975, 32.

41. "On Intelligence," *New York Times*, 13 January 1975, 28.

42. U.S. Senate, *Congressional Record* (27 January 1975), 94th Cong., 1st sess., 121, pt. 2:1417.

43. Ibid., 1418.

44. Ibid., 1428.

45. Ibid., 1426.

46. Ibid., 1423.

47. Ibid., 1419.

48. David Rosenbaum, "CIA-FBI Inquiry Voted by Senate," *New York Times*, 28 January 1975, 1. Some members of the White House staff tried to aid Stennis but were unsuccessful. See memo, Bud McFarlane to Brent Scowcroft, 10 January 1975, folder "William Spell," box 3, Brent Scowcroft Files, GRFL.

49. U.S. Senate, *Congressional Record* (27 January 1975), 94th Cong., 1st sess., 121, pt. 2:1430.

50. Mathias and Schweiker had solid liberal credentials: they were the only two Republican senators on Richard Nixon's enemies list.

51. Johnson, *Season of Inquiry*.

52. Barone, Ujifasa, and Matthews, *Almanac of American Politics, 1976*, 397, 438. Ratings are for 1974. The ADA ratings are the standard indicators of liberal beliefs in this period, but the group was also staunchly anticommunist.

53. Johnson, *Season of Inquiry*, 13.

54. For more background on Church, see LeRoy Ashby and Rod Gramer's excellent biography, *Fighting the Odds: The Life of Senator Frank Church* (Pullman: Washington State University Press, 1994); Johnson, *Season of Inquiry*, 20–22; and F. Forrester Church, *Father and Son: A Personal Biography of Senator Frank Church of Idaho* (New York: Harper and Row, 1985), 17–63, 105–14.

55. David Atlee Phillips, *The Night Watch* (New York: Atheneum, 1977), 291.

56. "Interview with Senator Frank Church," *Ramparts*, January 1965, 17–22.

57. Ashby and Gramer, *Fighting the Odds*, 394.

58. See ibid., 411–67.

59. Untitled draft in ser. 8.3, box 1, folder 36, Frank Church Collection, BSUL. *Family Weekly* informed Church that the article would be published on 3 October 1971, but there is no evidence it was ever published.

60. Letter, Frank Church to Gene McCarthy, 8 July 1964, ser. 3.2.2, box 4, folder 1, Frank Church Collection, BSUL.

61. Letter, Frank Church to David Underhill, 22 February 1967, ser. 3.2.2, box 4, folder 1, Frank Church Collection, BSUL.

62. Ashby and Gramer, *Fighting the Odds*, 472.

63. Letter, Joseph Napolitan to Frank Church, 20 January 1975, ser. 5.5, box 1, folder 19, Frank Church Collection, BSUL.

64. Joseph Napolitan, "Conceptual Campaign Plan," 11 August 1975, ser. 5.5, box 1, folder 19, Frank Church Collection, BSUL.

65. Campaign brochure, n.d., ser. 7.9, box 16, folder 1, Frank Church Collection, BSUL.

66. Untitled *Chicago Sun-Times* article distributed as press release, n.d., ser. 10.6, box 1, folder 21, Frank Church Collection, BSUL.

67. See, for example, Ashby and Gramer, *Fighting the Odds*, 71, 94, 318–24.

68. Memo, Vern Loen to Philip Buchen, 19 February 1975, folder "Intelligence—General," box 13, Vernon C. Loen and Charles Leppert Files, GRFL.

69. U.S. House, *Congressional Record* (19 February 1975), 94th Cong., 1st sess., 121, pt. 3:3612.

70. Ibid., 3612–13.

71. Ibid., 3616.

72. Barone, Ujifasa, and Matthews, *Almanac of American Politics, 1976*. The indexes were Dellums, ADA 96, NSI 10; Edwards, ADA 100, NSI 10; Giaimo, ADA 68, NSI 50; Harrington, ADA 100, NSI 10; McClory, ADA 24, NSI 70; Murphy, ADA 50, NSI 44; Nedzi, ADA 79, NSI 22; Stanton, ADA 90, NSI 8; and Treen, ADA 4, NSI 90. Kasten was newly elected and had not yet been rated.

73. U.S. House, *Congressional Record* (24 September 1974), 93d Cong., 2d sess., 120, pt. 24:32441–42.

74. James M. Naughton, "House Intelligence Inquiry Chief: Lucien Norbert Nedzi," *New York Times*, 22 February 1975, 14.

75. Frank J. Smist, Jr., *Congress Oversees the United States Intelligence Community, 1947–1989* (Knoxville: University of Tennessee Press, 1990), 150.

76. Rhodri Jeffreys-Jones, *The CIA and American Democracy* (New Haven: Yale University Press, 1989), 201; James M. Naughton, "Opposition Likely over Head of House CIA Inquiry," *New York Times*, 6 February 1975, 17; interview, Howard Baker, 27 March 1992.

77. Seymour Hersh, "Helms Disavows 'Illegal' Spying by the CIA in U.S.," *New York Times*, 25 December 1974, 1.

78. Colby, *Honorable Men*, 381.

79. Ibid., 346.

80. Interview, Lucien Nedzi, 26 March 1992.

Chapter Four

1. *CBS Evening News*, 28 February 1975, TNA.

2. William Colby with Peter Forbath, *Honorable Men: My Life in the CIA* (New York: Simon and Schuster, 1978), 410.

3. Loch Johnson, *A Season of Inquiry: Congress and Intelligence* (Chicago: Dorsey Press, 1988), 32.

4. Memo, Ron Nessen to Gerald Ford, 15 January 1975, folder "Jan. 16, 1975, Lunch with the *New York Times*," box 25, Ron Nessen Papers, GRFL.

5. Harrison E. Salisbury, *Without Fear or Favor: The New York Times and Its Times* (New York: Times Books, 1980), 537. For a firsthand account of the luncheon, see Tom Wicker, *On Press* (New York: Viking Press, 1978), 188–98.

6. Daniel Schorr, *Clearing the Air* (Boston: Houghton Mifflin, 1977), 144.

7. Salisbury, *Without Fear or Favor*, 538. There is no evidence that Ford's con-

fession to the *Times* was anything but a slip. Ford administration officials say the president simply made a mistake.

8. Ibid. Hersh was angry afterward that his editors had not informed him of the luncheon discussion. Interview, Seymour Hersh, 23 March 1992.

9. *New York Times*, 20 January 1975, 16. The movie Daniel cited was *Scorpio* (1973).

10. Schorr, *Clearing the Air*, 1–2.

11. Ibid., 3, 6, 66.

12. Ibid., 9. See also Barry Goldwater, *The Conscience of a Majority* (Englewood Cliffs, N.J.: Prentice-Hall, 1970), 179–81, and Sally Quinn, *We're Going to Make You a Star* (New York: Simon and Schuster, 1975), 42.

13. Daniel Schorr, "The FBI and Me," *Columbia Journalism Review*, November/December 1974, 8–14.

14. Schorr, *Clearing the Air*, 91.

15. William Barry Furlong, "Dan ('Killer') Schorr, the Great Abrasive," *New York Magazine*, 16 June 1975, 42.

16. Ibid.

17. Schorr, *Clearing the Air*, 103, 113.

18. Ibid., 117. The quote is Schorr's paraphrase of his remarks at the meeting.

19. Eric Sevareid, Walter Cronkite, and Dan Rather, "Letters," *New York Magazine*, 14 July 1975, 6.

20. Schorr, *Clearing the Air*, 118.

21. Ibid., 127.

22. Daniel Schorr, "My 17 Months on the CIA Watch," *Rolling Stone*, 8 April 1976, 32.

23. Schorr, *Clearing the Air*, 144–45; Colby, *Honorable Men*, 409–10.

24. Schorr, *Clearing the Air*, 144–45.

25. Ibid., 146.

26. Colby, *Honorable Men*, 410.

27. Daniel Schorr, "Assassination Is a Subject That Just Won't Go Away," *New York Times*, 4 May 1975, sect. 4, p. 3.

28. The Church committee ultimately concluded that the CIA had been involved in plots to kill Castro, Lumumba, Trujillo, Diem, and General Rene Schneider of Chile but either had not succeeded (as in the case of Castro) or had not been directly responsible for the deaths. See Chapter 5. See also U.S. Senate Select Committee to Study Governmental Operations with Respect to Intelligence Activities, *Alleged Assassination Plots Involving Foreign Leaders*, 94th Cong., 1st sess., 20 November 1975 (Washington, D.C.: Government Printing Office, 1975; reprint, New York: Norton, 1976).

29. Schorr, *Clearing the Air*, 147.

30. *CBS Evening News*, 28 April 1975, TNA. Helms later explained his outburst by saying that he had not expected to see Schorr that day; when he saw the reporter in the corridor, he exploded, releasing his suppressed anger at Schorr for reporting that the CIA had actually killed foreign leaders. "I probably shouldn't have said what I did, but I did say it," he commented. Interview, Richard Helms, 23 March 1992.

31. *CBS Evening News*, 29 April 1975, TNA; "CIA Plot to Kill Castro Described," *New York Times*, 30 April 1975, 9.

32. Transcript of telephone conversation between William Colby and General Brent Scowcroft, 20 February 1974, CIA doc. More than 200 pages of documents regarding the CIA's attempt to suppress the Project Jennifer story were released as a result of a 1977 Freedom of Information lawsuit brought against the CIA by the American Civil Liberties Union and the Public Citizen Litigation Project. Scholars can obtain copies of these documents by writing the Freedom of Information Office of the CIA in Washington, D.C.

33. James Phelan, *Howard Hughes: The Hidden Years* (New York: Random House, 1976), 191–92. Actually, the company discovered later that the thieves did *not* have the crucial memo outlining Project Jennifer. The burglars had dropped the memo on their way out, and the guard stuffed it in his pocket. In the excitement, he forgot to tell the police. Later he panicked and flushed the memo down the toilet.

34. For more details on Project Jennifer, see Phelan, *Howard Hughes*, 187–93; Donald L. Barlett and James B. Steele, *Empire: The Life, Legend, and Madness of Howard Hughes* (New York: Norton, 1979), 534–49; and Roy Varner and Wayne Collier, *A Matter of Risk: The Incredible Inside Story of the CIA's Hughes Glomar Explorer Mission to Raise a Russian Submarine* (New York: Random House, 1978).

35. Telegram by unnamed CIA official, 7 February 1975, CIA doc.

36. Ibid.

37. Quoted in Leonard Downie, Jr., *The New Muckrakers* (Washington, D.C.: New Republic Book Company, 1976), 90.

38. Telephone conversation between Seymour Hersh and unnamed CIA official, 10 February 1975, CIA doc.

39. Telephone conversation between William Colby and Seymour Hersh, 10 February 1975, CIA doc.

40. Telephone conversations between William Colby and Laurence Silberman and William Colby and Carl Duckett, both on 14 February 1975, CIA doc.

41. Colby, *Honorable Men*, 416.

42. Telephone conversation between William Colby and Brent Scowcroft, 21 February 1975, CIA doc.

43. Telephone conversation between William Colby and Katharine Graham, 13 February 1975, CIA doc.

44. Jack Anderson and Les Whitten, "Press Forgets Prime Responsibility," *Washington Post*, 25 March 1975, C21.

45. Seymour Hersh, "3 Panels in Congress Plan Inquiries into Sub Salvage," *New York Times*, 20 March 1975, 1.

46. The *Times* put this agreement with the CIA in writing. See letter, *New York Times* to William Colby, 3 March 1975, CIA doc.

47. Salisbury, *Without Fear or Favor*, 547.

48. Interview, Seymour Hersh, 23 March 1992.

49. Telephone conversation between William Colby and NBC official, 17 March 1975, CIA doc.

50. Telephone conversation between William Colby and Les Whitten, 18 March 1975, CIA doc.

51. Telephone conversation between William Colby and Brent Scowcroft, 14 March 1975, CIA doc.

52. Telephone conversation between William Colby and Carl Duckett, 13 March 1975, CIA doc. The stenographer was unsure whether Colby or Duckett spoke these particular words.

53. Telephone conversation between William Colby and *Los Angeles Times* editor, 27 February 1975, CIA doc.

54. Telephone conversation between William Colby and Brent Scowcroft, 14 March 1975, CIA doc.

55. "Querulous Quaker," *Time*, 13 December 1948, 70.

56. Douglas A. Anderson, *A "Washington Merry-Go-Round" of Libel Actions* (Chicago: Nelson-Hall, 1980), chaps. 1, 2; Jack Anderson with James Boyd, *Confessions of a Muckraker* (New York: Random House, 1979).

57. Jack Anderson and Les Whitten, "Being Spied on Has Benefits of Sorts," *Washington Post*, 31 January 1975, E17; Bob Woodward, "Hunt Told Associates of Orders to Kill Jack Anderson," *Washington Post*, 21 September 1975, A1. See also Gordon Liddy, *Will* (New York: St. Martin's Press, 1980), 207–10.

58. Telephone conversation, 18 March 1975, CIA doc., quoted in Howard Bray, *The Pillars of the Post* (New York: Norton, 1980), 153 (emphasis added). Whitten was not identified in the transcript but was identified by Bray.

59. Telephone conversation between William Colby and Jack Anderson, 18 March 1975, CIA doc.

60. Telephone conversation between William Colby and *Washington Post* official, 18 March 1975, CIA doc.

61. Of the twenty editorials surveyed by *Editorials on File*, only four were critical of Project Jennifer. *Editorials on File 1975* (New York: Facts on File, 1975), 311–17.

62. "The Glomar Explorer," *Washington Post*, 23 March 1975, B6.

63. "Project Jennifer," *New York Times*, 20 March 1975, 38.

64. "The Great Submarine Snatch," *Time*, 31 March 1975, 27.

65. "CIA's Mission Impossible," *Newsweek*, 31 March 1975, 32.

66. "The Spies in the Deep," *Los Angeles Times*, 20 March 1975, pt. 2, p. 6.

67. Seymour Hersh, "CIA Salvage Ship Brought Up Part of Soviet Sub Lost in 1968, Failed to Raise Atom Missiles," *New York Times*, 19 March 1975, 1; Anderson and Whitten, "Press Forgets Prime Responsibility."

68. *CBS Evening News*, 19 March 1975, TNA.

69. "The Case of the Sunken Sub," *Columbia Journalism Review*, May/June 1975, 6; "Salvaging the Sub Story," *Newsweek*, 31 March 1975, 66. The documents released in the 1977 Freedom of Information suit plainly show that this conspiracy theory is not true. In fact, Colby was worried about how the press would portray the project. At one point, he told Scowcroft that the media "are all just waiting to write that great, sanctimonious, sickening prose" (telephone conversation between William Colby and Brent Scowcroft, 14 March 1975, CIA doc.).

70. "The Glomar Explorer," *Washington Post*, 23 March 1975, B6 (emphasis added).

71. "Shivering from Overexposure," *Time*, 31 March 1975, 27.

72. "Show and Tell?," *Time*, 31 March 1975, 61.

73. Tom Wicker, "The Submarine Story," *New York Times*, 21 March 1975, 37.

74. Roger Wilkins, also a former editorial writer for the *Washington Post*, quoted in Bray, *Pillars of the Post*, 154.

75. Morton Kondracke, "The CIA and 'Our Conspiracy,' " *MORE*, May 1975, 10.

76. Anderson and Whitten, "Press Forgets Prime Responsibility."

77. Stephen Isaacs, "Withholding of Story Defended," *Washington Post*, 20 March 1975, A14.

78. William Greider, "Aftergate," *Esquire*, September 1975, 133.

79. "The Quiet Pulitzers," *Time*, 19 May 1975, 68.

80. Ibid.

81. Seymour Hersh, "Submarines of U.S. Stage Spy Missions inside Soviet Waters," *New York Times*, 25 May 1975, 1.

82. Bob Woodward again "exposed" the program in 1985, this time as an example of the secrets sold by Pelton. For Woodward's discussion of his "discovery" of this project and the CIA's attempt to censor him, see Bob Woodward, *Veil: The Secret Wars of the CIA, 1981–1987* (New York: Simon and Schuster, 1987), 447–63.

83. Meeting notes, "Mtg.—Buchen, A. G. Levi, Cheney," 28 May 1975, folder "Intelligence—*New York Times* Articles by Seymour Hersh, 5/75–6/75 (1)," box 6, Richard B. Cheney Files, GRFL. See also 29 May 1975 meeting notes in the same folder.

84. Memo, Bud McFarlane to Richard Cheney, 30 May 1975, and memo, Richard Cheney to Donald Rumsfeld, 31 May 1975, both in folder "Intelligence—*New York Times* Articles by Seymour Hersh, 5/75–6/75 (2)," box 6, Richard B. Cheney Files, GRFL.

85. Memo, Edward Levi to Gerald Ford, 29 May 1975, folder "Intelligence—*New York Times* Articles by Seymour Hersh, 5/75–6/75 (1)," box 6, Richard B. Cheney Files, GRFL.

86. Meeting notes, "Mtg.—Buchen, A. G. Levi, Cheney," 28 May 1975, folder "Intelligence—*New York Times* Articles by Seymour Hersh, 5/75–6/75 (1)," box 6, Richard B. Cheney Files, GRFL.

87. The reasons for the House committee crisis are explored in Chapter 6.

88. George Lardner, Jr., "CIA White House Infiltration Alleged," *Washington Post*, 10 July 1975, A1; John Crewdson, "File Said to Indicate CIA Had a Man in White House," *New York Times*, 10 July 1975, 1.

89. *CBS Evening News*, 9 July 1975, TNA.

90. For definitive discussions of the CIA practice of "detailing" employees, see U.S. House Select Committee on Intelligence, *U.S. Intelligence Agencies and Activities*, pt. 6, *Committee Proceedings, II*, 94th Cong., 2d sess., 4 February 1976, 2167–71, and *CIA: The Pike Report* (Nottingham: Spokesman Books, 1977), 225–26.

91. L. Fletcher Prouty, *The Secret Team: The CIA and Its Allies in Control of the United States and the World* (Englewood Cliffs, N.J.: Prentice-Hall, 1973), 339.

92. Sean Mitchell, "Stone, Writers Debate 'JFK' Fact, Fiction," *Los Angeles Times*, 5 March 1992, F8. Prouty also served as a "key adviser" to Stone on the film.

93. Narrative compiled from Stuart Loory, "The CIA's 'Man in the White

House,'" *Columbia Journalism Review*, September/October 1975; Charles Seib, "The Prouty-Butterfield Flap," *Washington Post*, 22 July 1975, A18; Schorr, *Clearing the Air*, 187; and *CBS Evening News*, 11 July 1975, TNA.

94. *CBS Evening News*, 15 July 1975, TNA.

95. George Lardner, Jr., "Butterfield Not CIA Spy, Church Says," *Washington Post*, 19 July 1975, A1.

96. "The Hustler," *Time*, 28 July 1975, 42–43.

97. Seib, "The Prouty-Butterfield Flap."

98. Loory, "The CIA's 'Man in the White House,' " 14.

99. Ibid.

100. Telephone interview, Daniel Schorr, 30 March 1992.

101. Tom Braden, "National Self Torture," *Washington Post*, 10 January 1976, A15. See also Schorr's response, "Daniel Schorr Replies," *Washington Post*, 17 January 1976, A14, and Braden's response to Schorr's reply, "The 'Revealing' of Information on TV," *Washington Post*, 24 January 1976, A19.

102. Salisbury, *Without Fear or Favor*, 549.

Chapter Five

1. David Belin, *Final Disclosure: The Full Truth about the Assassination of President Kennedy* (New York: Charles Scribner's Sons, 1988), 162.

2. Ibid., 163; interview, Roderick Hills, 27 March 1992.

3. Transcript of press conference, 6 June 1975, folder "June 6, 1975," box 9, Ron Nessen Papers, GRFL.

4. Carroll Kilpatrick, "Nessen and Press Clash," *Washington Post*, 7 June 1975, A8; Lou Cannon, "Nessen Attacks 'Mistrust' by Press," *Washington Post*, 27 June 1975, 1. Nessen was a former NBC correspondent.

5. John Osborne, *White House Watch: The Ford Years* (Washington, D.C.: New Republic Books, 1977), 147.

6. "No Time for Cover-Up," *New York Times*, 8 June 1975, sect. 4, p. 16.

7. For the complete report, see Commission on CIA Activities within the United States, *Report to the President by the Commission on CIA Activities within the United States* (Washington, D.C.: Government Printing Office, 1975).

8. Seymour Hersh, "Report on CIA Is Praised, but Recommendations Are Called Weak," *New York Times*, 12 June 1975, 23.

9. "Operation Chaos," *New York Times*, 11 June 1975, 42. Other news media also covered the report prominently. The *Washington Post* ran seven stories on the report the first day; *Newsweek* devoted its cover to the report; and CBS led its broadcast with the story for two days in a row.

10. Anthony Lewis, "The Teller of Truth," *New York Times*, 10 July 1975, 29. The *New Republic* also compared Hersh's charges to the Rockefeller report and concluded that Hersh had been vindicated. See Morton H. Halperin, "Led Astray by the CIA," *New Republic*, 28 June 1975, 8–16.

11. Transcript, "NPACT SPECIAL: The Rockefeller Commission Report on the CIA," 10 June 1975, ser. 7.9, box 4, folder 1, Frank Church Collection, BSUL.

12. Tom Wicker, "The Rocky Report: Better Than Expected," *New York Times*, 13 June 1975, 37.

13. Seymour Hersh, "At Its Best, How Good Is CIA in a Democracy?," *New York Times*, 15 June 1975, sect. 4, p. 1.

14. Hersh, "Report on CIA Is Praised."

15. Some staff members even believed that the assassination inquiry was a CIA ploy to divert the committee's attention from more important matters. Loch Johnson, *A Season of Inquiry: Congress and Intelligence* (Chicago: Dorsey Press, 1988), 54–55.

16. Linda Charlton, "Helms Says Search of Mail Was Illegal," *New York Times*, 23 October 1975, 1.

17. U.S. Senate Select Committee to Study Governmental Operations with Respect to Intelligence Activities, *Alleged Assassination Plots Involving Foreign Leaders*, 94th Cong., 1st sess., 20 November 1975 (Washington, D.C.: Government Printing Office, 1975; reprint, New York: Norton, 1976), 148, 151.

18. Johnson, *Season of Inquiry*, 47.

19. Quoted in Clifton Daniel, "The Assassination-Plot Rumors," *New York Times*, 6 June 1975, 66.

20. Adam Walinsky, "The Uses of Indifference," *New York Times*, 13 June 1975, 37. For another defense of the Kennedys, see the letter to the editor by Arthur Schlesinger, Jr., "Castro and the Kennedys," *New York Times*, 12 June 1975, 36.

21. Transcript of Church press conference, 13 June 1975, ser. 7.9, box 4, folder 1, Frank Church Collection, BSUL.

22. Lesley Oelsner, "Rockefeller Finds No Kennedy Link with Death Plots," *New York Times*, 16 June 1975, 1.

23. "The CIA: The Light of Day," *Newsweek*, 7 July 1975, 15.

24. John Crewdson, "Church Doubts Plot Links to Presidents," *New York Times*, 19 July 1975, 1.

25. John Tower, *Consequences: A Personal and Political Memoir* (Boston: Little, Brown, 1991), 134.

26. Memo, James Wilderotter to Phil Buchen and Rod Hills, 16 May 1975, folder "Justice—Intelligence," box 24, Philip W. Buchen Files, GRFL.

27. See, for example, Safire's columns of 15 September, 20 November, and 8 December 1975 in the *New York Times*.

28. Senator Tower disputed Safire, saying that Church "has bent over backward not to even give the appearance of covering up" the Kennedy mistress story. "No Cover-Up on Kennedy, Tower Says," *Washington Post*, 17 December 1975, A7.

29. Johnson, *Season of Inquiry*, 62; Frank J. Smist, Jr., *Congress Oversees the United States Intelligence Community, 1947–1989* (Knoxville: University of Tennessee Press, 1990), 65.

30. *CBS Evening News*, 5 February 1976, TNA.

31. Marquis Childs, "The CIA Puzzle," *Washington Post*, 8 July 1975, A17.

32. See Godfrey Hodgson, *America in Our Time* (New York: Vintage Books, 1978).

33. Garry Wills, "Controlling the Rogue Presidency," *Washington Post*, 25 January 1976, F1.

34. Russell Baker, "Our Uncle Is Now Dorian Sam," *New York Times*, 1 October 1974, 41.

35. Letter, Norma Wheeler to Frank Church, 1 November 1977, ser. 3.2.2, box 4, folder 2, Frank Church Collection, BSUL.

36. Lillian Hellman, "For Truth, Justice, and the American Way," *New York Times*, 4 June 1975, 39.

37. James E. Bryan, letter to the editor, *Washington Post*, 11 December 1975, A22.

38. Sue Clegg, letter to the editor, *Washington Post*, 10 July 1975, A19.

39. "The Road Home," *New York Times*, 23 November 1975, sect. 4, p. 16.

40. U.S. Senate Select Committee, *Alleged Assassination Plots*, 285.

41. William Colby with Peter Forbath, *Honorable Men: My Life in the CIA* (New York: Simon and Schuster, 1978), 392.

42. Martin Arnold, "Colby Tells Publishers That CIA Is Jeopardized by Sensational Headlines," *New York Times*, 8 April 1975, 10.

43. Colby did not personally believe that Helms had perjured himself, but, under pressure from mid-level officers, he thought he had a duty to advise the Justice Department to investigate. Helms eventually pleaded no contest to a charge of not "fully, completely and accurately" testifying to Congress. He received a two-year suspended sentence and a $2,000 fine, which was quickly paid for him by retired CIA officers. Colby, *Honorable Men*, 383–86; Thomas Powers, *The Man Who Kept the Secrets: Richard Helms and the CIA* (New York: Alfred A. Knopf, 1979), 13, 299–305.

44. Powers, *The Man Who Kept the Secrets*, 14. See Tom Mangold, *Cold Warrior: James Jesus Angleton, the CIA's Master Spy Hunter* (New York: Simon and Schuster, 1991), 311–16, for the details of Angleton's doubts about Colby's loyalties.

45. Colby, *Honorable Men*, 16.

46. Ibid., 440.

47. The CIA contended that the dart guns had never actually been used. See ibid., 441, and U.S. Senate Select Committee to Study Governmental Operations with Respect to Intelligence Activities, *Intelligence Activities: Senate Resolution 21*, vol. 1, *Unauthorized Storage of Toxic Agents*, 94th Cong., 1st sess., 16 September 1975, 19.

48. Johnson, *Season of Inquiry*, 74.

49. U.S. Senate Select Committee, *Intelligence Activities*, vol. 1, *Unauthorized Storage of Toxic Agents*, 16 September 1975, 32, 39.

50. Ibid., 44.

51. Ibid., 17 September 1975, 101.

52. Colby, *Honorable Men*, 442.

53. "Senate Anti-Toxin," *New York Times*, 17 September 1975, 44.

54. Tom Wicker, "Destroy the Monster," *New York Times*, 12 September 1975, 33.

55. In 1983, Church himself conceded that many observers had viewed the dart gun hearings as "an act of exhibitionism" by the committee and that his decision to focus on this topic first might have been a mistake. Quoted in Smist, *Congress Oversees the United States Intelligence Community*, 66.

56. Rowland Evans and Robert Novak, "Rebuilding the CIA," *Washington Post*, 25 September 1975, A19. Colby agreed that the dart gun hearings were "the last straw" for the White House (*Honorable Men*, 443).

57. U.S. Senate Select Committee, *Intelligence Activities*, vol. 1, *Unauthorized Storage of Toxic Agents*, 18 September 1975, 187.

58. For a detailed and perceptive discussion of the Huston plan, see Athan Theoharis, *Spying on Americans: Political Surveillance from Hoover to the Huston Plan* (Philadelphia: Temple University Press, 1978), chap. 1.

59. U.S. Senate Select Committee, *Intelligence Activities*, vol. 2, *Huston Plan*, 23 September 1975, 2.

60. Ibid., 24 September 1975, 93.

61. Ibid., 59.

62. Ibid., 72.

63. Ibid., 23 September 1975, 22.

64. Ibid., 24 September 1975, 87.

65. Ibid., 25 September 1975, 107.

66. Ibid., 107–8.

67. Ibid., 108.

68. Ibid., vol. 4, *Mail Opening*, 24 October 1975, 139.

69. Ibid., vol. 6, *Federal Bureau of Investigation*, 18 November 1975, 26.

70. Ibid., 31.

71. Ibid., 33. For the most complete examination of the FBI's harassment of King, see David Garrow, *The FBI and Martin Luther King, Jr.* (New York: Penguin Books, 1981).

72. U.S. Senate Select Committee, *Intelligence Activities*, vol. 6, *Federal Bureau of Investigation*, 3 December 1975, 157–65.

73. "Presidents and the FBI," *New York Times*, 8 December 1975, 30.

74. William Safire, "Orchestrating Outrage," *New York Times*, 8 December 1975, 31.

75. Tom Wicker, "Power and Corruption," *New York Times*, 5 December 1975, 39.

76. Johnson, *Season of Inquiry*, 153–55. For an example of Mondale's tough and well-prepared questioning of witnesses, see his exchange with Attorney General Levi in U.S. Senate Select Committee, *Intelligence Activities*, vol. 6, *Federal Bureau of Investigation*, 11 December 1975, 332.

77. U.S. Senate Select Committee, *Intelligence Activities*, vol. 6, *Federal Bureau of Investigation*, 19 November 1975, 64.

78. Shortly after the Church committee's most dramatic revelations, 80 percent of Americans agreed that "it was wrong for the FBI to send a note to Martin Luther King suggesting that he commit suicide," while 74 percent agreed that "it was wrong for the CIA to work out a deal with Mafia characters to try to assassinate Castro." Sixty-one percent agreed that "it was a violation of basic rights for the CIA and FBI to conduct spying on prominent Americans here at home." Louis Harris, "CIA, FBI Lose Faith of Public," *Chicago Tribune*, 22 January 1976, sect. 2, p. 4. For more discussion of this poll, see Chapter 6.

79. Rod MacLeish, "Conspiracy Theories," *Washington Post*, 5 August 1975, A16.

80. For examples of these charges, see Charles Colson on the *CBS Evening News*, 5 February 1975, TNA, and William Safire, "Murder Most Foul," *New York Times*, 22 December 1975, 29.

81. George Gallup, *The Gallup Poll: Public Opinion, 1972–1977*, vol. 1 (Wilmington, Del.: Scholarly Resources, 1978), 927–31.

82. Andrew Torchia, "Conspiracy Killed King, Widow Says," *Washington Post*, 28 November 1975, A1; Leon Dash, "Rights Leaders Ask Probe of Dr. King Assassination," *Washington Post*, 28 November 1975, A12.

83. "The King Review," *New York Times*, 27 November 1975, 32.

84. *Saginaw News*, 20 November 1975, in *Editorials on File 1975* (New York: Facts on File, 1975), 1427.

85. Mike Royko, "The FBI: How Low Can It Go?," *Washington Post*, 6 December 1975, A15.

86. Irving Wallace, *The R Document* (New York: Simon and Schuster, 1976); Robert Ludlum, *The Chancellor Manuscript* (New York: Dial Press, 1977).

87. Richard Gid Powers, *G-Men: Hoover's FBI in American Popular Culture* (Carbondale: Southern Illinois University Press, 1983), 260, 263. Columnist Russell Baker noted the shift in the FBI's popular image at the time. See Baker, "Black Hat for Uncle Sam," *New York Times*, 13 December 1975, 27.

88. "The Cointel Scandal," *Washington Post*, 22 November 1975, A14.

89. Helen Dewar, " 'Hoover' Building Irks Gude," *Washington Post*, 30 November 1975, A3.

90. W. H. Ferry, letter to the editor, *Washington Post*, 4 December 1975, A18. See also the *Post* op-ed and letters pages of 7, 8, and 13 December 1975.

91. The effort to rename the Hoover building remained alive throughout the 1980s and continued into the 1990s. See Sharon Waxman, "Erase Hoover, Reformer Asks, Cites King Slur," *Cleveland Plain Dealer*, 15 August 1984, 18A; Richard Cohen, "Has the Time Come to Remove Hoover's Name from the FBI?," *Sacramento Bee*, 29 September 1993, B7.

92. See, for example, Charles Collingwood, *The Defector* (New York: Harper and Row, 1970), and Victor Marchetti, *The Rope-Dancer* (New York: Grosset and Dunlap, 1971).

93. Another 1973 movie, *Executive Action*, suggested CIA complicity in John Kennedy's assassination.

94. Robert L. Duncan, *Dragons at the Gate* (New York: William Morrow and Company, 1975); Brian Garfield, *Hopscotch* (New York: M. Evans and Company, 1975); Jim Garrison, *The Star-Spangled Contract* (New York: McGraw-Hill, 1976). Although the television networks did not launch any regular series based on this new antispy genre, the heroic spies so prevalent in the 1960s no longer dominated the small screen. In contrast to the fourteen spy shows on the air in the 1960s, the 1970s saw just five, and only two of these (the *Six Million Dollar Man* and the *Bionic Woman*) became hits. John G. Cawelti and Bruce A. Rosenberg, *The Spy Story* (Chicago: University of Chicago Press, 1987), 244–45.

95. Compare James Grady, *Six Days of the Condor* (New York: Norton, 1974), with the screenplay, Lorenzo Semple, Jr., and David Rayfiel, *Three Days of the Condor* (Hollywood: Script City, 1975).

96. William F. Buckley, Jr., "Redford vs. the CIA," *New York Times*, 28 September 1975, sect. 2, p. 1. See also Dino de Laurentiis Corporation, "Dino de Laurentiis

Presents Three Days of the Condor," handbook of production information (Beverly Hills: Dino de Laurentiis Corporation, 1975).

97. Memo, the vice president, Henry A. Kissinger, James R. Schlesinger, Philip W. Buchen, and James T. Lynn to the president, 18 September 1975, folder "Intelligence Community Option Paper, 9/75," box 6, Richard B. Cheney Files, GRFL.

98. Memo, Edward Levi to Gerald Ford, October 1975, folder "National Security Intelligence (3)," box 30, Presidential Handwriting File, GRFL; interview, Howard Baker, 27 March 1992.

99. Interview, Mitchell Rogovin, 24 March 1992.

100. Seymour Hersh, "CIA's Work Unimpeded by Inquiries and Reports, Officials of Agency Assert," New York Times, 10 November 1975, 1.

101. U.S. Senate, Congressional Record (11 November 1975), 94th Cong., 1st sess., 121, pt. 28:35786–88.

102. David Rosenbaum, "Rep. Pike Accuses Intelligence Arm of Failing in Duty," New York Times, 29 September 1975, 1.

103. Johnson, Season of Inquiry, 28.

104. Interview, Mitchell Rogovin, 24 March 1992.

105. U.S. Senate Select Committee, Intelligence Activities, vol. 5, The National Security Agency and Fourth Amendment Rights, 29 October 1975, 3.

106. Johnson describes the internal committee disputes on the NSA hearings in Season of Inquiry, 91–96, 103–10.

107. For an account of the Abzug hearing that divulged details of the SHAMROCK program, see George Lardner, Jr., "U.S. Cables Monitored, House Told," Washington Post, 24 October 1975, A1. The Abzug hearings caused the White House to ease its opposition to hearings by the Church committee, which it viewed as more responsible. Memo, Jack Marsh to the president, 27 October 1975, folder "President 9/75–12/75," box 87, John O. Marsh Files, GRFL.

108. Johnson, Season of Inquiry, 121.

109. U.S. Senate Select Committee to Study Governmental Operations with Respect to Intelligence Activities, Covert Action in Chile, 1963–1973, 94th Cong., 1st sess., 18 December 1975, committee print. The committee concluded that the United States had tried unsuccessfully to foment a coup against the democratically elected Allende government in 1970 but had not been directly involved in the 1973 coup that finally forced Allende from office.

110. For the full text of the questions and Nixon's responses, see U.S. Senate Select Committee to Study Governmental Operations with Respect to Intelligence Activities, Final Reports, Book IV, Supplementary Detailed Staff Reports on Foreign and Military Intelligence, 94th Cong., 2d sess., 1976, 143–71.

111. Notes, "Meeting with president," 13 October 1975, folder "Meeting with the President, 10/13/75: Intelligence Reform," box 11, Michael Raoul-Duval Papers, GRFL.

112. Johnson, Season of Inquiry, 109.

113. The debate of the closed Senate session is described in ibid., 130–36.

114. Editorials on File 1975, 1408–17.

115. Ibid., 1409, 1411; "Murderous Diplomacy," New York Times, 22 November 1975, 28.

116. "... And More Than Murder," *New York Times*, 22 November 1975, 28.

117. U.S. Senate Select Committee, *Alleged Assassination Plots*, xvi.

118. *CBS Evening News*, 20 November 1975, TNA.

119. U.S. Senate Select Committee, *Alleged Assassination Plots*, 261.

120. Nicholas Horrock, " 'Leads' Reported in Inquiry on CIA," *New York Times*, 5 October 1975, 25.

121. U.S. Senate Select Committee, *Alleged Assassination Plots*, 263, 264.

122. Transcript of press conference, 20 November 1975, ser. 7.9, box 4, folder 2, Frank Church Collection, BSUL.

123. The next heading of the report read, "Administration officials failed to rule out assassination as a tool of foreign policy, to make clear to their subordinates that assassination was permissible or to inquire further after receiving indications that assassination was being considered." U.S. Senate Select Committee, *Alleged Assassination Plots*, 273.

124. Ibid., 285.

125. "The Assassination Report," *Washington Post*, 21 November 1975, A18.

126. Interview, Mitchell Rogovin, 24 March 1992.

127. U.S. Senate Select Committee, *Intelligence Activities*, vol. 1, *Unauthorized Storage of Toxic Agents*, 17 September 1975, 123.

128. U.S. Senate Select Committee, *Final Reports*, Book I, *Foreign and Military Intelligence*, 9 (emphasis added).

129. U.S. Senate Select Committee, *Alleged Assassination Plots*, 259.

130. Seymour Hersh, "CIA's Work Unimpeded by Inquiries."

Chapter Six

1. Interview, William Colby, 30 March 1992. Presidential counsel Jack Marsh agreed that "the experts" believed Pike asked much more important questions than Church. Interview, Jack Marsh, 27 March 1992.

2. Interview, Mitchell Rogovin, 24 March 1992.

3. Interview, Howard Baker, 27 March 1992.

4. Telephone interview, James Wilderotter, 28 March 1992.

5. Quoted in Loch Johnson, *A Season of Inquiry: Congress and Intelligence* (Chicago: Dorsey Press, 1988), 7.

6. Interview, Lucien Nedzi, 26 March 1992.

7. John Crewdson, "After 3 Months, House Committee Selects Lawyer to Head Intelligence Inquiry," *New York Times*, 14 May 1975, 27. By the end of the investigation, however, the liberal members of the committee had become great supporters of Field.

8. Nicholas Horrock, "Nedzi Is Said to Have Kept House in Dark on CIA Violations," *New York Times*, 5 June 1975, 26.

9. Interview, Lucien Nedzi, 26 March 1992.

10. Interview, Michael Harrington, 10 July 1992.

11. Nicholas Horrock, "Democrats Seeking to Oust Head of House CIA Unit," *New York Times*, 6 June 1975, 1.

12. George Lardner, Jr., "House Democrats Resolve Dispute on Nedzi Probe Role," *Washington Post*, 10 June 1975, A8.

13. Nicholas Horrock, "Nedzi Compromise on Inquiry of CIA," *New York Times*, 10 June 1975, 1.

14. George Lardner, Jr., "Nedzi Quitting CIA Unit," *Washington Post*, 13 June 1975, A1.

15. James M. Naughton, "Nedzi Quits CIA Panel; House Inquiry Is Delayed," *New York Times*, 13 June 1975, 1.

16. U.S. House, *Congressional Record* (16 June 1975), 94th Cong., 1st sess., 121, pt. 15:19054.

17. Ibid., 19055.

18. Ibid., 19057.

19. Forty-four members, including Nedzi, voted "present." For the entire debate, see ibid., 19054–61.

20. See Chapter 4.

21. Representative Anthony Toby Moffett quoted in U.S. House, *Congressional Record* (17 July 1975), 94th Cong., 1st sess., 121, pt. 18:23252. For other examples of House members' fears of a perceived cover-up, see George Lardner, Jr., "Intelligence Panel Survival Foreseen," *Washington Post*, 18 June 1975, A2.

22. For the entire debate, see U.S. House, *Congressional Record* (16, 17 July 1975), 94th Cong., 1st sess., 121, pt. 18:23098–113, 23241–56.

23. Michael Harrington, "Congress's CIA Cover-Up: Getting Out the Truth," *New Republic*, 26 July 1975, 16. See also Morton H. Halperin, "On Behalf of the Public's Right to Know," *New York Times*, 9 July 1975, 37.

24. For the debate over Harrington, see U.S. House, *Congressional Record* (17 July 1975), 94th Cong., 1st sess., 121, pt. 18:23245–55.

25. "Congressional Dilemma," *New York Times*, 19 July 1975, 22.

26. U.S. House Select Committee on Intelligence, *U.S. Intelligence Agencies and Activities*, pt. 5, *Risks and Control of Foreign Intelligence*, 94th Cong., 1st sess., 3 December 1975, 1660.

27. Oriana Fallaci, "Otis Pike and the CIA," *New Republic*, 3 April 1976, 9.

28. Richard L. Madden, "Investigator with Wit: Otis Grey Pike," *New York Times*, 19 July 1975, 51.

29. Richard L. Lyons, "A Congressman with Style," *Washington Post*, 21 September 1975, A4.

30. U.S. House Committee on Armed Services, Special Subcommittee on the U.S.S. Pueblo, *Inquiry into the U.S.S. Pueblo and EC-121 Plane Incidents*, 91st Cong., 1st sess., 28 July 1969, 1621. Pike had also been instrumental in revealing a military scandal in 1972. Tipped off by a source inside the government, Pike urged Seymour Hersh to investigate the retirement of air force general John Lavelle. After engaging in some enterprising reporting, Hersh disclosed that Lavelle had been relieved of command and demoted without a hearing for launching unauthorized bombing raids on North Vietnam and falsifying reports that the strikes were made in response to enemy attacks. Seymour Hersh, *The Price of Power: Kissinger in the Nixon White House* (New York: Summit Books, 1983), 507n.

31. U.S. House Select Committee, *U.S. Intelligence Agencies and Activities*, pt. 1, *Intelligence Costs and Fiscal Procedures*, 31 July 1975, 1.

32. Ibid., 6 August 1975, 262.

33. Ibid., 5 August 1975, 203.

34. Ibid., 1 August 1975, 85.

35. Ibid., 6 August 1975, 241.

36. Interview, Greg Rushford, 30 March 1992.

37. Interview, Mitchell Rogovin, 24 March 1992.

38. Quoted in Frank J. Smist, Jr., *Congress Oversees the United States Intelligence Community, 1947–1989* (Knoxville: University of Tennessee Press, 1990), 53.

39. Telephone interview, Jack Boos, 20 August 1992.

40. Telephone interview, Aaron Donner, 5 September 1992.

41. U.S. House Select Committee, *U.S. Intelligence Agencies and Activities*, pt. 1, *Intelligence Costs and Fiscal Procedures*, 31 July 1975, 49.

42. Ibid., pt. 2, *The Performance of the Intelligence Community*, 11 September 1975, 641.

43. Nicholas Horrock, "President Bars House Unit from Seeing Secret Data," *New York Times*, 13 September 1975, 1, and "House Inquiry Bids Ford Yield Secret Vietnam Data," *New York Times*, 14 September 1975, 27.

44. See Marvin Kalb and Bernard Kalb, *Kissinger* (Boston: Little, Brown, 1974), 454.

45. Meeting recounted in Walter Pincus, "Four Little Words and How They Grew," *Washington Post*, 28 September 1975, B2.

46. Interview, Mitchell Rogovin, 24 March 1992.

47. U.S. House Select Committee, *U.S. Intelligence Agencies and Activities*, pt. 2, *The Performance of the Intelligence Community*, 12 September 1975, 681.

48. Ibid., 671. The exchange was recorded on the *CBS Evening News*, 12 September 1975, TNA.

49. U.S. House Select Committee, *U.S. Intelligence Agencies and Activities*, pt. 2, *The Performance of the Intelligence Community*, 12 September 1975, 678.

50. Ibid., 680.

51. Telephone interview, Otis Pike, 15 June 1992.

52. Interview, Mitchell Rogovin, 24 March 1992.

53. Philip Shabecoff, "President Ready to Defy House Bid for Vietnam Data," *New York Times*, 17 September 1975, 1.

54. Interview, Mitchell Rogovin, 24 March 1992.

55. Shabecoff, "President Ready to Defy House Bid for Vietnam Data," 1. Columnist Anthony Lewis responded that Congress had a few more rights and responsibilities than a private citizen. Anthony Lewis, "Only Congress Itself," *New York Times*, 18 September 1975, 41.

56. Speech, Gerald R. Ford, 22 September 1975, folder "SP3-197 World Affairs Council, San Francisco, CA, 9/22/75," box 75, White House Central Files Subject File, GRFL.

57. David Rosenbaum, "Rep. Pike Accuses Intelligence Arm of Failing in Duty," *New York Times*, 29 September 1975, 1.

58. Letter, Otis Pike to Gerald Ford, 17 September 1975, folder "Intelligence—

House Select Committee: Handling and Release of Classified Documents," box 14, Vernon C. Loen and Charles Leppert Files, GRFL.

59. Hills now describes Pike as "a despicable man." Interview, Roderick Hills, 27 March 1992.

60. Anthony Lewis, "Only Congress Itself," 41.

61. "Son of Watergate," *New York Times*, 18 September 1975, 40.

62. Notes, "Meeting with president," 13 October 1975, folder "Meeting with the President, 10/13/75: Intelligence Reform," box 11, Michael Raoul-Duval Papers, GRFL. Other executive officials also wanted to compromise. Phil Buchen, the president's counsel, suggested that the administration should allow subordinate foreign service officers to testify but not force them to do so. The White House was very worried that not only the full House but also the courts would support Pike. Some aides believed that there was only a 50–50 chance that the courts would uphold Kissinger's position. Memo, Jack Marsh to Gerald Ford, 27 September 1975, folder "ND6 Intelligence 10/6/76," box 5, White House Central Files Subject File, GRFL.

63. Hersh, *The Price of Power*, 204. Hersh claimed that he wrote his critical biography of Kissinger in order to save "the honor of the press." "I resent the press falling all over and lying on its back and saying 'Scratch my stomach, Mr. Kissinger,' " he told an interviewer. Quoted in Anthony Marro, "It's Supersource!," *Columbia Journalism Review*, September/October 1983, 56. See also Walter Isaacson, *Kissinger: A Biography* (New York: Simon and Schuster, 1992), chap. 25.

64. "The Pursuit of Peace and Power," *Time*, 7 February 1972, 14; "Mr. Nixon's Secret Agent," *Newsweek*, 7 February 1972, 14.

65. Telephone interview, Aaron Donner, 5 September 1992. In his memoirs, Reston called Kissinger "one of the most intelligent, imaginative, and effective public servants of his time." James Reston, *Deadline: A Memoir* (New York: Random House, 1991), 420.

66. "Why High Noon?," *New York Times*, 28 September 1975, sect. 4, p. 16.

67. "Mr. Pike's Committee," *Washington Post*, 6 October 1975, A10.

68. "Pike's Pique," *Washington Star*, 29 September 1975, clipping in Robert McClory's personal files, courtesy of Doris McClory.

69. U.S. House Select Committee, *U.S. Intelligence Agencies and Activities*, pt. 2, *The Performance of the Intelligence Community*, 25 September 1975, 735.

70. Ibid., 736.

71. Stanley Kutler describes McClory's role in the impeachment hearings in *The Wars of Watergate* (New York: Alfred A. Knopf, 1990), 503, 519–29.

72. Robert McClory, letter to the editor, *Washington Star*, 15 October 1975, clipping in Robert McClory's personal files, courtesy of Doris McClory.

73. See, for example, memo, Charles Leppert to Jack Marsh, 25 September 1975, and memo, Charles Leppert to Jack Marsh, 30 September 1975, both in folder "House Select Committee—General," box 14, Vernon C. Loen and Charles Leppert Files, GRFL.

74. Memo, Charles Leppert to Jack Marsh, 19 September 1975, folder "House Select Committee—General," box 14, Vernon C. Loen and Charles Leppert Files, GRFL.

75. Memo, Charles Leppert to Jack Marsh, 20 September 1975, folder "House

Select Committee—General," box 14, Vernon C. Loen and Charles Leppert Files, GRFL.

76. Memo, Max Friedersdorf to Don Rumsfeld, 23 September 1975, folder "CIA Investigation (2)," box 10, Max L. Friedersdorf Files, GRFL.

77. See memo, Robert McClory to Gerald Ford, 23 September 1975, folder "National Security Intelligence (3)," box 30, Presidential Handwriting File, and transcript, GOP leadership meeting with the president, 24 September 1975, folder "Congressional Leadership Meetings: GOP, 9/24/75," box 2, Robert K. Wolthuis Files, both in GRFL.

78. U.S. House Select Committee, *U.S. Intelligence Agencies and Activities*, pt. 4, *Committee Proceedings*, 29 September 1975, 1237.

79. Ibid., 1238.

80. Ibid., 1253.

81. George Lardner, Jr., "CIA Bows to Pike, Yields Documents," *Washington Post*, 1 October 1975, A1.

82. U.S. House Select Committee, *U.S. Intelligence Agencies and Activities*, pt. 4, *Committee Proceedings*, 1 October 1975, 1281.

83. George Kennan, letter to the editor, "Support for Kissinger," *Washington Post*, 14 October 1975, A19.

84. David Binder, "Kissinger Backed in House Dispute," *New York Times*, 14 October 1975, 5.

85. Hersh was accused of using McCarthyite tactics when he wrote a negative story about one of the Rockefeller Commission members, Erwin Griswold. See William Safire, "The New McCarthyism," *New York Times*, 9 January 1975, 35, and Charles Edward Wyzanski, Jr., "The Case for Erwin N. Griswold," *New York Times*, 20 January 1975, 26. In July, *Time* magazine compared the CIA's problems to the State Department's problems during the 1950s. See "A 'Spy' in the White House?," *Time*, 21 July 1975, 14. The charges against Schorr appeared in Stuart Loory, "The CIA's 'Man in the White House,'" *Columbia Journalism Review*, September/October 1975, 14.

86. James Reston, "Chairman Pike's Pique," *New York Times*, 1 October 1975, 45.

87. "Neo-McCarthyism?," *New York Times*, 19 October 1975, 12.

88. U.S. House Select Committee, *U.S. Intelligence Agencies and Activities*, pt. 2, *The Performance of the Intelligence Community*, 31 October 1975, 843.

89. Ibid., 852.

90. See, for example, the report on the *CBS Evening News*, 31 October 1975, TNA.

91. Documents at the Ford library concerning possible replacements for Colby are dated as early as 10 July 1975. Bush was favored by only three of eight Ford advisers surveyed. Several other candidates, including former solicitor general Robert Bork, were preferred by the advisers. Presumably, the president's own friendship with Bush persuaded him to overrule his aides.

92. *CBS Evening News*, 3 November 1975, TNA.

93. U.S. House Select Committee, *U.S. Intelligence Agencies and Activities*, pt. 5, *Risks and Control of Foreign Intelligence*, 6 November 1975, 1585.

94. William Colby with Peter Forbath, *Honorable Men: My Life in the CIA* (New York: Simon and Schuster, 1978), 445.

95. U.S. House Select Committee, *U.S. Intelligence Agencies and Activities*, pt. 4, *Committee Proceedings*, 4 November 1975, 1311.

96. Ibid., 1312.

97. Ibid., 1319.

98. Ibid.

99. Ibid., 6 November 1975, 1333.

100. Ibid., 1332.

101. Ibid., 1341.

102. Ibid., 1352.

103. Ibid., 1343.

104. Ibid.

105. Columnist Joseph Kraft, a friend of Kissinger's, suggested a third possibility: that presidential counselor Jack Marsh deliberately tried to sabotage Kissinger by refusing to comply with the subpoenas and thus prompting the committee to cite him for contempt. Joseph Kraft, "Congress and Contempt Citations," *Washington Post*, 19 November 1975, A15.

106. Letter, Gerald Ford to Otis Pike, 19 November 1975, folder "Intelligence—House Select Committee: Subpoenas, Kissinger (2)," box 14, Vernon C. Loen and Charles Leppert Files, GRFL.

107. Memo, Jack Marsh to Gerald Ford, 13 November 1975, folder "National Security Intelligence (8)," box 31, Presidential Handwriting File, GRFL.

108. John Crewdson, "House Unit Seeks Contempt Order against Kissinger," *New York Times*, 15 November 1975, 1.

109. Marilyn Berger, "Intelligence Work Backed by Kissinger," *Washington Post*, 25 November 1975, A1.

110. Anthony Lewis, "The Light and the Dark," *New York Times*, 27 November 1975, 33.

111. John Crewdson, "Three-Count Contempt Citation of Kissinger Defended in House," *New York Times*, 18 November 1975, 15.

112. *Los Angeles Times*, 19 November 1975, in *Editorials on File 1975* (New York: Facts on File, 1975), 1423; *Tulsa Daily World*, 17 November 1975, in *Editorials on File 1975*, 1422.

113. William Safire, "The Blowsoft," *New York Times*, 4 December 1975, 41.

114. "Mr. Pike Goes Too Far," *Washington Post*, 19 November 1975, A14 (emphasis added).

115. Lewis, "The Light and the Dark."

116. *Worcester Telegram*, 21 November 1975, in *Editorials on File 1975*, 1424.

117. Letter, Otis Pike to House members, 5 December 1975, folder "Intelligence—House Select Committee: Subpoenas, Kissinger (3)," box 14, Vernon C. Loen and Charles Leppert Files, GRFL.

118. "Concurring Views of Otis G. Pike," November 1975, folder "Intelligence—House Select Committee: Subpoenas, Kissinger (1)," box 14, Vernon C. Loen and Charles Leppert Files, GRFL.

119. Memo, Charles Leppert to Jack Marsh, 8 December 1975, folder "Intelligence—House Select Committee: Subpoenas, Kissinger (3)," box 14, Vernon C. Loen and Charles Leppert Files, GRFL.

120. Memo, Charles Leppert to Jack Marsh, 18 November 1975, folder "Intelligence—House Select Committee: Subpoenas, Kissinger (2)," box 14, Vernon C. Loen and Charles Leppert Files, GRFL. Mahon's views are paraphrased in the memo.

121. "Dissenting Views of the Honorable Dale Milford," November 1975, folder "Intelligence—House Select Committee: Subpoenas, Kissinger (1)," box 14, Vernon C. Loen and Charles Leppert Files, GRFL.

122. The survey asked: "How would you rate the job being done by [fill in agency or committee name here]—excellent, pretty good, only fair, or poor?" The CIA's ratings were 32 percent positive, 49 percent negative, and 19 percent unsure. The FBI's ratings were 49 percent positive, 39 percent negative, and 12 percent unsure. The FBI's approval rating had been 84 percent ten years earlier. Louis Harris, "CIA, FBI Lose Faith of Public," *Chicago Tribune*, 22 January 1976, sect. 2, p. 4.

123. Ibid. The pollsters asked respondents whether they tended to agree or disagree with the following statements: "It was wrong for the FBI to send a note to Martin Luther King suggesting that he commit suicide" (80 percent agreed, 7 percent disagreed, 13 percent were unsure). "It was wrong for the CIA to work out a deal with Mafia characters to try to assassinate Castro" (74 percent agreed, 9 percent disagreed, 17 percent were unsure). "It was a violation of basic rights for the CIA and FBI to conduct spying on prominent Americans here at home" (61 percent agreed, 18 percent disagreed, 21 percent were unsure). "Both the CIA and FBI have learned their lessons and now will run things properly" (30 percent agreed, 41 percent disagreed, 29 percent were unsure).

124. Ibid. The survey asked: "How would you rate the job being done by [fill in agency or committee name here]—excellent, pretty good, only fair, or poor?"

125. Ibid. The pollsters asked if the respondents agreed with the following statements: "It would be a mistake to put tighter controls on the CIA and FBI because sometimes they know better than any outsider what is involved in an investigation" (48 percent agreed, 31 percent disagreed, 21 percent were unsure). "So much of the work of the CIA and FBI has been made public that soon they won't be able to do their jobs" (52 percent agreed, 33 percent disagreed, 15 percent were unsure).

126. J. William Fulbright, "Fulbright on the Press," *Columbia Journalism Review*, November/December 1975, 41. See Chapter 2.

127. Memo, Charles Leppert to Jack Marsh, 8 December 1975, folder "Intelligence—House Select Committee: Subpoenas, Kissinger (3)," box 14, Vernon C. Loen and Charles Leppert Files, GRFL.

128. Philip Shabecoff, "The House-Kissinger Battle over Contempt," *New York Times*, 15 December 1975, 25.

129. U.S. House Select Committee on Intelligence, *CIA: The Pike Report* (Nottingham: Spokesman Books, 1977), 188–89.

130. U.S. House Select Committee, *U.S. Intelligence Agencies and Activities*, pt. 2, *The Performance of the Intelligence Community*, 31 October 1975, 849, 855.

131. Ibid., 30 October 1975, 813.

132. Ibid., 4 November 1975, 1319.

133. U.S. House Select Committee, *CIA: The Pike Report*, 189.

134. Fallaci, "Otis Pike and the CIA," 10.

135. Johnson, *Season of Inquiry*, 98.

Chapter Seven

1. "Speakers' and Writers' Background Material," n.d., in unprocessed Ray Cline Collection, LC.

2. Letters, David A. Phillips to ARIO board members, 1 January, 1 February, 1976, Ray Cline Collection, LC.

3. Gerald R. Ford, "Address before a Joint Session of the Congress Reporting on United States Foreign Policy," 10 April 1975, in *Public Papers of Gerald R. Ford, 1975*, Book I (Washington, D.C.: Government Printing Office, 1977), 179 (emphasis added).

4. Memo, the vice president, Henry Kissinger, James Schlesinger, Philip Buchen, and James Lynn to the president, 18 September 1975, folder "Intelligence Community Options Paper, 9/75," box 6, Richard B. Cheney Files, GRFL.

5. For Kissinger's disagreements with other Ford administration officials, see John Osborne, *White House Watch: The Ford Years* (Washington, D.C.: New Republic Books, 1977), xxx–xxxi, 144–46, 172, 272; Joseph Kraft, "Congress and Contempt Citations," *Washington Post*, 19 November 1975, A15; and William Colby with Peter Forbath, *Honorable Men: My Life in the CIA* (New York: Simon and Schuster, 1978), 16.

6. Nicholas Horrock, "Administration Will Resist Curbs on Overseas Spying," *New York Times*, 19 October 1975, 29.

7. Memo, Mike Duval to John Marsh, 23 October 1975, folder "Draft Plan for ICG, 10/75," box 11, Michael Raoul-Duval Papers, GRFL.

8. For a discussion of the Hughes-Ryan amendment, see Chapter 3.

9. Mike Duval to John Marsh, 23 October 1975, folder "Draft Plan for ICG, 10/75," box 11, Michael Raoul-Duval Papers, GRFL.

10. Ibid.

11. Interview, Michael Harrington, 10 July 1992.

12. Ibid. Harrington himself is not sure that this was the case.

13. Richard D. Lyons, "Panel Drops Complaint on Leaks Filed against Rep. Harrington," *New York Times*, 7 November 1975, 14. The panel ruled that the meeting at which Colby had testified had itself violated House rules because no quorum was present and no public notice of the meeting was given. Thus the committee claimed that the session itself had violated House rules, and therefore any complaint about Harrington's conduct after the session was invalid. Harrington did not raise this technical defense himself, and observers speculated that the Democratic leadership had decided to squelch the investigation.

14. I. F. Stone, however, challenged this argument, claiming that the executive branch had more to gain by leaking information on the Kurdish operation and then blaming the committee for the leak. I. F. Stone, "The Schorr Case: The Real Dangers," *New York Review of Books*, 1 April 1976, 6–8.

15. Dick Clark, "Frustration," *New York Times*, 29 January 1976, 33.

16. Seymour Hersh, "CIA Is Reported to Give Anti-Reds in Italy $6 Million," *New York Times*, 7 January 1976, 1.

17. *CBS Evening News*, 19 November 1975, TNA; John Crewdson, "Colby Asks Panel to Drop 12 Names from Plot Report," *New York Times*, 20 November 1975, 1.

18. "Church Reads 10 Names That Colby Sought to Omit," *New York Times*, 21 November 1975, 54.

19. Philip Agee, *Inside the Company: CIA Diary* (New York: Stonehill Publishing Company, 1975).

20. Philip Agee, "Exposing the CIA," *Counterspy* 2, no. 2 (Winter 1975): 20.

21. John Marks, "How to Spot a Spook," *Washington Monthly*, November 1974, 5–11.

22. Excerpt from testimony of Morton Halperin before Subcommittee on Oversight of the House Committee on Intelligence, reprinted in *MORE*, February 1978, 22. The press did not know of the CIA's warning to Welch until nearly a year after his death.

23. *CBS Evening News*, 30 December 1975, TNA.

24. Phillips not only served as a source for numerous news stories about Welch but also soon wrote an entire book about the dead agent, the CIA, and what he believed were the excesses of the investigation. David Atlee Phillips, *The Night Watch* (New York: Atheneum, 1977).

25. Eugene L. Meyer, "Slain CIA Agent Receives Unusual Honor," *Washington Post*, 31 December 1975, 1.

26. Telephone interview, F. A. O. Schwarz, Jr., 25 August 1992. Otis Pike agreed that the CIA "played [the Welch death] like an organ." Telephone interview, Otis Pike, 15 June 1992.

27. The Revolutionary Organization of November 17, which took its name from the date of a bloody uprising against the Greek junta in 1973, later claimed responsibility for killing Welch, other American officials, and Greek conservatives. The group objected to American involvement in Greek politics, especially U.S. support for the repressive junta from 1967 to 1973. By 1986, the Greek police had attributed thirteen murders to the group but had not succeeded in arresting any suspects in these crimes. Steven V. Roberts, "One Year Later, the Murder of the CIA's Chief Officer in Athens Remains a Mystery without Solid Clues," *New York Times*, 26 December 1976, A8; Henry Kamm, "Slaying in Athens Linked to '75 Case," *New York Times*, 18 November 1983, A8.

28. Laurence Stern, "CIA Agent Welch Buried," *Washington Post*, 7 January 1976, A1.

29. Telephone interview, Aaron Donner, 5 September 1992.

30. "Year of Terror," *Time*, 5 January 1976, 24–26. See also *Editorials on File 1976* (New York: Facts on File, 1976), 7–10.

31. "Richard S. Welch," *Washington Post*, 29 December 1975, A16.

32. Transcript of press conference, 27 December 1975, folder "December 27, 1975," box 15, Ron Nessen Papers, GRFL.

33. Interview, Mitchell Rogovin, 24 March 1992.

34. U.S. Senate, *Congressional Record* (9 March 1976), 94th Cong., 2d sess., 122, pt. 5:5708.

35. News release, n.d., and news release, 17 January 1976, both in ser. 7.9, box 4, folder 3, Frank Church Collection, BSUL.

36. For examples of the press equating "unauthorized disclosures" from the committees with those from disaffected former agents, see "A Question of Leakage,"

Newsweek, 23 February 1976, 12, and John Crewdson, "Slaying of CIA Officer Stirs a Debate on Identity Disclosures," *New York Times*, 4 January 1976, 2. For letters from private citizens who blamed Church for Welch's death, see ser. 7.5, box 3, folder 10, and ser. 2.6, box 1, folder 8, Frank Church Collection, BSUL. Church, Pike, and other CIA critics received death threats after Welch's death.

37. "I Am a Spy for the CIA. . . . If You Print My Name I May Be Killed," *MORE*, February 1976, 14–15.

38. Charles Seib, "Media Manipulation," *Washington Post*, 16 January 1976, A19.

39. Quoted in Frank J. Smist, Jr., *Congress Oversees the United States Intelligence Community, 1947–1989* (Knoxville: University of Tennessee Press, 1990), 64.

40. Tristram Coffin, "A Cold War Coup D'Etat," *Washington Spectator*, 15 February 1976, 1, clipping in ser. 7.3, box 2, folder 12, Frank Church Collection, BSUL. Church himself discounted suggestions that there had been an executive branch conspiracy. See letter, Frank Church to Tristram Coffin, 27 February 1976, ser. 7.3, box 2, folder 12, Frank Church Collection, BSUL.

41. Telephone interview, A. Searle Field, 17 July 1992.

42. U.S. House Select Committee on Intelligence, *CIA: The Pike Report* (Nottingham: Spokesman Books, 1977), 249, 251.

43. "House Unit Seeking Release of Two CIA Reports," *New York Times*, 20 December 1975, 2.

44. U.S. House Select Committee, *CIA: The Pike Report*, 197. The committee did name Angola in the report because Congress had officially and publicly cut off CIA aid to that country.

45. Memo, John D. Morrison, Jr., to [name deleted], "Comments on House Select Committee Draft Final Report," 20 January 1976, CIA doc.

46. Memo, [name deleted] to [name deleted], "House Select Committee Report," 20 January 1976, CIA doc.

47. Memo, Paul Walsh to chief, review staff, "Draft Final Report of the House Select Committee," 20 January 1976, CIA doc.

48. Stone, "The Schorr Case," 6–11.

49. Stone's conspiracy theory has few adherents among staff or committee members today.

50. John Crewdson, "House Committee Report Finds CIA Understated Prices of Angolan Arms," *New York Times*, 20 January 1976, 1; Nicholas Horrock, "U.S. Role Hinted in Cypriot Coup," *New York Times*, 20 January 1976, 4; John Crewdson, "Pose as Journalists Laid to 11 in CIA," *New York Times*, 23 January 1976, 1.

51. U.S. House Committee on Standards of Official Conduct, *Investigation of Publication of Select Committee on Intelligence Report*, 94th Cong., 2d sess., 27 July 1976, 321.

52. Some journalists and staff members also suspected that Pike was trying to hurry the investigation because he was considering running for the Senate that year, though Pike denies this.

53. Technically, Pike asked for special permission to file the report on 30 January, a day when the House was not in session, and to file the minority views and committee recommendations on 11 February.

54. Testimony of Otis Pike in U.S. House Committee, *Investigation of Publication of Select Committee on Intelligence Report*, 19 July 1976, 58.

55. Because the minutes of the crucial meeting between Pike and the president are not in the Gerald R. Ford Library, it is impossible to determine whose interpretation was correct. The letter from Colby to Pike summarizing the agreement reached in the meeting does not mention the final report. No committee member mentioned the final report when the committee discussed the agreement. Seventeen years later, Pike said he did not remember the details of his meeting with the president or of the agreement. Ford also claimed in 1994 to have no memory of the meeting. Most likely, the final report was not discussed in the meeting, leading to future misunderstandings on this issue.

56. U.S. House Select Committee on Intelligence, *U.S. Intelligence Agencies and Activities*, pt. 6, *Committee Proceedings, II*, 94th Cong., 2d sess., 21 January 1976, 2044.

57. Ibid., 2045.

58. The vote went along the committee's usual lines, with conservative Democrat Dale Milford voting with the minority and Republican Jim Johnson joining the Democrats.

59. John Crewdson, "House Committee Finds Intelligence Agencies Generally Go Unchecked," *New York Times*, 26 January 1976, 1; Nicholas Horrock, "Panel Says Jackson Gave Secret Advice to CIA," *New York Times*, 26 January 1976, 1; "Inquiry Shows Secret Aid to Many Foreign Leaders," *New York Times*, 26 January 1976, 14; "Kurdish Rebels in Iraq Gave Three Rugs to Kissinger," *New York Times*, 26 January 1976, 14; John Crewdson, "Panel Says CIA Lets 85% of Its Contracts without Bidding," *New York Times*, 27 January 1976, 1; Alvin Schuster, "U.S. Paid $800,000 to Italian General; CIA Fought Move," *New York Times*, 30 January 1976, 1. The fact that the newspaper was the beneficiary of most of the committee's leaks did not stop it from editorializing against those leaks, however. See "How to Reform CIA," *New York Times*, 30 January 1976, 28.

60. *CBS Evening News*, 28 January 1976, TNA.

61. *CBS Evening News*, 25 January 1976, TNA.

62. Nicholas Horrock, "Intelligence Report Leaks Denounced by White House," *New York Times*, 27 January 1976, 1; *CBS Evening News*, 26 January 1976, TNA.

63. U.S. House Select Committee, *U.S. Intelligence Agencies and Activities*, pt. 6, *Committee Proceedings, II*, 28 January 1976, 2132.

64. "Report on CIA Blocked," *Washington Post*, 29 January 1976, A1.

65. U.S. House, *Congressional Record* (29 January 1976), 94th Cong., 2d sess., 122, pt. 2:1633.

66. Ibid., 1637.

67. Ibid., 1633.

68. Ibid., 1635.

69. Ibid., 1638.

70. J. Leiper Freeman, "Investigating the Executive Intelligence: The Fate of the Pike Committee," *Capitol Studies* 5 (Fall 1977): 113–14.

71. The final vote was 246–124, with 127 Democrats and 119 Republicans voting to suppress and 122 Democrats and 2 Republicans voting to publish.

72. David Rosenbaum, "House Prevents Releasing Report on Intelligence," *New York Times*, 30 January 1976, 1.

73. U.S. House Select Committee, *U.S. Intelligence Agencies and Activities*, pt. 6, *Committee Proceedings, II*, 3 February 1976, 2165.

74. Ibid., pt. 4, *Committee Proceedings*, 4 November 1975, 1305. The chairman was angry that one of the committee's most explosive discoveries—the American decision to aid, then abandon, the Kurds in Iraq—had been leaked to Schorr before the committee had decided whether to release the information.

75. Daniel Schorr, *Clearing the Air* (Boston: Houghton Mifflin, 1977), 195.

76. Ibid.

77. Telephone interview, Daniel Schorr, 30 March 1992.

78. Schorr, *Clearing the Air*, 198.

79. *CBS Evening News*, 10 February 1976, TNA; Schorr, *Clearing the Air*, 203. Schorr believed that CBS ran the story initially because the producers thought that the *New York Times* would run it the next morning. Then the *Times* inexplicably omitted Bill Paley's name in its article. Ironically, Schorr later said, "Paley's friends got to the *New York Times*" but they were not able to get to CBS. Telephone interview, Daniel Schorr, 30 March 1992.

80. Schorr, *Clearing the Air*, 198.

81. Ibid., 200.

82. Telephone interview, Daniel Schorr, 30 March 1992.

83. U.S. House Select Committee, *U.S. Intelligence Agencies and Activities*, pt. 6, *Committee Proceedings, II*, 10 February 1976, 2314.

84. Schorr, *Clearing the Air*, 204.

85. William Claiborne and Laurence Stern, "Part of Intelligence Report Published in N.Y. Tabloid: 'Voice' Melodrama," *Washington Post*, 12 February 1976, A1.

86. "How to Reform CIA," 28.

87. "Ford Offers Aid in Checking Leak," *New York Times*, 13 February 1976, 7; *CBS Evening News*, 12 February 1976, TNA.

88. Interview, Mitchell Rogovin, 24 March 1992.

89. Ethics Committee member Edward Hutchinson wrote a friend: "I sincerely hope that [the Schorr case] does not fail because of such technicalities" as those that hampered the Harrington inquiry. Letter, Edward Hutchinson to David W. Dennis, 25 February 1976, folder "Schorr, Daniel (1)," box 99, Edward Hutchinson Papers, GRFL.

90. Les Brown, "Affiliates Committee of CBS Radio Urged Dismissal of Schorr," *New York Times*, 11 March 1976, 69; Schorr, *Clearing the Air*, 212–13.

91. Letter, George Kryder to Robert Wood, 29 February 1976, folder "FG37 Select and Special Committees of the Senate and House," box 127, White House Central Files Subject File, GRFL.

92. Schorr, *Clearing the Air*, 217–22.

93. *Boston Globe*, 29 February 1976, in *Editorials on File 1976*, 305. Agnew, of course, was famous for his attacks on the press.

94. "Selling Secrets," *New York Times*, 15 February 1976, sect. 4, p. 12.

95. Charles Seib, "The Secret Report Caper," *Washington Post*, 29 February 1976, A19.

96. Stone, "The Schorr Case," 10. Stone noted that if the *Post* and the *Times* had acted like CBS, "the former would have suspended Woodward and Bernstein and the latter Seymour Hersh."

97. "Daniel in the Lion's Den," *Newsweek*, 8 March 1976, 55. See also "What Makes Danny Run?," *Newsweek*, 23 February 1976, 49.

98. For details of the Schorr–Reporters' Committee feud, see Bob Kuttner, "Look before You Leak," *MORE*, March 1976, 6–7.

99. Laurence Stern, "The Daniel Schorr Affair," *Columbia Journalism Review*, May/June 1976, 20–25; Daniel Schorr, " 'The Daniel Schorr Affair': A Reply," *Columbia Journalism Review*, July/August 1976, 48–49; Laurence Stern, "Schorr Affair: Author's Reply," *Columbia Journalism Review*, September/October 1976, 62–63.

100. Tom Wicker, "Defending Dan Schorr," *New York Times*, 24 February 1976, 35; Russell Baker, "Richard Milhous Congress," *New York Times*, 27 March 1976, 25.

101. William Safire, "Bill Paley's Big Secret," *New York Times*, 1 March 1976, 23. Schorr himself is wary of this theory. Telephone interview, Daniel Schorr, 30 March 1992.

102. Writer Nora Ephron, for example, said that many of his CBS colleagues had difficulty keeping "straight faces" when discussing Schorr's problems because they disliked him so much. Nora Ephron, "The Rain That Falls on Daniel Schorr's Parade," *Esquire*, June 1976, 50. See also Garry Wills, "A Hard Case," *New York Review of Books*, 24 November 1977, 6–9.

103. David Ignatius, "Dan Schorr: The Secret Sharer," *Washington Monthly*, April 1976, 20.

104. See Chapter 6. No poll was conducted after the Welch assassination and the leak.

105. Anthony Lewis, "Farce or Tragedy," *New York Times*, 2 February 1976, 23.

106. Ignatius, "Dan Schorr," 20.

107. "Schorr Intimates Trouble with CBS," *New York Times*, 26 February 1976, 13.

Chapter Eight

1. Richard Lyons, "Pike Charges CIA Effort at Retaliation for Findings," *New York Times*, 10 March 1976, 1; "Bush Denies CIA Leaked Report on Missing Data," *New York Times*, 17 March 1976, 10.

2. U.S. House Committee on Standards of Official Conduct, *Investigation of Publication of Select Committee on Intelligence Report*, 94th Cong., 2d sess., 20 July 1976, 121; 29 July 1976, 423.

3. Ibid., 29 July 1976, 398, 386, 392. Schorr denies that he told Stanton the identity of his source.

4. Ibid., 15 September 1976, 534.

5. Ibid., 566.

6. Charles B. Seib, "Protecting Sources—A Continuing Battle," *Washington Post*, 10 September 1976, A29.

7. U.S. House Committee on Standards of Official Conduct, *Report on Investiga-*

tion Concerning Unauthorized Publication of the Report of the Select Committee on Intelligence, 94th Cong., 2d sess., 1 October 1976, 43.

8. Ibid., 40.

9. Ibid., 49.

10. Telephone interview, Robert Giaimo, 9 March 1992.

11. U.S. House Committee, *Investigation of Publication of Select Committee on Intelligence Report*, 28 July 1976, 330.

12. The Church committee ratings were 38 percent positive, 40 percent negative, and 22 percent unsure. The Pike committee ratings were 36 percent positive, 40 percent negative, and 24 percent unsure. Louis Harris, "CIA, FBI Lose Faith of Public," *Chicago Tribune*, 22 January 1976, sect. 2, p. 4. For further discussion of this poll, see Chapter 6.

13. Loch Johnson, *A Season of Inquiry: Congress and Intelligence* (Chicago: Dorsey Press, 1988), 185.

14. No national polls on the intelligence investigations were conducted after December 1975.

15. Johnson, *Season of Inquiry*, 180.

16. Ibid., 194.

17. For a critique of Ford's proposals, see Morton H. Halperin, Jerry J. Berman, Robert L. Borosage, and Christine M. Marwick, *The Lawless State: The Crimes of the U.S. Intelligence Agencies* (New York: Penguin, 1981), 244–54. For another view, see John M. Oseth, *Regulating U.S. Intelligence Operations* (Lexington: University Press of Kentucky, 1985), 91–102.

18. "Ford's CIA Shake-Up," *Newsweek*, 1 March 1976, 18.

19. Martin Arnold, "Editors Fearful of Ford's Proposals," *New York Times*, 20 February 1976, 55.

20. Tom Wicker, "Protecting the Culprits, Punishing the Accusers," *New York Times*, 22 February 1976, sect. 4, p. 13.

21. "The President's Secrecy Legislation," *Washington Post*, 23 February 1976, A18.

22. See U.S. Senate Select Committee to Study Governmental Operations with Respect to Intelligence Activities, *Final Reports*, 94th Cong., 2d sess., 1976: *Foreign and Military Intelligence* (Book I); *Intelligence Activities and the Rights of Americans* (Book II); *Supplementary Detailed Staff Reports on Intelligence Activities and the Rights of Americans* (Book III); *Supplementary Detailed Staff Reports on Foreign and Military Intelligence* (Book IV); *The Investigation of the Assassination of President John F. Kennedy: Performance of the Intelligence Agencies* (Book V); and *Supplementary Reports on Intelligence Activities* (Book VI).

23. "Additional Views of Senators Walter F. Mondale, Gary Hart, and Philip Hart," in U.S. Senate Select Committee, *Final Reports*, Book I, *Foreign and Military Intelligence*, 567.

24. George Lardner, Jr., "The Intelligence Investigations: Congress Cops Out," *The Progressive*, July 1976, 16–17.

25. Nicholas Horrock, "Senate Intelligence Panel Calls for a Law to Curb Covert Action as Implement of Foreign Policy," *New York Times*, 27 April 1976, 1.

26. Telephone interview, F. A. O. Schwarz, Jr., 25 August 1992.

27. William Colby with Peter Forbath, *Honorable Men: My Life in the CIA* (New York: Simon and Schuster, 1978), 443.

28. U.S. Senate Select Committee, *Final Reports*, Book I, *Foreign and Military Intelligence*, 16, 445.

29. Ibid., Book II, *Intelligence Activities and the Rights of Americans*, 6.

30. Ibid., 427.

31. Ibid., 448. In contrast, the Pike committee only recommended congressional notification within forty-eight hours after the president approved the operations. See Chapter 7 for a discussion of the Pike committee recommendations.

32. Johnson, *Season of Inquiry*, 211.

33. Ibid., 227.

34. Cartoon in *Washington Post*, 28 April 1976, A12.

35. Walter Pincus, "Plan for Hill Intelligence Unit Assailed," *Washington Post*, 1 April 1976, A2.

36. For the debates, see U.S. Senate, *Congressional Record* (12, 13, 17–19 May 1976), 94th Cong., 2d sess., 122, pt. 11:13678–95, 13973–14002, pt. 12:14149–73, 14259–66, 14643–79.

37. Johnson, *Season of Inquiry*, 227–49, gives a detailed discussion of the parliamentary maneuvering for the oversight bill.

38. Frank J. Smist, Jr., *Congress Oversees the United States Intelligence Community, 1947–1989* (Knoxville: University of Tennessee Press, 1990), 214–15.

39. Pike, Ron Dellums, Robert Giaimo, and James Stanton were the Pike committee Democrats who voted against the bill. Conservative Republicans Robert McClory, David Treen, and Robert Kasten also voted against it because the membership was weighted against Republicans. Les Aspin, William Lehman, Dale Milford, and Morgan Murphy voted for the bill. For the debate, see U.S. House, *Congressional Record* (14 July 1977), 95th Cong., 1st sess., 123, pt. 18:22932–49. Harrington's quote appears on p. 22946.

40. J. Leiper Freeman, "Investigating the Executive Intelligence: The Fate of the Pike Committee," *Capitol Studies* 5 (Fall 1977): 116.

41. Strong defenders of the CIA are particularly bitter about Vice President Mondale's efforts to place restrictions on the intelligence agencies. See Barry Goldwater with Jack Casserly, *Goldwater* (New York: Doubleday, 1988), 298, and Ray Cline, *The CIA under Reagan, Bush, and Casey* (Washington, D.C.: Acropolis Books, 1981), 269–73.

42. For a critical analysis of Reagan's executive order on intelligence, see Stansfield Turner and George Thibault, "Intelligence: The Right Rules," *Foreign Policy* 48 (Fall 1982): 122–38.

43. The independent counsel investigating the Iran-contra scandal did not try to determine Casey's guilt or innocence since the CIA director died before he could answer the counsel's questions. However, Lawrence Walsh did state in his final report that Casey "played a role as a Cabinet-level advocate both in setting up the covert network to resupply the contras during the Boland funding cut-off, and in promoting the secret arms sales to Iran in 1985 and 1986." Although Casey tried to insulate himself and the CIA from any illegal activities, the report states, "there is evidence that he was involved in at least some of those [illegal] activities and may

have attempted to keep them concealed from Congress." Lawrence E. Walsh, *Iran-Contra: The Final Report* (New York: Times Books, 1994), 201.

44. Telephone interview, F. A. O. Schwarz, Jr., 25 August 1992.

45. W. Mark Felt and Edward Miller were convicted in November 1980. Another case against former acting director L. Patrick Gray was dropped by the prosecutors due to lack of evidence.

46. William Greider, *Who Will Tell the People?: The Betrayal of American Democracy* (New York: Simon and Schuster, 1992), 366; Ross Gelbspan, *Break-ins, Death Threats, and the FBI: The Covert War against the Central America Movement* (Boston: South End Press, 1991). See also U.S. House Committee on the Judiciary, *Break-ins at Sanctuary Churches and Organizations Opposed to Administration Policy in Central America*, 100th Cong., 1st sess., 19, 20 February 1987, and U.S. Senate Select Committee on Intelligence, *The FBI and CISPES*, 101st Cong., 1st sess., July 1989.

47. Johnson, *Season of Inquiry*, 265.

48. Smist, *Congress Oversees the United States Intelligence Community*, 275.

49. Bob Brauer, legislative assistant to Dellums during the Pike investigation as well as at the present time, says that he and Dellums believe that congressional oversight is now much better than it was before 1975. Telephone interview, Robert Brauer, 31 July 1992. Dellums's appointment to the permanent intelligence committee caused some controversy because of his leftist views. See Joshua Muravchik, "Dellums's Dilemma," *New Republic*, 11 March 1991, 14–16, and William F. Buckley, Jr., "To Look after Our Intelligence," *National Review*, 18 March 1991, 70. Dellums was appointed by Speaker Thomas Foley, who had served on the Ethics Committee during its inquiry into the Pike report leak. According to Brauer, Foley had been impressed by Dellums's work on the Pike committee. In 1993, Dellums gave up his intelligence committee assignment to become chairman of the House Armed Services Committee.

50. Interview, Michael Harrington, 10 July 1992.

51. Telephone interview, Philip W. Buchen, 16 June 1992.

52. Interview, Richard Helms, 23 March 1992.

53. John Prados, *Presidents' Secret Wars: CIA and Pentagon Covert Operations since World War II* (New York: William Morrow and Company, 1986), 412. See also Theodore Draper, *A Very Thin Line: The Iran-Contra Affairs* (New York: Hill and Wang, 1991), 596; Michael J. Glennon, *Constitutional Diplomacy* (Princeton: Princeton University Press, 1990), 296–303; John Ranelagh, *The Agency: The Rise and Decline of the CIA* (London: Weidenfeld and Nicolson, 1986), 598; and Anne Karalekas, "Intelligence Oversight: Has Anything Changed?," *Washington Quarterly* 6 (Summer 1982): 22–30.

54. Interview, Seymour Hersh, 23 March 1992. See Hersh, "Congress Is Accused of Laxity on CIA's Covert Activity," *New York Times*, 1 June 1978, A2, for Hersh's reporting on the weaknesses of congressional oversight two years after the investigations.

55. Lardner, "The Intelligence Investigations," 13–17; George Lardner, Jr., "The Case of the Missing Intelligence Charters," *The Nation*, 2 September 1978, 168–71.

56. Lardner, "The Case of the Missing Intelligence Charters," 171. For another

journalist's view of how the CIA emerged "the winner," see Taylor Branch, "The Trial of the CIA," *New York Times Magazine*, 12 September 1976, 35.

57. Interview, Charles Mathias, 23 March 1992.

58. U.S. Congress, *Report of the Congressional Committees Investigating the Iran-Contra Affair*, 100th Cong., 1st sess., 13 November 1987, 423.

59. Telephone interview, F. A. O. Schwarz, Jr., 25 August 1992. For Schwarz's views on the connections between the Church committee and Iran-contra, see his op-ed piece, "Recalling Major Lessons of the Church Committee," *New York Times*, 30 July 1987, 25.

60. President Reagan approved a "mental finding" and a retroactive finding and directed the CIA not to tell Congress about them. See Draper, *A Very Thin Line*, 203–63.

61. Harold Hongju Koh, *The National Security Constitution* (New Haven: Yale University Press, 1990), 3. Michael Schudson gives a different twist to the same argument in *Watergate in American Memory* (New York: Basic Books, 1992), 174–84. He agrees that Iran-contra was not an aberration but contends that the Iran-contra investigations were not unsuccessful because they significantly damaged the Reagan administration.

62. On the House intelligence committee's response to charges that Oliver North was violating the Boland amendment, see Draper, *A Very Thin Line*, 343–46. "Oversight was the right designation for the committee in more than one sense," Draper concludes.

63. Leslie Gelb, "Overseeing of CIA by Congress Has Produced Decade of Support," *New York Times*, 7 July 1986, A1.

64. I. F. Stone, "The Schorr Case: The Real Dangers," *New York Review of Books*, 1 April 1976, 10.

65. Rhodri Jeffreys-Jones, *The CIA and American Democracy* (New Haven: Yale University Press, 1989), 195.

66. Interview, William Colby, 30 March 1992. Stansfield Turner, President Carter's director of central intelligence, is also a strong proponent of the view that oversight helps the CIA make more judicious decisions while improving its public image. See Turner's book, *Secrecy and Democracy: The CIA in Transition* (Boston: Houghton Mifflin, 1985).

67. Quoted in Glennon, *Constitutional Diplomacy*, 309.

68. Colby, *Honorable Men*, 19.

69. Nicholas Horrock, "The Meaning of Congressional Intelligence Inquiries," *New York Times*, 30 April 1976, A20.

70. Schudson, *Watergate in American Memory*, chap. 6.

71. Tom Wicker, *On Press* (New York: Viking Press, 1978), 240.

72. See, for example, Max Kampelman, "The Power of the Press: A Problem for Our Democracy," *Policy Review* 6 (Fall 1978): 7–39; Irving Kristol, "Is the Press Misusing Its Growing Power?," *MORE*, January 1975, 28, 26; and Joseph Kraft, "The Imperial Media," *Commentary* 71 (May 1981): 36–47.

73. John Hohenberg, *A Crisis for the American Press* (New York: Columbia University Press, 1978), 287.

74. John B. Oakes, "Confidence in the Press," *New York Times*, 5 May 1976, 41.

75. Wicker, *On Press*, 260.

76. Daniel Hallin, "The Media, the War in Vietnam, and Political Support: A Critique of the Thesis of an Oppositional Media," *Journal of Politics* 46 (February 1984): 2–24, and *The "Uncensored War": The Media and Vietnam* (New York: Oxford University Press, 1986).

77. Ben Bagdikian, "The Fruits of Agnewism," *Columbia Journalism Review*, January/February 1973, 9–21.

78. Anthony Lewis, "Farce or Tragedy," *New York Times*, 2 February 1976, 23.

79. Harry Howe Ransom, "Congress and Reform of the CIA," *Policy Studies Journal* 5 (Summer 1977): 479.

80. Garry Wills, "Controlling the Rogue Presidency," *Washington Post*, 25 January 1976, F1.

81. Michael Schudson discusses the implications of the omission of the Cambodia article in *Watergate in American Memory*, 49–50.

82. Aaron Wildavsky, ed., *The Presidency* (Boston: Little, Brown, 1969), 230–43; Draper, *A Very Thin Line*, 580–98. For debates on Wildavsky's thesis, see Steven A. Shull, ed., *The Two Presidencies: A Quarter Century Assessment* (Chicago: Nelson-Hall, 1991).

83. Mary McGrory, "Sen. Church's Topic: The Nation's Soul," *Washington Star*, 1 December 1975.

84. Anthony Downs, "Up and Down with Ecology: The 'Issue-Attention' Cycle," *Public Interest* 28 (Summer 1972): 38.

85. Nicholas Horrock, "Intelligence Inquiries in Capitol Focus on Legitimacy of Covert Espionage," *New York Times*, 18 May 1975, 42.

86. "Jack Anderson Lives," *Washington Post*, 22 October 1975, A22.

87. Meg Greenfield, "No Matter How You Slice It," *Newsweek*, 8 December 1975, 108.

88. Thomas Powers, *The Man Who Kept the Secrets: Richard Helms and the CIA* (New York: Alfred A. Knopf, 1979), 6.

89. Schudson, *Watergate in American Memory*, 160.

90. Russell Baker, "Our Uncle Is Now Dorian Sam," *New York Times*, 1 October 1974, 41.

91. Interview, Richard Helms, 23 March 1992.

92. *Dayton Daily News*, 23 November 1975, in *Editorials on File 1975* (New York: Facts on File, 1975), 52. See also Anthony Lewis, "The Honorable, Murderous Gentlemen of a Secret World," *New York Times*, 23 November 1975, sect. 4, p. 1, and "Not a Nut or a Bolt," *New York Times*, 24 November 1975, 35.

93. Paul Λ. Francis, letter to the editor, *Washington Post*, 6 February 1976, A18.

94. Rod MacLeish, "Intelligence and Democracy," *Washington Post*, 2 February 1976, A17.

95. Paul M. Sniderman, W. Russell Neuman, Jack Citrin, Herbert McCloskey, and J. Merrill Shanks, "Stability of Support for the Political System: The Initial Impact of Watergate," *American Politics Quarterly* 3 (October 1975): 437–57; Arthur R. Miller, Edie N. Goldenberg, and Lutz Erbring, "Type-Set Politics: Impact of Newspapers on Public Confidence," *American Political Science Review* 73 (March 1979): 67–84.

96. Letter, E. I. Watson to Gerald Ford, 5 January 1975, folder "FG 6-2 1/1/75–12/31/75," box 20, White House Central Files Subject File, GRFL.

Epilogue

1. LeRoy Ashby and Rod Gramer, *Fighting the Odds: The Life of Senator Frank Church* (Pullman: Washington State University Press, 1994), 487.

2. Letter, Burns W. Roper to Frank Church, 2 July 1976, ser. 5.5, box 8, folder 9, Frank Church Collection, BSUL. Church actually came in second to California governor Jerry Brown in Roper's poll, but Roper assured Church that "Carter has made it pretty clear that he is not about to pick Brown." Mondale tied for eleventh place in the poll.

3. F. Forrester Church, *Father and Son: A Personal Biography of Senator Frank Church of Idaho* (New York: Harper and Row, 1985), 120–23. Church's former legislative assistant, Loch Johnson, believes that the senator's reputation as a somewhat sanctimonious loner was more likely the deciding factor. Church's colleagues on Capitol Hill told Carter's "talent scouts" that Church was not a team player, whereas Mondale was easygoing and popular. Loch Johnson, *A Season of Inquiry: Congress and Intelligence* (Chicago: Dorsey Press, 1988), 251.

4. Campaign brochure, National Conservative Political Action Committee, "Frank Church's Record of Shame," ser. 5.5, box 2, folder 1, Frank Church Collection, BSUL.

5. Newsletter, "The ABC [Anybody But Church] Informant," April 1979, Carl Burke Papers, box 2, folder 71, Frank Church Collection, BSUL.

6. For the attacks on Schorr, see Merrill Panitt, "First Amendment: No License to Steal," *TV Guide*, 16 October 1976, A5–6, and Henry Fairlie, "The Harlot's Prerogative, Continued: Profit without Honor," *New Republic*, 7 May 1977, 16–19. For Schorr's response, see Daniel Schorr, "Daniel Schorr Strikes Back," *MORE*, September 1977, 46–48.

7. Joseph C. Goulden, *Fit to Print: A. M. Rosenthal and His Times* (Secaucus, N.J.: Lyle Stuart, 1988), 192.

8. Ibid., 298. Hersh did complete the biography. See Seymour Hersh, *The Price of Power: Kissinger in the Nixon White House* (New York: Summit Books, 1983).

9. Michael O'Neil quoted in James Aronson, *The Press and the Cold War* (New York: Monthly Review Press, 1990), 312.

10. James Boylan, "Declarations of Independence," *Columbia Journalism Review*, November/December 1986, 44.

Selected Bibliography

Manuscript Sources

Ann Arbor, Michigan
  Gerald R. Ford Library
    Philip W. Buchen Files
    James M. Cannon Papers
    Richard B. Cheney Files
    Leo Cherne Papers
    James E. Connor Files
    Dorothy E. Downton Files
    Gerald Ford Congressional Papers
    Jay T. French Files
    Max L. Friedersdorf Files
    David R. Gergen Files
    Robert T. Hartmann Files
    Edward Hutchinson Papers
    Jerry H. Jones Files
    William T. Kendall Files
    Vernon C. Loen and Charles Leppert Files
    John O. Marsh Files
    Ron Nessen Papers
    Patrick E. O'Donnell and Joseph S. Jenckes Files
    President Ford Committee Campaign Records
    Presidential Handwriting File
    Michael Raoul-Duval Papers
    A. James Reichley Interview Transcripts
    Edward J. Savage Files
    Edward C. Schmults Files
    Brent Scowcroft Files
    White House Central Files Subject File
    Robert K. Wolthuis Files
Boise, Idaho
  Boise State University Library
    Frank Church Collection
Washington, D.C.
  Library of Congress
    Ray Cline Collection
    David Atlee Phillips Papers

Videotape Collection

CBS Evening News. October 1974–May 1976. Television News Archive, Vanderbilt University, Nashville, Tennessee.

Interviews

All interviews were conducted by the author.

Congressional Investigators

Senator Howard Baker (member, Church committee), Washington, D.C., 27 March 1992.

Jack Boos (chief investigator, Nedzi and Pike committees), telephone, 20 August 1992.

Robert Brauer (legislative assistant to member, Nedzi and Pike committees), telephone, 31 July 1992.

Aaron Donner (chief counsel, Pike committee), telephone, 5 September 1992.

A. Searle Field (chief of staff, Nedzi and Pike committees), telephone, 17 July 1992.

The Honorable Robert Giaimo (member, Nedzi and Pike committees), telephone, 9 March 1992.

The Honorable Michael Harrington (member, Nedzi committee), Salem, Massachusetts, 10 July 1992.

The Honorable James P. Johnson (member, Pike committee), telephone, 20 August 1992.

Doris McClory (widow of Robert McClory, ranking minority member, Nedzi and Pike committees), Washington, D.C., 28 March 1992.

Senator Charles Mathias (member, Church committee), Washington, D.C., 23 March 1992.

The Honorable Lucien Nedzi (chairman, Nedzi committee), Washington, D.C., 26 March 1992.

The Honorable Otis Pike (chairman, Pike committee), telephone, 15 June 1992.

Greg Rushford (staff member, Pike committee), Washington, D.C., 30 March 1992.

F. A. O. Schwarz, Jr. (chief counsel, Church committee), telephone, 25 August 1992.

Executive Branch Officials

Philip W. Buchen (counsel to the president), telephone, 16 June 1992.

William Colby (director, Central Intelligence Agency), Washington, D.C., 30 March 1992.

President Gerald R. Ford, telephone, 4 April 1994.

Richard Helms (director, Central Intelligence Agency), Washington, D.C., 23 March 1992.

Roderick Hills (deputy counsel to the president), Washington, D.C., 27 March 1992.

Jack Marsh (counsel to the president), Washington, D.C., 27 March 1992.

Michael Raoul-Duval (executive director, White House Intelligence Coordinating Group), telephone, 29 August 1994.

Mitchell Rogovin (special counsel, Central Intelligence Agency), Washington, D.C., 24 March 1992.

James Wilderotter (associate counsel to the president), telephone, 28 March 1992.

Journalists

Ben Bradlee (editor, *Washington Post*), Washington, D.C., 30 March 1992.

Seymour Hersh (reporter, *New York Times*), Washington, D.C., 23 March 1992.

George Lardner, Jr. (reporter, *Washington Post*), Washington, D.C., 24 March 1992.
Daniel Schorr (correspondent, CBS News), telephone, 30 March 1992.

Government Documents

Hearings

U.S. House Committee on Standards of Official Conduct. *Investigation of Publication of Select Committee on Intelligence Report.* 94th Cong., 2d sess., 1976.

U.S. House Select Committee on Intelligence. *U.S. Intelligence Agencies and Activities.* 94th Cong., 1st sess., 1975, 2d sess., 1976 (6 parts). *Intelligence Costs and Fiscal Procedures* (part 1); *The Performance of the Intelligence Community* (part 2); *Domestic Intelligence Programs* (part 3); *Committee Proceedings* (part 4); *Risks and Control of Foreign Intelligence* (part 5); *Committee Proceedings, II* (part 6).

U.S. Senate Select Committee to Study Governmental Operations with Respect to Intelligence Activities. *Intelligence Activities: Senate Resolution 21.* 94th Cong., 1st sess., 1975 (7 vols.). *Unauthorized Storage of Toxic Agents* (vol. 1); *Huston Plan* (vol. 2); *Internal Revenue Service* (vol. 3); *Mail Opening* (vol. 4); *The National Security Agency and Fourth Amendment Rights* (vol. 5); *Federal Bureau of Investigation* (vol. 6); *Covert Action* (vol. 7).

Interim and Final Reports

Commission on CIA Activities within the United States. *Report to the President by the Commission on CIA Activities within the United States.* Washington, D.C.: Government Printing Office, 1975.

U.S. House Committee on Standards of Official Conduct. *Report on Investigation Concerning Unauthorized Publication of the Report of the Select Committee on Intelligence.* 94th Cong., 2d sess., 1 October 1976.

U.S. House Select Committee on Intelligence. *CIA: The Pike Report.* Nottingham: Spokesman Books, 1977.

U.S. Senate Select Committee to Study Governmental Operations with Respect to Intelligence Activities. *Alleged Assassination Plots Involving Foreign Leaders.* 94th Cong., 1st sess., 20 November 1975. Washington, D.C.: Government Printing Office, 1975. Reprint, New York: Norton, 1976.

——. *Covert Action in Chile, 1963–1973.* 94th Cong., 1st sess., 18 December 1975.

——. *Final Reports.* 94th Cong., 2d sess., 1976 (6 books). *Foreign and Military Intelligence* (Book I); *Intelligence Activities and the Rights of Americans* (Book II); *Supplementary Detailed Staff Reports on Intelligence Activities and the Rights of Americans* (Book III); *Supplementary Detailed Staff Reports on Foreign and Military Intelligence* (Book IV); *The Investigation of the Assassination of President John F. Kennedy: Performance of the Intelligence Agencies* (Book V); *Supplementary Reports on Intelligence Activities* (Book VI).

Newspapers and Periodicals (December 1974–May 1976)

Columbia Journalism Review
Newsweek

New York Times
Time
Washington Post

Books and Articles

Agee, Philip. *Inside the Company: CIA Diary*. New York: Stonehill Publishing Company, 1975.

Anderson, Douglas A. *A "Washington Merry-Go-Round" of Libel Actions*. Chicago: Nelson-Hall, 1980.

Anderson, Jack, with James Boyd. *Confessions of a Muckraker*. New York: Random House, 1979.

Aronson, James. *The Press and the Cold War*. New York: Monthly Review Press, 1990.

Ashby, LeRoy. "Frank Church Goes to the Senate." *Pacific Northwest Quarterly* 78 (January–April 1987): 17–31.

Ashby, LeRoy, and Rod Gramer. *Fighting the Odds: The Life of Senator Frank Church*. Pullman: Washington State University Press, 1994.

Bagdikian, Ben. *The Media Monopoly*. Boston: Beacon Press, 1987.

Bamford, James. *The Puzzle Palace*. Boston: Houghton Mifflin, 1982.

Barnouw, Erik. *Tube of Plenty: The Evolution of American Television*. New York: Oxford University Press, 1975.

Belin, David. *Final Disclosure: The Full Truth about the Assassination of President Kennedy*. New York: Charles Scribner's Sons, 1988.

Berman, Jerry J., and Morton H. Halperin. "The Fight over Oversight." *New Republic*, 8 May 1976, 11–14.

Bernstein, Barton J. "The Road to Watergate and Beyond: The Growth and Abuse of Executive Authority since 1940." *Law and Contemporary Problems* 40 (Spring 1976): 58–86.

Bernstein, Carl. "The CIA and the Media." *Rolling Stone*, 20 October 1977, 55–67.

Black, Jay, Bob Steele, and Ralph Barney. *Doing Ethics in Journalism: A Handbook with Case Studies*. Greencastle, Ind.: Sigma Delta Chi and the Society of Professional Journalists, 1992.

Braden, Tom. "What's Wrong with the CIA?" *Saturday Review*, 5 April 1975, 14–18.

Branch, Taylor. "The Trial of the CIA." *New York Times Magazine*, 12 September 1976, 35, 115–26.

Branch, Taylor, and George Crile III. "The Kennedy Vendetta." *Harper's*, August 1975, 49–63.

Bray, Howard. *The Pillars of the Post*. New York: Norton, 1980.

Cawelti, John G., and Bruce A. Rosenberg. *The Spy Story*. Chicago: University of Chicago Press, 1987.

Church, F. Forrester. *Father and Son: A Personal Biography of Senator Frank Church of Idaho*. New York: Harper and Row, 1985.

Cline, Ray. *The CIA under Reagan, Bush, and Casey*. Washington, D.C.: Acropolis Books, 1981.

Cohen, Jacob. "Conspiracy Fever." *Commentary* 60 (October 1975): 33–42.

Colby, William, with Peter Forbath. *Honorable Men: My Life in the CIA*. New York: Simon and Schuster, 1978.

Cook, Fred J. *The FBI Nobody Knows*. New York: Macmillan, 1964.

Cornwell, Elmer E., Jr. *Presidential Leadership of Public Opinion*. Bloomington: Indiana University Press, 1965.

Corson, William R. *Armies of Ignorance: The Rise of the American Intelligence Establishment*. New York: Dial Press/James Wade, 1977.

Crabb, Cecil V., Jr., and Pat M. Holt. *Invitation to Struggle: Congress, the President, and Foreign Policy*. Washington, D.C.: Congressional Quarterly Press, 1989.

Davis, Deborah. *Katharine the Great: Katharine Graham and the Washington Post*. New York: Harcourt Brace Jovanovich, 1979.

Diamond, Edwin. *Behind the Times: Inside the "New" New York Times*. New York: Villard Books, 1993.

Donner, Frank. *The Age of Surveillance*. New York: Alfred A. Knopf, 1980.

Dorman, William A., and Mansour Fahrang. *The U.S. Press and Iran: Foreign Policy and the Journalism of Deference*. Berkeley: University of California Press, 1987.

Downie, Leonard, Jr. *The New Muckrakers*. Washington, D.C.: New Republic Book Company, 1976.

Downs, Anthony. "Up and Down with Ecology: The 'Issue-Attention' Cycle." *Public Interest* 28 (Summer 1972): 38–50.

Draper, Theodore. *A Very Thin Line: The Iran-Contra Affairs*. New York: Hill and Wang, 1991.

Editorials on File 1975. New York: Facts on File, 1975.

Elliff, John T. "Congress and the Intelligence Community." In *Congress Reconsidered*, edited by Laurence C. Dodd and Bruce I. Oppenheimer, 193–206. New York: Praeger, 1977.

Entman, Robert. "The Imperial Media." In *Politics and the Oval Office: Towards Presidential Governance*, edited by Arnold J. Meltsner, 79–101. San Francisco: Institute for Contemporary Studies, 1981.

Epstein, Edward Jay. *News from Nowhere*. New York: Random House, 1973.

Eszterhas, Joe. "The Toughest Reporter in America." *Rolling Stone*, 10 April 1975, 48–52, 73–81; 24 April 1975, 45–47, 62–72.

Fallaci, Oriana. "Otis Pike and the CIA." *New Republic*, 3 April 1976, 8–12.

Felsenthal, Carol. *Power, Privilege, and the Post: The Katharine Graham Story*. New York: G. P. Putnam's Sons, 1993.

Ford, Gerald R. *A Time to Heal*. New York: Harper and Row, 1979.

Franck, Thomas M., and Edward Weisband. *Foreign Policy by Congress*. New York: Oxford University Press, 1979.

Franck, Thomas M., ed. *The Tethered Presidency: Congressional Restraints on Executive Power*. New York: New York University Press, 1981.

Freeman, J. Leiper. "Investigating the Executive Intelligence: The Fate of the Pike Committee." *Capitol Studies* 5 (Fall 1977): 103–18.

Fulbright, J. William. "Fulbright on the Press." *Columbia Journalism Review*, November/December 1975, 39–45.

Furlong, William Barry. "Dan ('Killer') Schorr, the Great Abrasive." *New York Magazine*, 16 June 1975, 41–44.

Gallup, George. *The Gallup Poll: Public Opinion, 1935–1971*. Vol. 3. New York: Random House, 1972.

——. *The Gallup Poll: Public Opinion, 1972–1977*. Vol. 1. Wilmington, Del.: Scholarly Resources, 1978.

Galnoor, Itzhak, ed. *Government Secrecy in Democracies*. New York: New York University Press, 1977.

Garment, Suzanne. *Scandal: The Culture of Mistrust in American Politics*. New York: Times Books, 1991.

Garrow, David. *The FBI and Martin Luther King, Jr.* New York: Penguin Books, 1981.

Gelb, Leslie. "The CIA and the Press." *New Republic*, 22 March 1975, 13–16.

Gelbspan, Ross. *Break-ins, Death Threats, and the FBI: The Covert War against the Central America Movement*. Boston: South End Press, 1991.

Gentry, Curt. *J. Edgar Hoover: The Man and the Secrets*. New York: Norton, 1991.

Glennon, Michael J. *Constitutional Diplomacy*. Princeton: Princeton University Press, 1990.

Goldwater, Barry. *Goldwater*. New York: Doubleday, 1988.

Goulden, Joseph C. *Fit to Print: A. M. Rosenthal and His Times*. Secaucus, N.J.: Lyle Stuart, 1988.

Graber, Doris A. *Mass Media and American Politics*. Washington, D.C.: Congressional Quarterly Press, 1980.

Grady, James. *Six Days of the Condor*. New York: Norton, 1974.

Graham, Katharine. "The Press after Watergate: Getting Down to New Business." *New York Magazine*, 4 November 1974, 69–72.

Greene, John Robert. *The Limits of Power: The Nixon and Ford Administrations*. Bloomington: Indiana University Press, 1992.

Greider, William. "Aftergate." *Esquire*, September 1975, 99–102, 133–34.

——. *Who Will Tell the People?: The Betrayal of American Democracy*. New York: Simon and Schuster, 1992.

Grossman, Michael Baruch, and Martha Joynt Kumar. *Portraying the President: The White House and the News Media*. Baltimore: Johns Hopkins University Press, 1981.

Halberstam, David. *The Powers That Be*. New York: Alfred A. Knopf, 1979.

Hallin, Daniel. "The Media, the War in Vietnam, and Political Support: A Critique of the Thesis of an Oppositional Media." *Journal of Politics* 46 (February 1984): 2–24.

——. *The "Uncensored War": The Media and Vietnam*. New York: Oxford University Press, 1986.

Halperin, Morton H. "Led Astray by the CIA." *New Republic*, 28 June 1975, 8–16.

Halperin, Morton H., Jerry J. Berman, Robert L. Borosage, and Christine M. Marwick. *The Lawless State: The Crimes of the U.S. Intelligence Agencies*. New York: Penguin, 1981.

Harrington, Michael. "Congress's CIA Cover-Up: Getting Out the Truth." *New Republic*, 26 July 1975, 14–17.

Harris, Louis. *The Harris Survey Yearbook of Public Opinion, 1973*. New York: Louis Harris and Associates, 1976.

Hart, Gary. *The Good Fight: The Education of an American Reformer*. New York: Random House, 1993.

Hartmann, Robert. *Palace Politics*. New York: McGraw-Hill, 1980.

Herman, Edward S., and Noam Chomsky. *Manufacturing Consent: The Political Economy of the Mass Media*. New York: Pantheon, 1988.

Hersh, Seymour. *The Price of Power: Kissinger in the Nixon White House*. New York: Summit Books, 1983.

———. *The Reporter's Obligation: An Address*. Tucson: University of Arizona Press, 1975.

Hertsgaard, Mark. *On Bended Knee: The Press and the Reagan Presidency*. New York: Farrar Straus Giroux, 1988.

Hess, Stephen. *The Washington Reporters*. Washington, D.C.: Brookings Institution, 1981.

Hinckle, Warren, and William Turner. *The Fish Is Red: The Story of the Secret War against Castro*. New York: Harper and Row, 1981.

Hodgson, Godfrey. *America in Our Time*. New York: Vintage Books, 1978.

Hohenberg, John. *A Crisis for the American Press*. New York: Columbia University Press, 1978.

Hougan, Jim. *Secret Agenda: Watergate, Deep Throat, and the CIA*. New York: Random House, 1984.

Huntington, Samuel P. *American Politics: The Promise of Disharmony*. Cambridge: Harvard University Press, 1981.

———. "The Democratic Distemper." *Public Interest* 41 (Fall 1975): 9–38.

Ignatius, David. "Dan Schorr: The Secret Sharer." *Washington Monthly*, April 1976, 6–20.

Immerman, Richard H. *The CIA in Guatemala: The Foreign Policy of Intervention*. Austin: University of Texas Press, 1982.

Isaacson, Walter. *Kissinger: A Biography*. New York: Simon and Schuster, 1992.

Jeffreys-Jones, Rhodri. *American Espionage: From Secret Service to CIA*. New York: Free Press, 1977.

———. *The CIA and American Democracy*. New Haven: Yale University Press, 1989.

Johnson, Loch. *America's Secret Power: The CIA in a Democratic Society*. New York: Oxford University Press, 1989.

———. *A Season of Inquiry: Congress and Intelligence*. Chicago: Dorsey Press, 1988.

———. "The U.S. Congress and the CIA: Monitoring the Dark Side of Government." *Legislative Studies Quarterly* 5 (November 1980): 477–99.

Jones, Gordon S., and John A. Marini, eds. *The Imperial Congress: Crisis in the Separation of Powers*. New York: Pharos Books, 1988.

Kampelman, Max. "The Power of the Press: A Problem for Our Democracy." *Policy Review* 6 (Fall 1978): 7–39.

Karalekas, Anne. "Intelligence Oversight: Has Anything Changed?" *Washington Quarterly* 6 (Summer 1982): 22–30.

Keller, William W. *The Liberals and J. Edgar Hoover*. Princeton: Princeton University Press, 1989.

Koh, Harold Hongju. *The National Security Constitution*. New Haven: Yale University Press, 1990.

Kondracke, Morton. "The CIA and 'Our Conspiracy.' " *MORE*, May 1975, 10–12.

Kraft, Joseph. "The Imperial Media." *Commentary* 71 (May 1981): 36–47.

Kristol, Irving. "Is the Press Misusing Its Growing Power?" *MORE*, January 1975, 28, 26.

Kutler, Stanley. *The Wars of Watergate*. New York: Alfred A. Knopf, 1990.

Kuttner, Bob. "Look before You Leak." *MORE*, March 1976, 6–7.

Kwitny, Jonathan. *Endless Enemies: The Making of an Unfriendly World*. New York: Congdon and Weed, 1984.

Lang, Gladys Engel, and Kurt Lang. *The Battle for Public Opinion: The President, the Press, and the Polls during Watergate*. New York: Columbia University Press, 1983.

Langman, Larry, and David Ebner. *Encyclopedia of American Spy Films*. New York: Garland Publishing, 1990.

Lardner, George, Jr. "The Case of the Missing Intelligence Charters." *The Nation*, 2 September 1978, 168–71.

———. "The Intelligence Investigations: Congress Cops Out." *The Progressive*, July 1976, 13–17.

Lefever, Ernest W., and Roy Godson. *The CIA and the American Ethic: An Unfinished Debate*. Washington, D.C.: Ethics and Public Policy Center of Georgetown University, 1979.

Leffler, Melvyn P. *A Preponderance of Power: National Security, the Truman Administration, and the Cold War*. Stanford: Stanford University Press, 1992.

Lipset, Seymour Martin, and William Schneider. *The Confidence Gap: Business, Labor, and Government in the Public Mind*. Baltimore: Johns Hopkins University Press, 1987.

Loory, Stuart. "The CIA's 'Man in the White House.' " *Columbia Journalism Review*, September/October 1975, 11–14.

———. "The CIA's Use of the Press: A 'Mighty Wurlitzer.' " *Columbia Journalism Review*, September/October 1974, 9–18.

Mangold, Tom. *Cold Warrior: James Jesus Angleton, the CIA's Master Spy Hunter*. New York: Simon and Schuster, 1991.

Marchetti, Victor, and John Marks. *The CIA and the Cult of Intelligence*. New York: Alfred A. Knopf, 1974.

Marks, John. "How to Spot a Spook." *Washington Monthly*, November 1974, 5–11.

———. *The Search for the Manchurian Candidate: The CIA and Mind Control*. New York: Times Books, 1979.

Mayhew, David R. *Divided We Govern: Party Control, Lawmaking, and Investigations, 1946–1990*. New Haven: Yale University Press, 1991.

Miller, Arthur R., Edie N. Goldenberg, and Lutz Erbring. "Type-Set Politics: Impact of Newspapers on Public Confidence." *American Political Science Review* 73 (March 1979): 67–84.

Moynihan, Daniel Patrick. "The Presidency and the Press." *Commentary* 51 (March 1971): 41–52.

Nessen, Ron. *It Sure Looks Different from the Inside*. Chicago: Playboy Press, 1978.

Ogul, Morris. *Congress Oversees the Bureaucracy*. Pittsburgh: University of Pittsburgh Press, 1976.

Osborne, John. *White House Watch: The Ford Years*. Washington, D.C.: New Republic Books, 1977.

Oseth, John M. *Regulating U.S. Intelligence Operations*. Lexington: University Press of Kentucky, 1985.

Paletz, David L., and Robert M. Entman. *Media Power Politics*. New York: Free Press, 1981.

Paterson, Thomas G. *Meeting the Communist Threat: Truman to Reagan*. New York: Oxford University Press, 1988.

Persico, Joseph. *Casey: From the OSS to the CIA*. New York: Viking Press, 1990.

Phillips, David Atlee. *The Night Watch*. New York: Atheneum, 1977.

Pincus, Walter. "Covering Intelligence." *New Republic*, 1 February 1975, 10–12.

Pollard, James E. *The Presidents and the Press*. New York: Macmillan, 1947.

Powers, Richard Gid. *G-Men: Hoover's FBI in American Popular Culture*. Carbondale: Southern Illinois University Press, 1983.

———. *Secrecy and Power: The Life of J. Edgar Hoover*. New York: Free Press, 1987.

Powers, Thomas. *The Man Who Kept the Secrets: Richard Helms and the CIA*. New York: Alfred A. Knopf, 1979.

Prados, John. *Presidents' Secret Wars: CIA and Pentagon Covert Operations since World War II*. New York: William Morrow and Company, 1986.

Ranelagh, John. *The Agency: The Rise and Decline of the CIA*. London: Weidenfeld and Nicolson, 1986.

Ransom, Harry Howe. "Congress and Reform of the CIA." *Policy Studies Journal* 5 (Summer 1977): 476–80.

———. "Congress and the Intelligence Agencies." In *Congress against the President*, edited by Harvey C. Mansfield, 153–66. New York: Praeger, 1975.

———. *The Intelligence Establishment*. Cambridge: Harvard University Press, 1970.

———. "The Politicization of Intelligence." In *Intelligence and Intelligence Policy in a Democratic Society*, edited by Stephen J. Cimbala, 25–46. Dobbs Ferry, N.Y.: Transnational, 1987.

———. "Secret Intelligence Agencies and Congress." *Society* 12 (March/April 1975): 33–38.

———. "The Uses (and Abuses) of Secret Power." *Worldview*, May 1975, 11–15.

Reston, James. *The Artillery of the Press: Its Influence on American Foreign Policy*. New York: Harper and Row, 1967.

Roberts, Chalmers. *In the Shadow of Power: The Story of the Washington Post*. Cabin John, Md.: Seven Locks Press, 1989.

Rubenstein, Leonard. *The Great Spy Films*. Secaucus, N.J.: Citadel Press, 1979.

Rushford, Gregory. "Making Enemies: The Pike Committee's Struggle to Get the Facts." *Washington Monthly*, July/August 1976, 42–52.

Sabato, Larry J. *Feeding Frenzy: How Attack Journalism Has Transformed American Politics*. New York: Free Press, 1991.

Salisbury, Harrison E. *Without Fear or Favor: The New York Times and Its Times*. New York: Times Books, 1980.

Schlesinger, Arthur M., Jr. *The Imperial Presidency*. Boston: Houghton Mifflin, 1973.

Schorr, Daniel. *Clearing the Air*. Boston: Houghton Mifflin, 1977.

———. "The FBI and Me." *Columbia Journalism Review*, November/December 1974, 8–14.

———. "My 17 Months on the CIA Watch." *Rolling Stone*, 8 April 1976, 32–38, 80–98.

Schudson, Michael. *Discovering the News: A Social History of American Newspapers*. New York: Basic Books, 1978.

———. *Watergate in American Memory*. New York: Basic Books, 1992.

Schwarz, F. A. O., Jr. "Intelligence Activities and the Rights of Americans." Speech to the American Bar Association, 16 November 1976.

Semple, Lorenzo, Jr., and David Rayfiel. *Three Days of the Condor*. Hollywood: Script City, 1975.

Shull, Steven A., ed. *The Two Presidencies: A Quarter Century Assessment*. Chicago: Nelson-Hall, 1991.

Siebert, Fred, Theodore Peterson, and Wilbur Schramm. *Four Theories of the Press*. Urbana: University of Illinois Press, 1956.

Smist, Frank J., Jr. *Congress Oversees the United States Intelligence Community, 1947–1989*. Knoxville: University of Tennessee Press, 1990.

Smith, Hedrick. *The Power Game*. New York: Random House, 1988.

Sniderman, Paul M., W. Russell Neuman, Jack Citrin, Herbert McCloskey, and J. Merrill Shanks. "Stability of Support for the Political System: The Initial Impact of Watergate." *American Politics Quarterly* 3 (October 1975): 437–57.

Spear, Joseph C. *The Presidents and the Press: The Nixon Legacy*. Cambridge: MIT Press, 1984.

Stafford, David. *The Silent Game: The Real World of Imaginary Spies*. Athens: University of Georgia Press, 1991.

Stern, Laurence. "The Daniel Schorr Affair." *Columbia Journalism Review*, May/June 1976, 20–25.

———. "Exposing the CIA (Again)." *Columbia Journalism Review*, March/April 1975, 55–56.

Stockwell, John. *In Search of Enemies: A CIA Story*. New York: Norton, 1978.

Stone, I. F. "The Schorr Case: The Real Dangers." *New York Review of Books*, 1 April 1976, 6–11.

Sundquist, James L. *The Decline and Resurgence of Congress*. Washington, D.C.: Brookings Institution, 1981.

Szulc, Tad. "Shaking Up the CIA." *New York Times Magazine*, 29 July 1979, 13, 21, 33–35, 45–46.

Taylor, Richard Norton. *In Defence of the Realm?: The Case for Accountable Security Services*. London: Civil Liberties Trust, 1990.

Theoharis, Athan. *Spying on Americans: Political Surveillance from Hoover to the Huston Plan*. Philadelphia: Temple University Press, 1978.

Theoharis, Athan, and John Stuart Cox. *The Boss: J. Edgar Hoover and the Great American Inquisition*. Philadelphia: Temple University Press, 1988.

Thompson, Kenneth W. *The Ford Presidency: Twenty-two Intimate Perspectives of Gerald R. Ford*. Lanham, Md.: University Press of America, 1988.

Tower, John. *Consequences: A Personal and Political Memoir.* Boston: Little, Brown, 1991.

Treverton, Gregory F. *Covert Action: The Limits of Intervention in the Postwar World.* New York: Basic Books, 1987.

Turner, Stansfield. *Secrecy and Democracy: The CIA in Transition.* Boston: Houghton Mifflin, 1985.

Turner, Stansfield, and George Thibault. "Intelligence: The Right Rules." *Foreign Policy* 48 (Fall 1982): 122–38.

Varner, Roy, and Wayne Collier. *A Matter of Risk: The Incredible Inside Story of the CIA's Hughes Glomar Explorer Mission to Raise a Russian Submarine.* New York: Random House, 1978.

Walters, Vernon. *Silent Missions.* Garden City, N.Y.: Doubleday, 1978.

Wark, Wesley K., ed. *Spy Fiction, Spy Films, and Real Intelligence.* London: Frank Cass, 1991.

Weaver, Paul H. "The New Journalism and the Old: Thoughts after Watergate." *Public Interest* 35 (Spring 1974): 67–88.

Whitfield, Stephen J. *The Culture of the Cold War.* Baltimore: Johns Hopkins University Press, 1991.

Wicker, Tom. *On Press.* New York: Viking Press, 1978.

Wise, David. *The American Police State.* New York: Random House, 1976.

Wise, David, and Thomas B. Ross. *The Invisible Government.* New York: Random House, 1964.

Wolfe, Alan. "The Emergence of the Dual State." *The Nation,* 29 March 1975, 363–69.

Woodward, Bob. *Veil: The Secret Wars of the CIA, 1981–1987.* New York: Simon and Schuster, 1987.

Index

committee; Colby, William; Ford administration; "Rogue elephant" metaphor

Cheney, Richard, 49, 75–76

Childs, Marquis, 88

Church, Frank, 2, 42, 70, 78, 81–82, 134, 153, 154, 173, 181, 214 (n. 55); presidential ambitions, 3, 7, 55, 93, 108–9, 186, 191–92, 236 (n. 2); contrasted with Pike, 8, 103, 105, 111–12, 118, 119, 127, 133, 181; background and ideology, 53–55; attacked as partisan, 86, 87–88. *See also* Church committee; "Rogue elephant" metaphor

Church committee, 2, 46, 148; members appointed, 52–53; contrasted with Nedzi and Pike committees, 56–57, 110, 113, 133, 136, 140, 142–43, 172, 174–75, 181; CIA assassination plots inquiry and report, 60, 66, 85–91, 105–10, 145, 150, 181; toxin hearings, 91–94; Huston plan hearings, 94–97; COINTELPRO hearings, 97–99, 101; NSA hearings, 104–5; covert action hearings, 105; final report, 169, 174–75; recommendations, 175. *See also* Church, Frank

Clark, Dick, 150

Clark, Mark, 198 (n. 7)

Clark, Ramsey, 113

Clark amendment, 150, 179–80

COINTELPRO, 95, 97–99

Colby, William, 29, 46, 47, 48, 76–77, 134, 148, 150, 152, 154, 169, 175, 181, 214 (n. 43), 222 (n. 91); and Hersh exposé, 12, 24, 35; and CIA in Chile, 17, 105, 149; and "family jewels," 30, 58, 114; and CIA assassination plots story, 60, 65–66; and Project Jennifer story, 68–74, 210 (n. 69); strategy for congressional hearings, 91–94; and Pike committee, 112, 119, 120, 122, 124, 125, 130–31, 135, 137, 159

Cold War consensus, 4, 14, 19–22, 185, 187–89; effect of Vietnam War on, 23, 44, 89–90, 113

Columbia Journalism Review, 26, 34, 39, 78, 166

Congress, U.S.: reluctance to challenge secret government, 5, 42, 106, 112, 160–61, 170, 182–83, 185–86, 193; Ninety-fourth, 48, 185. *See also* Church committee; Nedzi committee; Pike committee

Connor, John, 50

Cook, Fred, 36

Counterspy, 151, 154

Crewdson, John, 161

Cronkite, Walter, 23, 64

Daniel, Clifton, 61, 62

Dean, John, 34

Defense Intelligence Agency, 94, 136, 163

Dellums, Ron, 57, 76–77, 113–15, 117, 122, 131, 133, 135–36, 163, 171, 172, 178, 232 (n. 39), 233 (n. 49)

Détente, 23

Dillon, Douglas, 49, 83

Donner, Aaron, 121, 127, 153

Doolittle committee report, 13–14, 109–10, 185

Downie, Leonard, Jr., 59

Downs, Anthony, 186

Draper, Theodore, 186

Dulles, Allen, 22, 77

Dulles, John Foster, 132

Durenberger, David, 181

Eagleburger, Lawrence, 126, 128

Eagleton, Tom, 44–45

Editor and Publisher, 171

Edwards, Don, 57, 116

Eisenhower, Dwight, 13–14, 43, 86, 108, 185, 198 (n. 7), 199 (n. 21)

Ellsberg, Daniel, 16, 24, 166

Ethics Committee, House: probe of Michael Harrington, 56, 149, 164,

225 (n. 13); probe of Daniel Schorr, 164–65, 170–72

Evans, Rowland, 46, 94

Federal Bureau of Investigation (FBI), 16, 63, 76, 82, 94–96, 155, 163, 173, 184; *Washington Post* exposé of, 2, 36–37; in popular culture, 14–15, 99, 100–101, 187; public opinion ratings of, 17, 99, 140; COINTELPRO, 97–99; and Church report, 174–75; Reagan administration reforms, 177–78. *See also* King, Martin Luther, Jr.

Felker, Clay, 162

Felt, W. Mark, 233 (n. 45)

Field, A. Searle, 113, 155

Fifth Estate, 151

Fleming, Ian, 14, 73

Foley, Thomas, 172, 233 (n. 49)

Ford, Gerald, 7, 16–17, 36, 46, 55, 70, 105–6, 124, 133–34, 228 (n. 55); attitude toward CIA and FBI, 47–49; appoints Rockefeller Commission, 49–50; slip about CIA assassination plots, 60–62, 65; and executive privilege, 138–41. *See also* Ford administration

Ford administration: response to investigations by press and Congress, 12, 49–50, 75–76, 82–85, 93–94, 103–6, 122–41, 147–56, 164; and Hughes-Ryan amendment, 46, 148; and Pike report leak, 156–61, 164; reforms of intelligence community, 173–74

Foreign Intelligence Surveillance Act (1978), 177

Frankel, Max, 61

Freeman, J. Leiper, 160

Friedersdorf, Max, 129

Friendly, Fred, 63

Fulbright, J. William, 39, 44, 140

Gelb, Leslie, 38, 39, 180

Giaimo, Robert, 57, 117, 119, 129, 131, 135–36, 172, 232 (n. 39)

Giancana, Sam, 99

Glomar Explorer, 60, 67–74, 79, 183, 184

Goldwater, Barry, 48, 52, 63, 87, 88, 93, 98, 150, 176

Grady, James, 102

Graham, Daniel, 154

Graham, Katharine, 25, 26, 70

Graham, Phil, 19, 22, 37

Gray, L. Patrick, 16, 233 (n. 45)

Greenfield, Meg, 187

Greider, William, 27, 74

Griswold, Erwin, 49, 222 (n. 85)

Gruson, Sydney, 20

Gude, Gilbert, 101

Halberstam, David, 23, 33

Haldeman, Bob, 16, 63

Hallin, Daniel, 5–6, 19, 23, 184

Harrington, Michael, 17, 56, 57, 113–17, 149, 176, 178, 181, 188, 200 (nn. 25, 26), 225 (n. 13)

Harris, Fred, 2

Hart, Gary, 52

Hart, Philip, 52, 53

Hayes, Philip, 117, 136

Hébert, Edward, 57–58, 185

Hellman, Lillian, 90

Helms, Richard, 3, 16, 22, 30, 39, 41, 86–87, 91, 93, 96, 109, 134, 178, 187, 188; confrontation with Daniel Schorr, 66–67, 107–8, 162, 165, 208 (n. 30); perjury investigation, 92, 214 (n. 43)

Hersh, Seymour, 6, 27, 62, 67, 79, 110, 131, 165, 166, 167, 178–79, 191, 192–93, 208 (n. 8), 219 (n. 30), 222 (n. 85); domestic spying exposé, 1, 2, 3, 7, 8, 11–13, 24, 29–36, 38–39, 41, 46–47, 57, 66, 81, 84–85, 146, 173–74, 181, 183; Chile exposé, 7, 17, 45, 46, 200 (n. 25); Pulitzer Prize competition, 35, 75; and Project Jennifer, 67–71, 73, 74; and Holystone, 75–76

Hills, Roderick, 83, 125

Hodgson, Godfrey, 4, 89

Schudson, Michael, 6, 18, 183, 187–88
Schwarz, F. A. O., Jr., 120, 152, 174, 177, 179
Schweiker, Richard, 51, 52, 86, 87
Scorpio (movie), 101
Scott, Hugh, 52
Scowcroft, Brent, 70, 134, 210 (n. 69)
Secret Team, The (Prouty), 77
Seib, Charles B., 38, 78, 154, 165, 171
Senate Select Committee to Study Governmental Operations with Respect to Intelligence Activities. *See* Church committee
Sevareid, Eric, 35, 64
Shannon, Edgar, 50
Small, Bill, 65
Smist, Frank, Jr., 3, 178
Stanton, James, 57, 117, 135, 171, 232 (n. 39)
Steele, James, 75
Stennis, John, 52, 58, 113, 176, 185
Stern, Laurence, 34, 44, 163–64, 165–66, 200 (n. 25)
Stone, I. F., 19–20, 156, 165, 180–81, 225 (n. 14)
Sullivan, William, 97
Sulzberger, Arthur, 61
Sundquist, James, 43–44
Symington, Stuart, 58
Szulc, Tad, 21

Thomas, William, 69
Three Days of the Condor (book and movie), 102
Time, 23, 25, 29, 34, 36, 38, 73–74, 75, 78, 127, 198 (n. 22)
Tower, John, 52, 87, 176, 193, 213 (n. 28)
Treen, David, 57, 117, 158, 160, 232 (n. 39)
Trujillo, Rafael, 66, 107, 208 (n. 28)
Tufo, Peter, 162

Udall, Morris, 2
U-2 spy flights, 20–21, 48

Vietnam War, 4, 12, 22–23, 39, 44, 53, 57, 89, 113, 115, 180, 181, 182, 184, 185, 186, 187
Village Voice, 162–63, 171

Walinsky, Adam, 87
Walsh, Lawrence, 232 (n. 43)
Walsh, Paul, 156
War Powers Bill, 44–45
Washington Post, 22, 23, 42, 66, 67, 70, 76, 90, 101, 108, 130, 131, 141, 153, 187; exposé of FBI, 2, 8, 36–37; Watergate and, 24, 25, 26–27; desire to appear responsible, 27, 36, 73, 128, 139, 174; response to Hersh's domestic spying stories, 34–36; rivalry with *New York Times*, 37, 38; and Pike report leak, 163–64, 165, 171
Washington Star, 66, 128
Watergate scandal, 1, 4, 12, 15–16, 44, 89, 102, 113, 115, 124, 139, 143, 155, 167, 180, 181, 185–86, 187, 189; effect on press, 24, 26, 182, 183–85; changing perceptions of, 39, 86, 91, 98
Weaver, Paul, 25
Weicker, Lowell, 50, 155
Welch, Richard, 151–55, 160, 167, 172, 173, 174, 175, 182, 226 (n. 27)
White, Theodore, 11
Whitten, Les, 72
Wicker, Tom, 19, 24, 25–26, 32, 61, 62, 74, 85, 93, 98, 125, 166, 174, 183, 184
Wildavsky, Aaron, 186
Wilderotter, James, 112
Wills, Garry, 89, 90, 185
Wisner, Frank, 22
Woodward, Bob, 24, 26, 27, 31, 60, 183, 211 (n. 82)

Zumwalt, Elmo, 137